Dan Sater's
Ultimate European
HOME PLANS COLLECTION

106 Alluring Designs
Including English, French, Italian, Spanish & Tuscan Styles

A DESIGNS DIRECT PUBLISHING BOOK

Presented by

The Sater Design Collection, Inc.
The Center at the Springs
25241 Elementary Way, Suite 102, Bonita Springs, FL 34135

Dan F. Sater, II - CEO and Author

Dan F. Sater, II - Editor in Chief

Alma Mezzell - Senior Editor

Dana Lee Gibson - Art Director / Production Manager

Contributing Illustrators
Sean DiVincenzo / Lone Wolf Drafting & Design
CG Render Visualization Studio, Inc.
Dave Jenkins

Contributing Photographers
CJ Walker, Larry Taylor, M.E. Parker, Doug Thompson, Kim Sargent,
Michael Lowry, Jerry Willis, Richard Leo Johnson, William Minarich,
Danielle Sater

Contributing Writters
Marla Ottenstein, Laura Hurst Brown, Alan Lopuszynski

Printed by: Toppan Printing Co., China
Second Printing: June 2015
10 9 8 7 6 5 4 3 2

Porto Velho

Plan #6950 ~ Page 108

Contents

San Filippo

Plan #8055 ~ Page 88

In creating this series of designs, my interest was not to replicate European designs, but rather to capture the essence of the classic beauty inherent in each archetype. Classical Old-World architecture significantly influenced early American residential design in several ways. Admirers of great masters, such as Thomas Jefferson, brought back these ideas and design elements and early sought to incorporate them into a truly American style. It is with the same passion that we bring you "Ultimate European" home plans, the New-World portfolio of distinctively American homes representing not replicas, but new designs that borrow from the character and magic of these masterpieces. We have integrated history-rich exteriors with plans that include all of the state-of-the-art conveniences and amenities one would expect in the modern American home.

For this collection, I selected five regions of European influence: English, French, Italian, Spanish and Tuscan Styles. Each of these archetypes have played an important role in the development of American residential design.

I hope you will find in these home plans a sense of heritage, not only in timeless exterior elevations, but also in well-planned interiors that incorporate thoughtful intimate spaces with ultra-functional modern amenities.

Thanks for purchasing this book. I hope you find your dream home within.

Blessings,

Dan F. Sater II, AIBD, CPBD, CGP

Hebrews 3:4

Tuscan | *Massimo 8057*

Tuscan architecture is a pre-classical Italianate style of rustic villas and farmhouses that evolved from readily available materials found in the Tuscan hillside and fields: such as fieldstone, rough-hewn wood and terra-cotta clay. Paramount to the design is the rapport between the interior and exterior living areas, as manifest in the prevalence of open courtyards, walkways and loggias. Warm, vibrant "earth-toned" colors, evocative of the sun-kissed hillside, are characteristic of a Tuscan-themed home, as in the use of textured wall finishes, rough-hewn wooden flooring, natural stone tiles and rustic beamed ceilings.

Decorative elements, such as stone columns, arches and cornices, as well as terra-cotta roofs, cobblestone walkways, richly painted stucco façades with wrought-iron accents, play an important role in creating the comfortable, Old-World ambience that is associated with Tuscan design.

Italian | *Bartolini 8022*

No country has more profoundly influenced residential architecture than Italy. Great masters such as Vignola, Palladio and Bernini employed great skill in practicing their craft. No one, however, impacted residential design like Palladio, who understood the importance of the relationship between the home and its site.

Classical architects also understood the relationship of the home to its occupants. In fact, classical architecture may be construed as an embodiment of the human form, seeking to relate building proportions to human scale. The Italians developed a mastery of these techniques, and in addition gave us a mix of grand porticos and turrets, trefoil windows, cut-stone masonry, carved eaves brackets and spiral columns.

American styles that reflect direct Italian influences are Renaissance, Tuscan and Baroque.

French | *Brittany 8040*

French architecture extended the concepts of scale and sight relative to houses with a heightened sense of grandeur and luxe detail. Residential design reached its greatest heights under the tutelage of French kings who, impressed by Italian life and art, sought to emulate the rich aesthetics and translate them into a French style. Great French architects such as Philibert de l'Orame and Jacques Androuet du Cereceau, and later François Mansart, defined this style by focusing on the use of ornaments over form. French kings and the "nouveau riche" built many grand mansions, incorporating art as architecture and adding new features such as porte-cocheres, galleries and grand staircases. The new use of steeply pitched roofs punctuated with ornamented dormers, flared eaves, rusticated pilasters and quoins became common elements in crowning French homes. Use of columns divorced from arches was also a departure from the Roman influence, and became an important part of French classical architecture.

American styles that reflect French influences are Chateauesque, Beaux Arts, French Provincial (Country) and Second Empire.

English | *Brittany 8040*

England was also greatly influenced by Italian design aesthetics, as well as French architecture. Yet British architects such as Inigo Jones and his contemporaries developed their own unique style by implementing Palladian concepts with a decidedly British flair. Rugged exterior textures, stately gables and pediments, cornerstone arches and plentiful multi-pane windows created welcoming façades reminiscent of the English countryside. Aside from the obvious, it is easy to understand the direct English influence on American architecture. With transcontinental waves of immigrants came a wealth of variants on the dominant British styles. Benjamin Latrobe, the first professional architect to practice in America, was born in Yorkshire and trained in London. He drew plans for the White House and other notable public buildings, and later influenced a generation of leading American designers. American styles influenced by the British Isles are Georgian, Colonial Revival, Gothic (Tudor), Victorian and Classical Revival, to name a few.

Spanish | *Martelli 8061*

Spanish architecture was influenced not only by elements of Italian and French design, but by Moorish styles as well. Coupled with Native American building techniques, the eclectic dialects of the Spanish vernacular led to a truly unique archetype in home design. Elaborate entry turrets, quatrefoil windows, low-pitched rooflines, carved balustrades and rounded arches became a few of the style's defining traits. Andalusian and Moorish influences altered the home's relationship with nature, with such residential features as courtyards, interior fountains and arched loggias. The use of brightly colored tile mosaics for decoration on sculpted stucco and stone façades extended the Spanish vernacular and is practiced with artful skill in modern revivals.

American styles that reflect Spanish influences are Mediterranean, Spanish Colonial and Monterey.

Leighton

Plan No. 8070

Front Elevation

© Sater Design Collection, Inc.

An Unforgettable Façade

Quiet elegance is found throughout Leighton, a stunning British Colonial home that boasts multiple outdoor living spaces, specialty ceiling treatments and state-of-the-art amenities. Details both romantic and practical are found around every corner, like the living room's striking bow windows.

A soaring portico and stately turret create an unforgettable façade. Inside, the foyer opens to views of a grand staircase, formal dining room and a wide-open living room that is as impressive for its soaring two-story ceiling as it is for the gorgeously detailed, two-sided fireplace that it shared with the study.

But Leighton's treasures don't end there. The master suite encompasses one whole side of the plan and delights with an art niche foyer, private lanai access, dual walk-in closets and dual vanities in a luxurious bath overlooking a private master garden.

A casual living zone is on the opposite side of the first floor arranged in an open layout. The gourmet kitchen is open to a dining nook and leisure room with built-ins

Through French doors on the far side of the leisure room, a lanai with a full outdoor kitchen and fireplace beckons.

The second story echoes the classic elegance of the first floor with tray and vaulted ceilings in the bedrooms, walk-in closets and overlooks to both the living and leisure rooms. ❖

PHOTO ABOVE: Whether your plans include entertaining friends and family or simply a quiet evening alone, Leighton's design extends the interior to several outdoor living areas. A fully equipped kitchen, roaring fireplace and many intimate details help set the scene.

PHOTO LEFT: Just inside the foyer, stately columns and a tray ceiling define the intimate dining room. This creates an open, but warm, gathering place conveniently located near the wet bar and kitchen.

PHOTO FAR LEFT: View upon entering breakfast nook with arch to kitchen on right, with loft above, and family room in the background.

PHOTO LEFT: From late night snacks to full-scale dinner parties, the kitchen is where it all happens. This open design includes a wraparound eating bar and provides quick and easy access to the home's large leisure room and nook. A center island with prep sink provides another helpful advantage.

PHOTO FAR LEFT: The formal living room, with its dramatic two-story, coffered ceiling, is filled with light and views thanks to the wall of bow windows that display the home's outdoor living areas. The striking fireplace, crafted in handsome detail, provides a grand and comfortable centerpiece.

PHOTO BELOW: The spacious loft overlooks the leisure room. Perfect as a game area or relaxation space.

PHOTO ABOVE: The master suite combines exquisite elegance with quiet solitude, creating a welcome retreat. Resplendent in its details, the suite features a step-up tray ceiling and arched entryways with stately columns to access the lanai. (Photo reflects customer modified sitting room).

PHOTO RIGHT: To create a romantic ambiance, the luxurious master bath is flooded with views from wide, beautiful windows with arched transoms over the whirlpool tub.

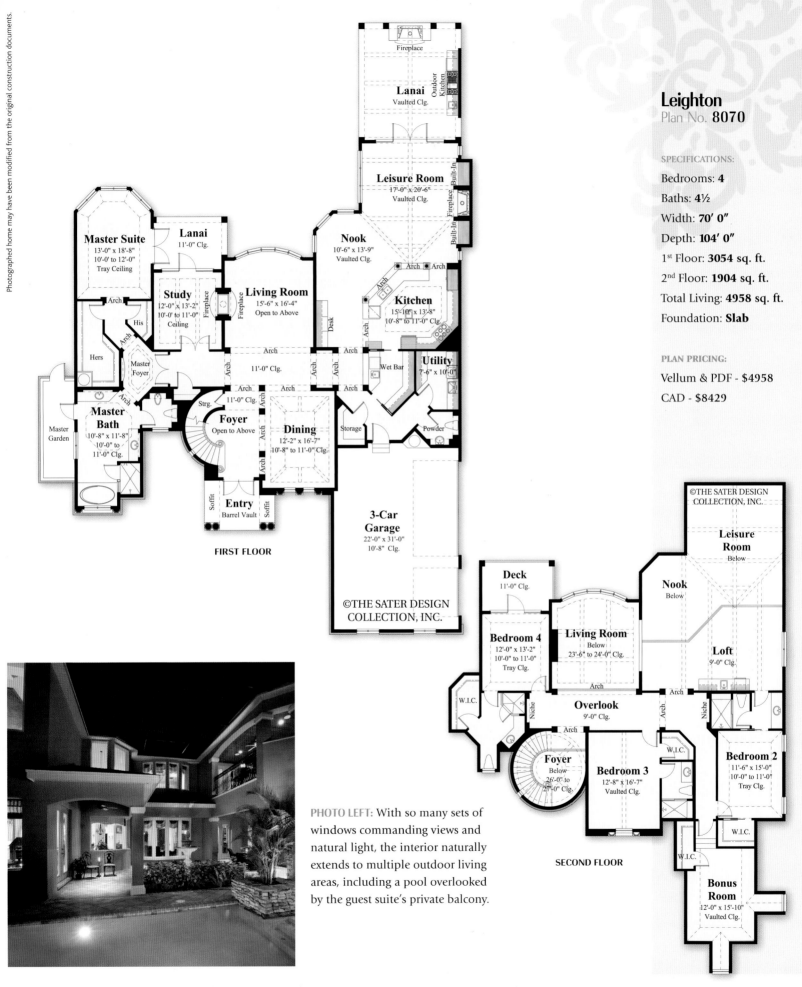

FIRST FLOOR

Master Suite
13'-0" x 18'-8"
10'-0" to 12'-0"
Tray Ceiling

Lanai
11'-0" Clg.

Study
12'-0" x 13'-2"
10'-0" to 11'-0"
Ceiling

Living Room
15'-6" x 16'-4"
Open to Above

Lanai
Vaulted Clg.

Outdoor Kitchen

Fireplace

Leisure Room
17'-0" x 20'-6"
Vaulted Clg.

Built-In

Fireplace

Built-In

Nook
10'-6" x 13'-9"
Vaulted Clg.

Arch   Arch

His

Hers

Master Foyer

Arch

Arch

Kitchen
15'-10" x 13'-8"
10'-8" to 11'-0" Clg.

Arch

Master Bath
10'-8" x 11'-8"
10'-0" to 11'-0" Clg.

Master Garden

Arch   11'-0" Clg.   Arch   Arch

Desk

Wet Bar

Utility
7'-6" x 10'-0"

Arch   11'-0" Clg.   Arch   Arch

Strg.

Foyer
Open to Above

Dining
12'-2" x 16'-7"
10'-8" to 11'-0"' Clg.

Storage

Powder

Soffit   Entry
Barrel Vault   Soffit

3-Car Garage
22'-0" x 31'-0"
10'-8" Clg.

©THE SATER DESIGN
COLLECTION, INC.

SECOND FLOOR

©THE SATER DESIGN
COLLECTION, INC.

Leisure Room
Below

Deck
11'-0" Clg.

Nook
Below

Bedroom 4
12'-0" x 13'-2"
10'-0" to 11'-0"
Tray Clg.

Living Room
23'-6" to 24'-0" Clg.
Below

Loft
9'-0" Clg.

W.I.C.

Niche

Overlook
9'-0" Clg.

Arch

Arch

Niche

Bedroom 2
11'-6" x 15'-0"
10'-0" to 11'-0"
Tray Clg.

Arch

Foyer
Below
26'-0" to
27'-0"

Bedroom 3
12'-8" x 16'-7"
Vaulted Clg.

W.I.C.

W.I.C.

W.I.C.

Bonus Room
12'-0" x 15'-10"
Vaulted Clg.

Leighton
Plan No. **8070**

SPECIFICATIONS:

Bedrooms: **4**

Baths: **4½**

Width: **70' 0"**

Depth: **104' 0"**

1st Floor: 3054 sq. ft.

2nd Floor: 1904 sq. ft.

Total Living: 4958 sq. ft.

Foundation: **Slab**

PLAN PRICING:

Vellum & PDF - $4958

CAD - $8429

PHOTO LEFT: With so many sets of windows commanding views and natural light, the interior naturally extends to multiple outdoor living areas, including a pool overlooked by the guest suite's private balcony.

Andros Island

Plan No. 6927

British West Indies Flavor

From hues and architectural lines that mimic the natural landscape, to disappearing walls and a spectacular courtyard that has an indoor feel, the intent of this home is to embrace the outdoors. The dining room, guest suite and study at the front of the home accomplish this with floor-to-ceiling bay windows. In the living room, retreating glass walls create flawless indoor-outdoor transitions. The kitchen flows into a leisure room that also has disappearing sliders to the lanai and courtyard.

Custom details, including a corner entertainment unit in the leisure room and sunburst-laden transoms above the kitchen bar, infuse the home with individuality. The master suite reveals elegant respite starting with the entry foyer and continuing into a walk-in shower that merges with a private outdoor garden. The second-level bonus room offers a substantial flexible space that includes a full bathroom and balcony.

PHOTO ABOVE: The possibilities for entertaining are endless in this captivating courtyard adjacent to the lanai. Columns, tray ceilings and tile floors exude an indoor feel, while the island-inspired fireplace, fully appointed kitchen and hearty furniture embrace any climactic changes.

PHOTO LEFT: An octagonal tray ceiling and bay windows illuminate the expansive space of the dining room and lend sophistication to every meal. A built-in buffet fits elegantly into a lighted wall niche that's perfect for a treasured piece of artwork.

PHOTO FAR LEFT: Foyer with corbeled ceiling, recessed niche and inlaid mosaic tile medallion floor.

PHOTO ABOVE: Zero-corner glass walls disappear to expand the living room onto the lanai. The layered moulding adds flair and the room's unique shape is a creative setting for flexible seating.

PHOTO RIGHT: The lateral arrangement between the leisure room and kitchen, with nearby breakfast nook, creates a casual zone—a great place for relaxing with friends and snacks.

PHOTO LEFT: The richly appointed kitchen with butcher block capped island is perfect for preparing gourmet meals or serving parties.

PHOTO BELOW: The quaint bonus room makes a perfect guest retreat complete with Juliet's balcony.

PHOTO ABOVE: This intimate master suite is
made complete with the adjoining sitting area
featured here for reading a good book or writing
a note to an old friend.

PHOTO RIGHT: A meandering lanai follows the
unusual lines of the back of the home, where
a circular glass-walled breakfast nook and
disappearing glass walls in the living room blur
the lines between indoors and out.

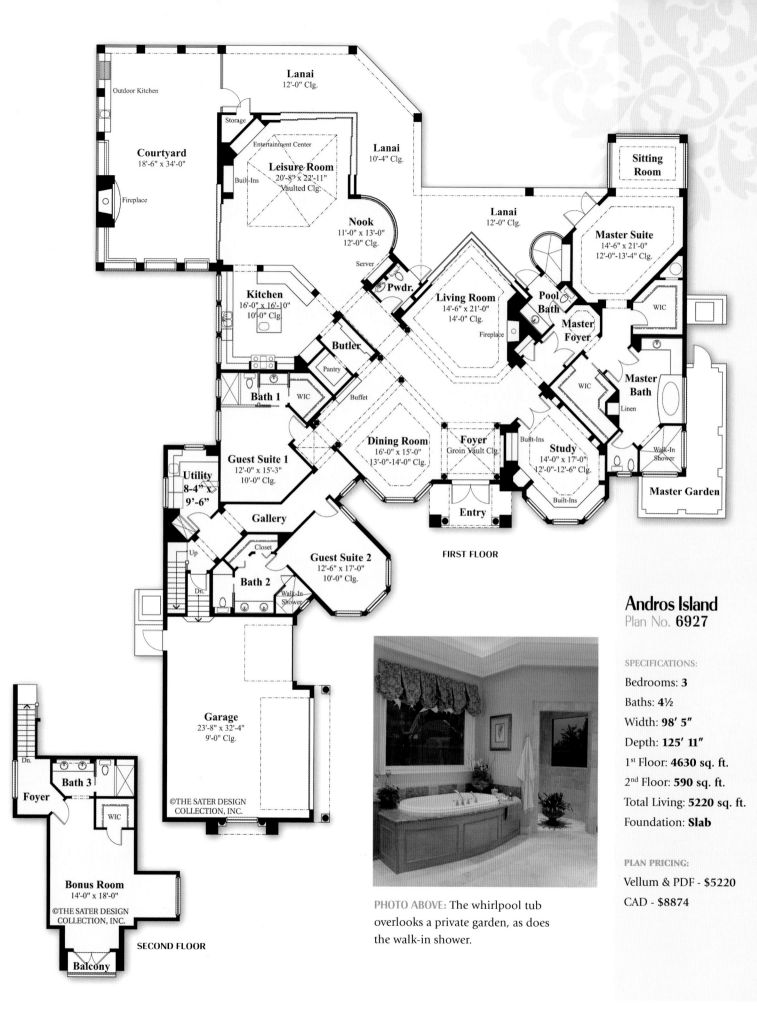

Courtyard
18'-6" x 34'-0"

Outdoor Kitchen

Fireplace

Storage

Lanai
12'-0" Clg.

Entertainment Center

Leisure Room
20'-8" x 22'-11"
Vaulted Clg.

Built-Ins

Lanai
10'-4" Clg.

Nook
11'-0" x 13'-0"
12'-0" Clg.

Server

Kitchen
16'-0" x 16'-10"
10'-0" Clg.

Pwdr.

Lanai
12'-0" Clg.

Living Room
14'-6" x 21'-0"
14'-0" Clg.

Fireplace

Sitting Room

Master Suite
14'-6" x 21'-0"
12'-0"-13'-4" Clg.

WIC

Pool Bath

Master Foyer

Butler

Pantry

Bath 1

WIC

Buffet

Master Bath

WIC

Linen

Guest Suite 1
12'-0" x 15'-3"
10'-0" Clg.

Dining Room
16'-0" x 15'-0"
13'-0"-14'-0" Clg.

Foyer
Groin Vault Clg.

Built-Ins

Study
14'-0" x 17'-0"
12'-0"-12'-6" Clg.

Walk-In Shower

Utility
8-4" x 9'-6"

Gallery

Closet

Entry

Built-Ins

Master Garden

FIRST FLOOR

Up

Bath 2

Guest Suite 2
12'-6" x 17'-0"
10'-0" Clg.

Walk-In Shower

Dn.

Garage
23'-8" x 32'-4"
9'-0" Clg.

©THE SATER DESIGN COLLECTION, INC.

SECOND FLOOR

Dn.

Bath 3

Foyer

WIC

Bonus Room
14'-0" x 18'-0"

©THE SATER DESIGN COLLECTION, INC.

Balcony

Andros Island
Plan No. **6927**

SPECIFICATIONS:

Bedrooms: **3**

Baths: **4½**

Width: **98' 5"**

Depth: **125' 11"**

1st Floor: **4630 sq. ft.**

2nd Floor: **590 sq. ft.**

Total Living: **5220 sq. ft.**

Foundation: **Slab**

PLAN PRICING:

Vellum & PDF - **$5220**

CAD - **$8874**

PHOTO ABOVE: The whirlpool tub overlooks a private garden, as does the walk-in shower.

Cordillera
Plan No. 6953

© Sater Design Collection, Inc.

Mediterranean Revival Estate

A desire to create a home that paid homage to Palm Beach's great Spanish-influenced villas while at the same time embracing contemporary design ideas and technologies was the inspiration behind Dan Sater's award-winning design *Cordillera*. The recipient of both a 2006 Aurora and AIBD award, *Cordillera* incorporates modern amenities and elements such as corner-less disappearing sliding-glass walls, clubrooms, outdoor living spaces and full-house automation.

This villa-style plan opens traditionally boxed spaces to satisfying views of the landscape. The vaulted foyer opens through the front gallery to the formal core of the home: a series of three view-oriented rooms designed to encourage intimate gatherings.

To the right of the home, the casual living zone incorporates a spacious leisure room that links with a nook and kitchen. Upstairs, a balcony bridge connects a game room, pub and home theater with two guest suites.

PHOTO ABOVE: The outdoor retreat wraps the leisure room, nook and kitchen with a perfect space for entertaining. Interior and exterior living areas mix seamlessly via retreating glass doors.

PHOTO LEFT: Shapely columns and arches create a fluid boundary between the pool deck and solana, and shelter the outside living area from the midday sun.

PHOTO FAR LEFT: View looking down gallery from home's foyer.

PHOTO LEFT: Connected to the living room at the center of the plan, the dining room takes in views of the pool and lakefront. A stunning stepped ceiling adds a touch of drama to its formality.

PHOTO FAR LEFT: The grand living room with stunning stone fireplace. Straight ahead of the main entry, a series of three French doors open to a spectacular pool setting, offering brilliant views both day and night.

PHOTO BELOW: The ultimate entertainment room—a wet bar, home theater and French doors opening to a private deck round out the media room's many amenities.

PHOTO LEFT: The club room's media alcove allows for a full theater experience for some while others can look on while playing cards or shooting pool.

PHOTO FAR LEFT: Closely linked to the living area via a shared fireplace, the study offers a quiet environment for talks and planning. Adjacent to the master wing, the study easily converts to a work space, reading room or home office. Double doors open to the sun terrace and pool, offering an easy transition from work to play.

PHOTO BELOW: Retreating glass doors provide a seamless connection from the leisure room to the solana, lanai and courtyard. High-end electronics integrated into the design provide surround-sound, advanced security systems and soft, subtle lighting.

PHOTO RIGHT: Palm trees and beds of poppy-red geraniums in cut-stone planters border the freshwater lap pool, designed to extend the eye out to the lake beyond. An extensive sun terrace connects the outdoor living areas with a solana, spa and outdoor kitchen.

PHOTO FAR RIGHT: The dramatic lanai features 12-foot ceilings and wraps along the entire back of the house and around the pool for first-class outdoor living and entertaining.

PHOTO BELOW: Exquisite details enrich the central hip roof that dominates the rear perimeter of the home: an arcature caps the rusticated surround and massive pilasters frame the archway in complementary styles. A row of French doors opens the interior to the outside living area, which overlooks the sun terrace and pool. To the left, the solana dissolves the boundaries of outer and inner spaces and features a fireplace and alfresco kitchen.

PHOTO ABOVE: Floor-to-ceiling windows permit natural light to permeate the master bedroom. Curved moldings, a coffered ceiling and a flattened arch lend dimension, depth and texture to the room, which leads outside to the sun terrace, pool and spa.

PHOTO RIGHT: Framed by twin Tuscan columns, a sculpted Persian-red marble tub surround subdues the grand scale of the master bath. Past the tall muntin window and fanlight is a glimpse of the private garden.

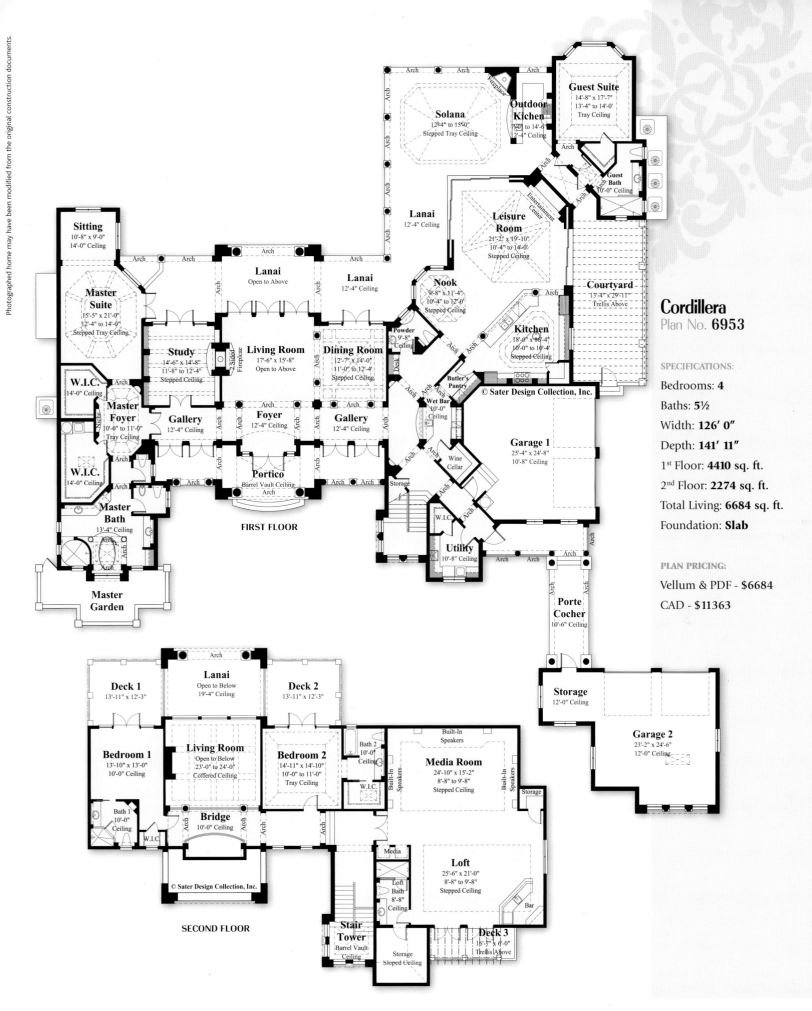

FIRST FLOOR

Sitting
10'-8" x 9'-0"
14'-0" Ceiling

Master
Suite
15'-5" x 21'-0"
12'-4" to 14'-0"
Stepped Tray Ceiling

W.I.C.
14'-0" Ceiling

Master
Foyer
10'-0" to 11'-0"
Tray Ceiling

W.I.C.
14'-0" Ceiling

Master
Bath
13'-4" Ceiling

Master Garden

Study
14'-6" x 14'-8"
11'-8" to 12'-4"
Stepped Ceiling

Gallery
12'-4" Ceiling

Living Room
17'-6" x 15'-8"
Open to Above

Foyer
12'-4" Ceiling

Portico
Barrel Vault Ceiling
Arch

Lanai
Open to Above

Lanai
12'-4" Ceiling

Dining Room
12'-7" x 14'-0"
11'-0" to 12'-4"
Stepped Ceiling

Gallery
12'-4" Ceiling

Nook
9'-8" x 11'-4"
10'-4" to 12'-0"
Stepped Ceiling

Powder
9'-8" Ceiling

Wet Bar
10'-0" Ceiling

Butler's Pantry

Wine Cellar

Storage

Utility
10'-8" Ceiling

Solana
12'-4" to 15'-0"
Stepped Tray Ceiling

Outdoor Kitchen
7'-0" to 14'-6"

Lanai
12'-4" Ceiling

Leisure Room
21'-2" x 19'-10"
10'-4" to 14'-0"
Stepped Ceiling

Entertainment Center

Kitchen
18'-0" x 10'-4"
10'-0" to 10'-4"
Stepped Ceiling

Garage 1
25'-4" x 24'-8"
10'-8" Ceiling

Guest Suite
14'-8" x 17'-7"
13'-4" to 14'-0"
Tray Ceiling

Guest Bath
10'-0" Ceiling

Courtyard
13'-4" x 29'-11"
Trellis Above

W.I.C.

© Sater Design Collection, Inc.

Porte Cocher
10'-6" Ceiling

SECOND FLOOR

Deck 1
13'-11" x 12'-3"

Bedroom 1
13'-10" x 13'-0"
10'-0" Ceiling

Bath 1
10'-0" Ceiling

W.I.C.

Lanai
Open to Below
19'-4" Ceiling

Living Room
Open to Below
23'-0" x 24'-0"
Coffered Ceiling

Bridge
10'-0" Ceiling

Deck 2
13'-11" x 12'-3"

Bedroom 2
14'-11" x 14'-10"
10'-0" to 11'-0"
Tray Ceiling

W.I.C.

Bath 2
10'-0" Ceiling

Media
Room
24'-10" x 15'-2"
8'-8" to 9'-8"
Stepped Ceiling

Built-In Speakers

Media

Loft Bath
8'-8" Ceiling

Loft
25'-6" x 21'-0"
8'-8" to 9'-8"
Stepped Ceiling

Bar

Stair Tower
Barrel Vault Ceiling

Storage
Sloped Ceiling

Deck 3
15'-7" x 6'-0"
Trellis Above

Storage
12'-0" Ceiling

Garage 2
23'-2" x 24'-6"
12'-0" Ceiling

© Sater Design Collection, Inc.

Cordillera
Plan No. 6953

SPECIFICATIONS:

Bedrooms: **4**

Baths: **5½**

Width: **126' 0"**

Depth: **141' 11"**

1st Floor: **4410 sq. ft.**

2nd Floor: **2274 sq. ft.**

Total Living: **6684 sq. ft.**

Foundation: **Slab**

PLAN PRICING:

Vellum & PDF - **$6684**

CAD - **$11363**

Padova
Plan No. 6962

Front Elevation

© Sater Design Collection, Inc.

Spanish Inspired Luxury Estate

This home is the ultimate destination for relaxation and entertainment! You'll immediately feel like you are arriving at a luxurious resort when you drive up under the dramatic porte cochere. Upon entering the grand entry doors you are greeted by a two story grand salon with a stone fireplace and curved glass wall that overlooks the pool and view beyond. Ideally positioned between the formal living areas and the leisure areas is the island wet bar for parties small and large.

The casual wing of the home is perfect for leisure. Starting with the open leisure room featuring disappearing, corner-less and pocketed sliding glass doors which embrace the wrap-around Veranda. The island kitchen with walk-in pantry overlooks the leisure room and dining nook beyond.

The luxurious master suite features a bayed sitting area, his/hers walk-in-closets, all surmounted by an elegant master bath with columned whirlpool tub and walk-in shower.

Two spacious guest suites are remotely located on the first floor for maximum comfort and privacy for guests.

Ascending the grand circular staircase to the entertainment zone of the home, guests are treated to an overview of the barrel ceilinged dining room and grand salon below. The loft is the perfect place for a game of billiards or quietly reading a good book. Grab a drink from the wet bar and make your way to the theater room to watch a movie. This level has another spacious guest suite as well as a fifth bedroom that is perfect as a bunk room for visiting grandchildren. ❖

PHOTO ABOVE: The striking wrought iron entry doors and surround set the stage for the barrel vaulted foyer and two-story living room beyond, which is accented by a carved stone fireplace. Perfect for entertaining two or twenty people.

PHOTO LEFT: Guests are greeted upon entering the home by the living room's dramatic two story ceiling and curved wall of glass beyond. The living room is defined by two Tuscan stone columns.

PHOTO FAR LEFT: Wrought iron railings overlooking the dining room and stair vestibule below. The elegant circular stairway is highlighted by the unique inverted dome ceiling above.

The beautiful carved limestone fireplace surround is the centerpiece of the home's living room. A floor to ceiling curved glass wall of segmented windows brings the outdoors in.

PHOTO LEFT: The home's kitchen is the hub of entertainment. Whether you are a gourmet chef or just a gourmand, you will love the kitchen's open and well appointed layout. The kitchen features a walk-in pantry, island counter and raised serving counter.

PHOTO BELOW: Ideally located between the formal and informal areas is the home's wet bar. In the foreground is the living room with the foyer, dining room, and circular stairway beyond.

PHOTO ABOVE: Located near the second floor loft and home's game area is the dedicated theater room, which is complete with coffered ceilings, backlit glass panels and platformed theater seating.

PHOTO FAR RIGHT: Situated under a paneled barrel vaulted ceiling is the home's formal dining room. The home's circular staircase makes a stunning backdrop to this already beautiful setting.

PHOTO RIGHT: The spacious loft area overlooks the formal areas of the home through arched openings. This space is just as perfectly suited as a game area or quiet sitting area.

PHOTO ABOVE: Padova's master suite is both roomy and intimate and includes a bay windowed sitting area and stepped tray ceiling. The French door provides easy access to outdoor areas.

PHOTO RIGHT: Pampering it's owners is what this home's master bath does best. The columned and arch wrapped master tub is a visual delight and looks out upon a private wall garden. In the background is the walk-In shower.

PHOTO FAR RIGHT: Pictured is a night time view of the home's impressive rear elevation.

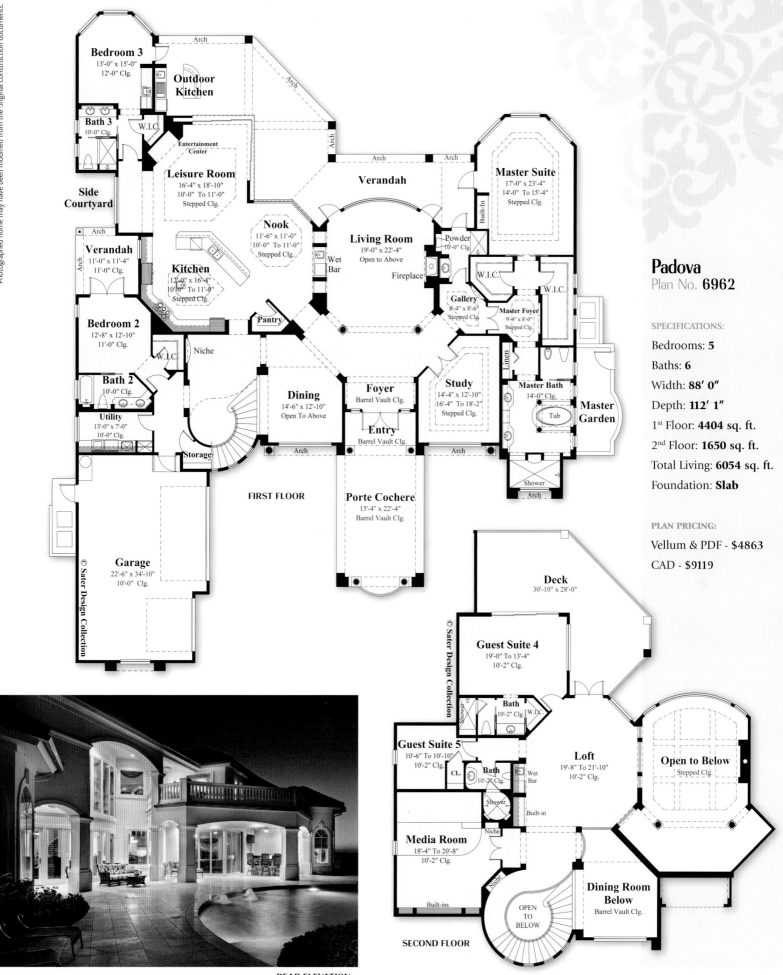

Bedroom 3
13'-0" x 15'-0"
12'-0" Clg.

Outdoor Kitchen

Arch

Arch

Arch

Bath 3
10'-0" Clg.

W.I.C.

Master Suite
17'-0" x 23'-4"
14'-0" To 15'-4"
Stepped Clg.

Arch   Arch

Entertainment Center

Leisure Room
16'-4" x 18'-10"
10'-0" To 11'-0"
Stepped Clg.

Verandah

Built-In

Side Courtyard

Nook
11'-6" x 11'-0"
10'-0" To 11'-0"
Stepped Clg.

Living Room
19'-0" x 22'-4"
Open to Above

Powder
10'-0" Clg.

Arch

Verandah
11'-0" x 11'-4"
11'-0" Clg.

Kitchen
12'-0" x 16'-4"
10'-0" To 11'-0"
Stepped Clg.

Wet Bar

Fireplace

W.I.C.

W.I.C.

Gallery
8'-4" x 8'-6"
Stepped Clg.

Master Foyer
9'-4" x 8'-0"
Stepped Clg.

Pantry

Bedroom 2
12'-8" x 12'-10"
11'-0" Clg.

W.I.C. Niche

Linen

Bath 2
10'-0" Clg.

Dining
14'-6" x 12'-10"
Open To Above

Foyer
Barrel Vault Clg.

Study
14'-4" x 12'-10"
16'-4" To 18'-2"
Stepped Clg.

Master Bath
14'-0" Clg.

Tub

Master Garden

Utility
13'-0" x 7'-0"
10'-0" Clg.

Storage

Entry
Barrel Vault Clg.

Arch   Arch

Shower

Arch

FIRST FLOOR

Porte Cochere
15'-4" x 22'-4"
Barrel Vault Clg.

Garage
22'-6" x 34'-10"
10'-0" Clg.

© Sater Design Collection

Padova
Plan No. **6962**

SPECIFICATIONS:

Bedrooms: **5**

Baths: **6**

Width: **88' 0"**

Depth: **112' 1"**

1st Floor: **4404 sq. ft.**

2nd Floor: **1650 sq. ft.**

Total Living: **6054 sq. ft.**

Foundation: **Slab**

PLAN PRICING:

Vellum & PDF - **$4863**

CAD - **$9119**

Deck
30'-10" x 28'-0"

Guest Suite 4
19'-0" To 13'-4"
10'-2" Clg.

© Sater Design Collection

Bath
10'-2" Clg.

W.I.C.

Guest Suite 5
10'-6" To 10'-10"
10'-2" Clg.

Loft
19'-8" To 21'-10"
10'-2" Clg.

Open to Below
Stepped Clg.

CL.

Bath
10'-2" Clg.

Wet Bar

Shower

Built-in

Niche

Media Room
18'-4" To 20'-8"
10'-2" Clg.

Built-ins

Niche

OPEN TO BELOW

Dining Room Below
Barrel Vault Clg.

SECOND FLOOR

REAR ELEVATION

Villa Sabina
Plan No. 8068

© Sater Design Collection, Inc.

FRONT ELEVATION

Stunning Award-Winning Home

Stone arches, corbels and cornice details accentuate the façade of this Italian-inspired home, which includes a magnificent limestone-sheathed tower and cupola. The two-story foyer, living and dining rooms invite the outdoors inside through myriad windows and glass-fronted doors. Astute architectural detailing, including several unique ceiling applications, punctuates the design premise of the home.

To the right of the foyer, a stunning staircase ascends to the second-floor loft and guest suites. The kitchen, café and family room open onto an expansive verandah with retreating glass walls. The study and master retreat are adjacent to the foyer, with easy access to the verandah.

On the optional lower level, a fully equipped kitchen and family room transition to the loggia and pool area. The rear façade is a profusion of columns, arches and a balustrade-enhanced loggia, which emphasizes the connection between the interior and outside.

PHOTO ABOVE: This spacious leisure room with arched built-ins has an open dialog with the kitchen and nook beyond.

PHOTO LEFT: This beautiful duet of wrought iron railed circular stairs is surmounted by a beautiful chandelier and radial spoked ceiling.

PHOTO FAR LEFT: Breathtaking views from the loggia, shown here with optional walkout basement.

Tall, arched windows gradually decrease in size as the spiral staircase ascends to the second floor. Scrolled, wrought-iron grillwork adorns the banister, while a beamed a appliqué-enhanced cove ceiling adds balance and depth to the space.

The two-story dining room is an amalgamation of a striking backlit coffered ceiling and scallop-edged loft overlook. A deep-set niche and glass-fronted French doors bring more intimate proportions to the room.

PHOTO LEFT: While the centerpiece of the European-styled kitchen is the appliqué- and listello-embellished cut-stone hood, the center preparation island, expansive breakfast bar, custom cabinetry and stunningly tiled backsplash all play an important role in the overall design.

PHOTO FAR LEFT: Floor-to-ceiling, veneered limestone walls complement the stone flooring and decorative cast-stone tiles that surround the tub and vanities. Dual reflections of his-and-hers vanities, with their custom milled cabinetry, are captured in separate mirrors, adding depth to the room.

PHOTO BELOW: A pair of French doors invites guests into the masculine study. A series of custom-designed built-ins have been superbly fitted into a wall of three arched niches. The fireplace, with its hand-cut, arched marble façade, comes to life against the textured, suede walls.

PHOTO ABOVE: A spiral staircase descends to the lower level, which boasts an enormous game room large enough for a variety of concurrent activities. An expansive bay-shaped wall of large paned windows reinforces the eternal connection between the indoors and outdoors.

PHOTO RIGHT: The curved loft overlooking living room and foyer is a great spot to curl up and read that favorite book.

The centerpiece of the living room is the wall of elongated windows and corresponding arched transoms, which offer incredible lake views through an exterior arched opening. The curvature of the bay window is manifest in two column-supported entryways, the ceiling's ornate circular soffit design and in the corbel-enhanced fireplace façade.

PHOTO ABOVE: In addition to the spectacular bathroom and enormous closets, the luxurious master suite boasts a morning kitchen and spacious sitting room, which opens onto the covered verandah. To spatially differentiate the room, a unique, quadruple-tiered step ceiling cloaks the sitting area, while a triple-tiered coffered ceiling blankets the bedroom area.

PHOTO RIGHT: The focal point of the gloriously appointed master bath is the elevated tub, which is enhanced by two intricately tiled steps, a pair of decorative columns and an arched stone wall. A triptych of windows draws the eye outward to the private garden. A three-paneled coffered ceiling complements the window configuration.

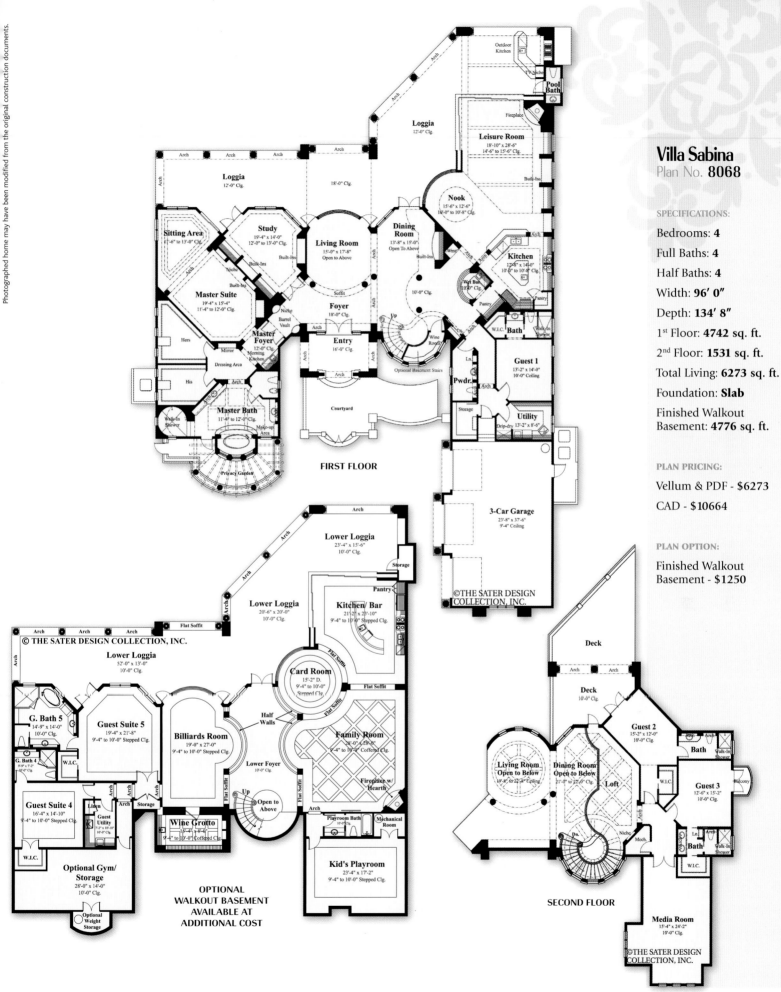

Photographed home may have been modified from the original construction documents.

Loggia
12'-0" Clg.

Loggia
12'-0" Clg.

18'-0" Clg.

Sitting Area
11'-6" to 13'-0" Clg.

Study
19'-4" x 14'-0"
12'-0" to 13'-0" Clg.

Living Room
15'-0" x 17'-8"
Open to Above

Dining Room
13'-8" x 15'-0"
Open to Above

Nook
15'-6" x 12'-6"
10'-0" to 10'-8" Clg.

Kitchen
12'-8" x 14'-0"
10'-0" to 10'-8" Clg.

Soffit

Master Suite
19'-4" x 15'-4"
11'-4" to 12'-0" Clg.

Wet Bar
10'-0" Clg.

Foyer
18'-0" Clg.

Master Foyer
12'-0" Clg.
Morning Kitchen

Dressing Area

Mirror

Entry
16'-0" Clg.

Up

Wine Room

Optional Basement Stairs

W.I.C.

Bath

Walk-In Shower

Guest 1
13'-2" x 14'-0"
10'-0" Ceiling

His

Master Bath
11'-4" x 12'-0" Clg.

Walk-In Shower

Make-up Area

Courtyard

Pwdr.

Ln.

Storage

Utility
13'-2" x 8'-6"
Drip-dry

Privacy Garden

FIRST FLOOR

Outdoor Kitchen

TV Niche

Pool Bath

Fireplace

Leisure Room
18'-10" x 28'-6"
14'-6" x 15'-6" Clg.

Built-Ins

3-Car Garage
23'-8" x 37'-6"
9'-4" Ceiling

©THE SATER DESIGN COLLECTION, INC.

Villa Sabina
Plan No. 8068

SPECIFICATIONS:

Bedrooms: **4**

Full Baths: **4**

Half Baths: **4**

Width: **96′ 0″**

Depth: **134′ 8″**

1st Floor: **4742 sq. ft.**

2nd Floor: **1531 sq. ft.**

Total Living: **6273 sq. ft.**

Foundation: **Slab**

Finished Walkout Basement: **4776 sq. ft.**

PLAN PRICING:

Vellum & PDF - $6273

CAD - $10664

PLAN OPTION:

Finished Walkout Basement - $1250

© THE SATER DESIGN COLLECTION, INC.

Lower Loggia
23'-4" x 15'-6"
10'-0" Clg.

Lower Loggia
20'-6" x 20'-0"
10'-0" Clg.

Storage

Pantry

Kitchen/ Bar
21'-2" x 23'-10"
9'-4" to 10'-0" Stepped Clg.

Flat Soffit

Lower Loggia
52'-0" x 13'-0"
10'-0" Clg.

Flat Soffit

Card Room
15'-2" D.
9'-4" to 10'-0" Stepped Clg.

Flat Soffit

G. Bath 5
14'-9" x 14'-0"
10'-0" Clg.

Guest Suite 5
19'-4" x 21'-8"
9'-4" to 10'-0" Stepped Clg.

Half Walls

Billiards Room
19'-0" x 27'-0"
9'-4" to 10'-0" Stepped Clg.

Family Room
28'-0" x 28'-0"
9'-4" to 10'-0" Coffered Clg.

G. Bath 4
9'-0" x 7'-2"
10'-0" Clg.

W.I.C.

Guest Suite 4
16'-4" x 14'-10"
9'-4" to 10'-0" Stepped Clg.

Linen

Guest Utility
7'-2" x 10'-0"
10'-0" Clg.

Storage

Up

Lower Foyer
10'-0" Clg.

Open to Above

Fireplace w/ Hearth

W.I.C.

Optional Gym/ Storage
28'-0" x 14'-0"
10'-0" Clg.

Optional Weight Storage

Wine Grotto
15'-4" x 8'-6"
9'-4" to 10'-0" Coffered Clg.

Playroom Bath
10'-0" Clg.

Mechanical Room

Kid's Playroom
23'-4" x 17'-2"
9'-4" to 10'-0" Stepped Clg.

OPTIONAL WALKOUT BASEMENT AVAILABLE AT ADDITIONAL COST

Deck

Deck
10'-0" Clg.

Living Room
Open to Below
19'-8" to 22'-8" Ceiling

Dining Room
Open to Below
21'-2" to 22'-0" Clg.

Loft

Guest 2
15'-2" x 12'-0"
10'-0" Clg.

Bath

Walk-In Shower

W.I.C.

Guest 3
12'-6" x 15'-2"
10'-0" Clg.

Balcony

Dn.

Niche

Mech.

Ln.

Bath

Walk-In Shower

W.I.C.

SECOND FLOOR

Media Room
15'-4" x 24'-2"
10'-0" Clg.

©THE SATER DESIGN COLLECTION, INC.

Ferretti
Plan No. 6786

Right Elevation

© Sater Design Collection, Inc.

A Secret Oasis Awaits Within

With its terra-cotta hued barrel roof tiles, limestone sheathed walls, stone accents and golden-hued stucco façade this is a quintessential Tuscan-inspired home. After entering the courtyard through a pair of wrought iron gates, a loggia of stone-covered pillars and arched openings travels the length of the home. Myriad windows and glass doors grace the interior walls resulting in an instant and irrevocable synergy that connects the interior and exterior spaces.

To the left of the foyer, the master suite faces the pool and seemingly draws the outdoors inward. The library is located near the foyer and adjacent to the airy kitchen, dining

and great room, which naturally transition outward onto the covered loggia and ensuing pool area. Facing the enclosed courtyard, two second-story guest suites share a common loft that opens up onto a covered balcony and pergola-shaded deck. Anchored on one side by a private guesthouse, a privacy wall encloses the courtyard, enhancing the home's oasis-like ambiance.

PHOTO ABOVE: A balcony accessed from the second-floor loft and third guest suite provides a quiet respite from a harried day to enjoy wide views of lush scenery.

PHOTO LEFT: This home features a warming outdoor fireplace adjacent to the built-in grille and outdoor kitchen, all oriented to accommodate a swim-up eating bar for swimmers enjoying the refreshing pool.

PHOTO FAR LEFT: View overlooking home's stairway landing from above.

PHOTO LEFT: The spacious kitchen and dining area, with its large center island and extended breakfast bar, transitions easily into the great room, which opens out onto the covered lanai and subsequent pool deck. Modern amenities will delight aspiring chefs; conveniences like the pot-filling spigot above the range and prep sink on the center island anticipate needs.

PHOTO FAR LEFT: Adjacent to the dining room and kitchen, the great room, with its repeating arches, beamed coffered ceiling and carved mantel, ties together like a perfectly accessorized outfit.

PHOTO BELOW: Arched niches flank the coffer ceilinged great room's fireplace. The graceful wrought iron stair rail and landing add light and interest to the space.

PHOTO ABOVE: An expansive wall of glass-fronted doors connects the master suite, with its softly hued walls and elegantly tiered ceiling, to the stunningly designed pool and spa area.

PHOTO RIGHT: The master retreat begins with an elegant foyer and boasts a spacious walk-in closet, but the crowning jewel is this luxurious master bath, spaciously designed to enhance functionality.

FIRST FLOOR

Lanai
13'-0" x 7'-0"
10'-0" Clg.

W.I.C.

Sun Tunnel

Master Foyer

10'-0" Ceiling

Skylight

Master Bath

Whirlpool

Garden

Walk-In Shower

Study/Library
12'-8" x 15'-8"
10'-8" To 12'-0"
Stepped Clg.

Niche

Foyer
12'-4" x 11'-4"
11'-0" To 12'-0"
Stepped Clg.

Master Suite
18'-4" x 16'-4"
10'-8" To 12'-0"
Stepped Clg.

Arch

Pantry

Kitchen
13'-4" x 13'-0"
10'-8" To 12'-0"
Stepped Clg.

Dining
10'-10" x 12'-5"
10'-8" To 12'-0"
Stepped Clg.

Arch

Arch

Arch

Planter

Pool

Fountain

Built-Ins

Great Room
20'-0" x 19'-8"
11'-4" To 12'-8"
Stepped Clg.

Fireplace

Built-Ins

Loggia
9'-4" x 36'-0"
10'-0" Clg.

Planter

Spa

Planter

Arch

Up

Stor.

Pwdr./Cabana

Lin.

Walk-In Shower

Portico
9'-10" x 11'-4"
10'-0" Clg.

Guest Suite
13'-0" x 11'-0"
9'-4" To 10'-0"
Tray Clg.

Outdoor Grille

Utility
10'-0" Clg.

Service/Family Entrance

Walk-In Shower

Bath
9'-0" Clg.

W.I.C.

©THE SATER DESIGN COLLECTION, INC.

Garage
20'-0" x 23'-0"
10' 0" Clg.

SECOND FLOOR

Deck
10'-4" x 11'-10"

A/C

Mech.
20'-0" x 8'-4"
7'-0" Clg.

A/C

Skylights

©THE SATER DESIGN COLLECTION, INC.

Balcony
18'-0" x 6'-0"

Loft
10'-2" x 16'-10"
9'-4" To 10'-0"
Stepped Clg.

Guest Suite 3
13'-0" x 11'-0"
9'-4" To 10'-0"
Stepped Clg.

Dn.

Bath
9'-4" Clg.

Shower

Balconette

Shower

Bath
9'-4" Clg.

W.I.C.

Guest Suite 2
13'-7" x 13'-4"
9'-4" To 10'-0"
Stepped Clg.

Ferretti
Plan No. **6786**

SPECIFICATIONS:

Bedrooms: **4**

Baths: **5**

Width: **45' 0"**

Depth: **95' 8"**

1st Floor: **2254 sq. ft.**

2nd Floor: **777 sq. ft.**

Total Living: **3031 sq. ft.**

Foundation: **Slab**

PLAN PRICING:

Vellum & PDF - $1516

CAD - $2728

PHOTO RIGHT: Essential to the home's design are the visual and physical associations that connect each interior space, including those in the detached guesthouse and second-story guest wing, to the outdoors.

La Serena
Plan No. 8076

Front Elevation

© Sater Design Collection, Inc.

Blend of Classical and Contemporary

Hipped rooflines, carved eave brackets and varied gables evoke a sense of the past in this Italianate-style design. Inside, an engaging blend of old and new prevails where beamed and coffered ceilings play counterpoint to modern amenities—cutting-edge appliances in the kitchen, a state-of-the-art utility room and retreating glass walls in the leisure room.

Past the dramatic entryway, columns line the formal rooms and foyer. The hand-carved fireplace is nestled between built-in cabinetry and lies underneath the cove-lit coffered-ceiling. Nearby, the leisure room is an open and comfortable retreat for family and guests. Centrally located between the main living areas, snacks are just a few feet away in the kitchen, retreating glass walls open up to the lanai—making indoor/outdoor entertaining a breeze and a fun-filled game room lays just beyond the art-niche foyer.

A split-bedroom floor plan ensures privacy to the master wing of the home. A generous walk-in closet provides ample storage while the master bath features luxe amenities. On the opposite wing, three guest bedrooms offer plenty of space for overnight guests.

PHOTO ABOVE: Sitting under an octagonal coffered ceiling, the leisure room is an open and comfortable retreat for family and guests. Centrally located between the main living areas, snacks are just a few feet away in the kitchen. Retreating-glass doors open up to the lanai—making indoor/outdoor entertaining a breeze.

PHOTO LEFT: The disappearing corner-less sliding glass doors open the leisure room to the pool and outdoor dining on veranda.

PHOTO FAR LEFT: Light streams in to the foyer through the sleek curved sidelights surrounding the elegant paneled door. Hand-carved Crema Maya stone columns and arches define the space, creating a fluid movement into the formal rooms.

Hand-carved Crema Maya stone columns, weighing over one-ton apiece, line the formal living room and foyer. A stunning focal point, the hand-carved fireplace surround is nestled between built-in cabinetry and lies underneath the cove-lit coffered-ceiling.

PHOTO LEFT: Towering cherry finished bookshelves frame the study's bayed windows with transoms. A perfect space to read a book or conduct business in comfort.

PHOTO BELOW: Beveled-glass surrounds the breakfast nook, and brings the outdoors in (without the bugs). From the nook are clear views of the outdoor fireplace featuring hand-painted mosaic-tile and Crema Maya stone. Repeating arches and columns line the spacious lanai.

PHOTO ABOVE: A split-bedroom floor plan provides privacy to the master wing of the home. Muted lighting creates a relaxing environment while the sitting nook provides a quiet spot for reading. A step-tray ceiling adds an elegant touch to the spacious room.

PHOTO RIGHT: To create a warm and organic feel, earth-toned slate tiles flow throughout the entire master bath. A cove-lit tray ceiling, his-and-hers vanities, spa-style tub and walk-in shower complete the luxurious retreat.

La Serena
Plan No. **8076**

WIC

Game Room
13'-6" x 15'-8"
12'-10" to 13'-6"
Stepped Clg.

Veranda
13'-6" Clg.

Walk-In Shower

Outdoor Grille

Bath 1
10'-0" Clg.

WIC

Leisure Room
19'-10" x 19'-0"
12'-0" to 13'-6"
Coffered Clg.

Nook
12'-0" Clg.

Veranda
13'-6" Clg.

Outdoor Fireplace

Sitting Area
6'-9" x 9'-8"
10'-0" Clg.

Bedroom 2
13'-4" x 13'-0"
10'-0" Clg.

Built-In Entertainment Center

Bedroom 3
13'-8" x 12'-0"
10'-0" Clg.

Kitchen
13'-8" x 13'-0"
12'-0" to 13'-6"
Stepped Clg.

Living Room
14'-10" x 20'-4"
13'-6" to 15'-0"
Coffered Clg.

Built-In

Fireplace

Built-In

Powder Bath

Master Suite
13'-10" x 20'-4"
10'-0" to 11'-0"
Stepped Clg.

Pantry

Bath 2
9'-4" Clg.

Gallery

Art Niche

WIC

Bedroom 4
11'-10" x 11'-10"
10'-0" Clg.

Ducts

Coat Closet

Utility
10'-0" x 7'-8"
10'-0" Clg.

Built-in Iron

Dining Room
11'-0" x 11'-4"
14'-0" to 15'-0"
Stepped Clg.

Foyer
13'-6" Barrel Vault

Study
19'-8" x 10'-8"
12'-0" to 13'-0"
Stepped Clg.

Lin.

Master Bath
10'-0" to 11'-4"
Tray Clg.

Storage

Entry
13'-6" Barrel Vault

Built-In

Make-Up Area

Whirlpool

Walk-In Shower

Garage 1
26'-0" x 20'-8"
10'-0" Clg. A.F.F.

FIRST FLOOR

Garage 2
11'-8" x 20'-8"
10'-0" Clg. A.F.F.

Arabella
Plan No. 6799

Front Elevation w/ Entry Gate

© Sater Design Collection, Inc.

Old World Courtyard Villa

The *Arabella's* Old World Tuscan styling is unmistakable, from its stone walled entry courtyard with bougainvillea draped trellis and wrought iron gateway, to the towering circular entry portico. This 3,433 square foot living area home plan features three bedrooms and three and a half baths. Upon entering the home's expansive coffer ceilinged foyer, one is invited to the formal dining room with its French doors that open onto another small side courtyard. Stepping through the foyer, one enters into the great room with kitchen and nook. This spacious area overlooks the veranda and views beyond.

The master suite is accessed off the foyer and features his and hers closet, as well as a third closet for storing winter clothes or perhaps maybe house those special shoes and handbags. The master bath has a walk-in shower, whirlpool tub, his/her vanities and a private dressing vanity. The master suite itself includes a sitting area and overlooks the veranda and its outdoor sitting area with fireplace.

Rounding out the home's spaces is a roomy study which overlooks the front courtyard and is accessed via double doors. The two guest suites each have walk-in closets and private baths and look out onto adjacent patio or courtyards. The conveniently located powder bath and ample utility room complete this well appointed and thoughtfully laid out floor plan.

PHOTO ABOVE: The views from the great room overlooking the expansive veranda and optional pool beyond lend to the bright airy feeling of this space. It is highlighted by a herringbone detailed beamed ceiling.

PHOTO LEFT: This open multi-purpose space lends itself to casual living. The kitchen beyond features a walk-in pantry and stone cooktop hood and is open to the casual nook that overlooks the veranda.

PHOTO FAR LEFT: A close-up view of master sitting area.

PHOTO ABOVE: The *Arabella* is just as beautiful from the rear featuring a trio of hip rooflines, the center one with a sculpted archway and hewn-wood corbels. An optional pool is shown to showcase the home's inclusivity to outdoor living.

PHOTO RIGHT: This luxurious master suite has a sitting area that overlooks the veranda and view beyond. It is highlighted by a stepped tray ceiling.

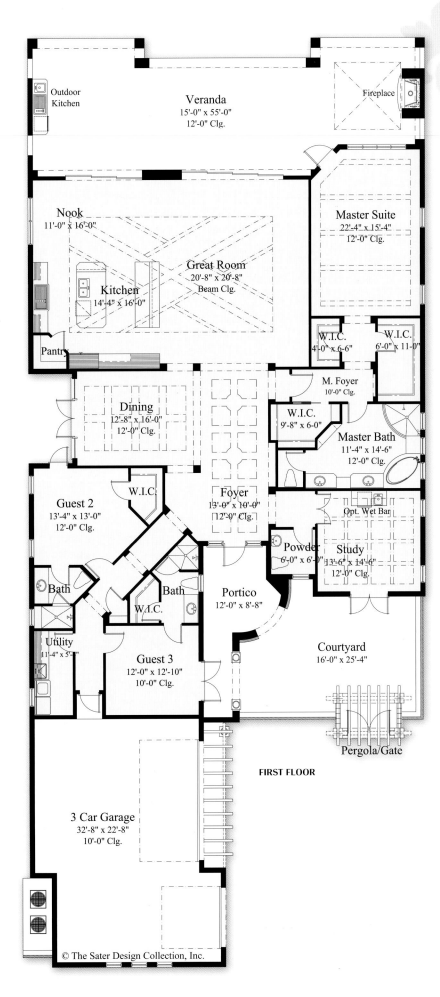

Outdoor Kitchen

Veranda
15'-0" x 55'-0"
12'-0" Clg.

Fireplace

Nook
11'-0" x 16'-0"

Master Suite
22'-4" x 15'-4"
12'-0" Clg.

Great Room
20'-8" x 20'-8"
Beam Clg.

Kitchen
14'-4" x 16'-0"

W.I.C.
4'-0" x 6'-6"

W.I.C.
6'-0" x 11'-0"

Pantry

M. Foyer
10'-0" Clg.

W.I.C.
9'-8" x 6'-0"

Dining
12'-8" x 16'-0"
12'-0" Clg.

Master Bath
11'-4" x 14'-6"
12'-0" Clg.

Guest 2
13'-4" x 13'-0"
12'-0" Clg.

W.I.C.

Foyer
13'-0" x 10'-0"
12'-0" Clg.

Opt. Wet Bar

Bath

Bath

Powder
6'-0" x 6'-0"

Study
13'-6" x 14'-6"
12'-0" Clg.

W.I.C.

Portico
12'-0" x 8'-8"

Utility
11'-4" x 5'-0"

Guest 3
12'-0" x 12'-10"
10'-0" Clg.

Courtyard
16'-0" x 25'-4"

Pergola/Gate

FIRST FLOOR

3 Car Garage
32'-8" x 22'-8"
10'-0" Clg.

© The Sater Design Collection, Inc.

Arabella
Plan No. **6799**

SPECIFICATIONS:

Bedrooms: **3**

Baths: **3½**

Width: **55′ 0″**

Depth: **124′ 8″**

1st Floor: **3433 sq. ft.**

Total Living: **3433 sq. ft.**

Foundation: **Slab**

PLAN PRICING:

Vellum & PDF - **$2231**

CAD - **$3948**

Gabriella

Plan No. **6961**

Italian Styling, Casual Living

This Mediterranean inspired estate home reflects the best in elegant yet casual living. It's turreted and varied tiled rooflines recall Old-World imagery. One is greeted by the home's combined great room and dining room upon entering. This room's soaring coffered ceiling space with pocketing sliders that open onto the home's outdoor veranda brings in plenty of natural light. A pleasant surprise is the overlooking Juliet's balcony from the loft above. Looking out upon the veranda and its outdoor fireplace and kitchen area is the home's well appointed kitchen.

The master wing with it's spacious master suite that incorporates a morning kitchen, as well as sitting room that overlooks the veranda and outdoors. The master bath features his and her closets and vanities, island whirlpool tub and walk-in shower.

The main level is rounded out with home office or optional 6th bedroom, powder bath, utility room and a detached guest cabana suite.

Upstairs is an expansive loft with three adjoining bedrooms each with it's own bath. Perfect for children or guests.

PHOTO ABOVE: This beautiful dining room and adjacent great room makes for great family gatherings and for entertaining. A pass-thru serving counter from the kitchen makes for buffet-style entertaining. Both rooms open to the outdoor veranda and pool beyond.

PHOTO LEFT: Draped columns accentuate the expansive veranda, complete with outdoor fireplace and kitchen beyond. This is easily accessible to the adjacent main kitchen.

PHOTO FAR LEFT: This wet bar is conveniently located between the dining room and kitchen for ease of entertaining.

The granite countered island with guest seating is the centerpiece of this gourmet kitchen, which overlooks the great room beyond. Wet bar is conveniently located nearby.

PHOTO LEFT: The pass-thru serving counter between kitchen and dining room is great for buffet service or for additional seating for large gatherings.

PHOTO BELOW: Dual chandeliers grace the dining room table. The arched serving counter opens to gourmet kitchen and dining nook beyond.

PHOTO LEFT: Outdoor living at its finest is accommodated by the spacious veranda complete with outdoor fireplace and kitchen beyond.

PHOTO FAR LEFT: Imagine being serenaded from the piano located in the loft above adjacent to the Juliet's balcony, which overlooks the two-story great room below. The large seating area overlooks the veranda via tall pocketing sliding glass doors and transom above.

PHOTO RIGHT:
The great room is highlighted by arched built-in TV niche and bookshelves. The full-sized over mirror resonates the homes ambiance.

Tray ceilings and bed niche accentuates the spacious master suite. The intimate sitting area is accessed through the stone columned archway and affords it's owners panoramic views of pool and view beyond.

Optional Pool Enclosure

Guest Suite
15'-4" x 15'-2"
12'-0" Clg.

W.I.C.

Pool Bath

Flat Soffit

Flat Soffit

Flat Soffit

Outdoor Shower

Exercise
9'-4" x 9'-10"
Pyramid Vault Clg.

Flat Soffit

Arch

Veranda
16'-0" x 34'-4"
11'-6" to 12'-4" Clg.

Veranda
11'-2" x 25'-2"
14'-2" Clg.

Arch

Flat Soffit

Master Suite
20'-8" x 13'-6"
12'-0" to 13'-0" Clg.

Nook
8'-0" x 10'-6"
11'-4" Clg.

Kitchen
20'-0" x 17'-8"
11'-4" to 12'-0" Clg.

Built-Ins

Living Room
19'-11" x 21'-4"
Open to Above

Dining Room
19'-10" x 9'-0"
12'-0" Clg.

Arch

W.I.C.

W.I.C.

Island

Arch

Arch

Niche

Arch   Arch   Arch   Arch   Arch   Arch

Arch

Linen

Arch

Foyer
16'-0" Clg.

Arch

Arch

Arch

Wine Cellar

Family Valet

Arch

Arch

Pwdr. Bath
9'-4" Clg.

Study/ Bedroom 5
18'-4" x 12'-0"
11'-0" Clg.

Master Bath
17'-0" x 14'-8"
12'-0" to 12'-8" Clg.

Seat

Make-up Area

Arch   Arch   Arch

Portico
6'-10" x 11'-0"
13'-4" Clg.

Arch

Arch

Arch

Closet

Desk

Utility
7'-8" x 12'-0"
10'-0" Clg.

FIRST FLOOR

4 Car Garage
46'-2" x 24'-0"
10'-0" Clg.

Covered Balcony
8'-4" x 18'-4"
9'-4" Clg.

Deck

Bath 1
13'-0" x 9'-3"
9'-4" Clg.

W.I.C.

Bedroom 1
17'-4" x 12'-0"
9'-4" Clg.

Bedroom 2
17'-7" x 12'-0"
9'-4" Clg.

Bath 2
10'-0" x 5'-10"
9'-4" Clg.

W.I.C.

Open to Below

Arch

Loft/Game Room
28'-0" x 20'-10"
9'-4" Clg.

Bath 3
9'-8" x 6'-0"
9'-4" Clg.

W.I.C.

© The Sater Design Collection, Inc.

Arch

Dn

Built-Ins

Bedroom 3
17'-0" x 12'-4"
9'-4" Clg.

SECOND FLOOR

© The Sater Design Collection, Inc.

Gabriella
Plan No. **6961**

SPECIFICATIONS:

Bedrooms: **6**

Baths: **5½**

Width: **80' 4"**

Depth: **150' 0"**

1st Floor: **3702 sq. ft.**

2nd Floor: **1612 sq. ft.**

Total Living: **5314 sq. ft.**

Foundation: **Slab**

PLAN PRICING:

Vellum & PDF - **$5314**

CAD - **$9034**

PHOTO LEFT: The pool is overlooked by a balcony that serves two of the homes upstairs guest suites.

Dimora
Plan No. 6954

Front Elevation

© Sater Design Collection, Inc.

French Influenced Resort Home

Corbelled cornices, decorative quoin elements and keystone enhanced arches, coupled with a capriciously gabled roofline reinforce the home's French inspired design. The true essence of the home is the amalgamation of interior and exterior spaces, thus maximizing the spatiality and functionality of the home. While myriad windows and glass doors strengthen the constant connection between the inside and outdoors, the study, dining and living rooms transition freely into one another.

To the left of the foyer, the wet bar differentiates the informal and formal venues. In the kitchen and family room, retreating glass walls open onto the covered lanai and pool deck, creating a "room without walls." To the right of the foyer, the master suite, with its large sitting alcove, oversized walk-in closet and luxuriously appointed bath and private courtyard, is a serene milieu that is unsurpassed.

PHOTO ABOVE: Retreating glass walls seemingly pull the outdoors inside toward the family room, kitchen and nook, creating a large, wide-open living space. Enhanced by custom millwork elements, the family room's exaggerated sloped tray ceiling creates a cozy ambiance.

PHOTO LEFT: Custom designed, floor-to-ceiling built-ins enhance the study's distinctly understated, yet masculine character. Bordering the master suite, the focal point of the room is the triple-tiered, octagonal-shaped ceiling, into which a dropped soffit detail has been skillfully introduced.

PHOTO FAR LEFT: With its generously curved, two-tiered granite countertop and stone-enhanced art niche, the wet bar serves as an anchor, joining the casual family room and kitchen to the formal living and dining areas.

PHOTO LEFT: The detailed, triple-tiered ceiling envelops the magnificent dining room. From the large art niche to the glass-fronted French doors, which effortlessly travel outdoors, every detail comes together as one, creating a picture-perfect design.

PHOTO FAR LEFT: An enormous, three-panel mitered window accentuates the curvature of the room, drawing the eye toward the pool's spectacularly conceived water feature. The highly crowned, triple-tiered ceiling mimics the shape of the room strengthening the rapport between the interior and exterior elements.

PHOTO RIGHT: The kitchen, with its octagonal-shaped, beamed coffered ceiling and center prep island, opens up into the family room and nook. The angled breakfast bar and arched side entries define the exclusivity of the separate spaces while at the same time joining them as one.

PHOTO ABOVE: Through a row of windows in the bay-shaped sitting alcove, as well as through a pair of adjacent French doors, a profusion of sunlight explodes in the luxuriously detailed master suite. The double-tiered coffered ceiling adds depth and interest, resulting in a peaceful owners' retreat.

PHOTO RIGHT: Set back into an arched niche, a large mirror captures reflections of the adjoining private courtyard. In the center of the room, the tile surround and deck of the oval-shaped tub incorporates the same intricate detailing as in the stunning walk-in shower.

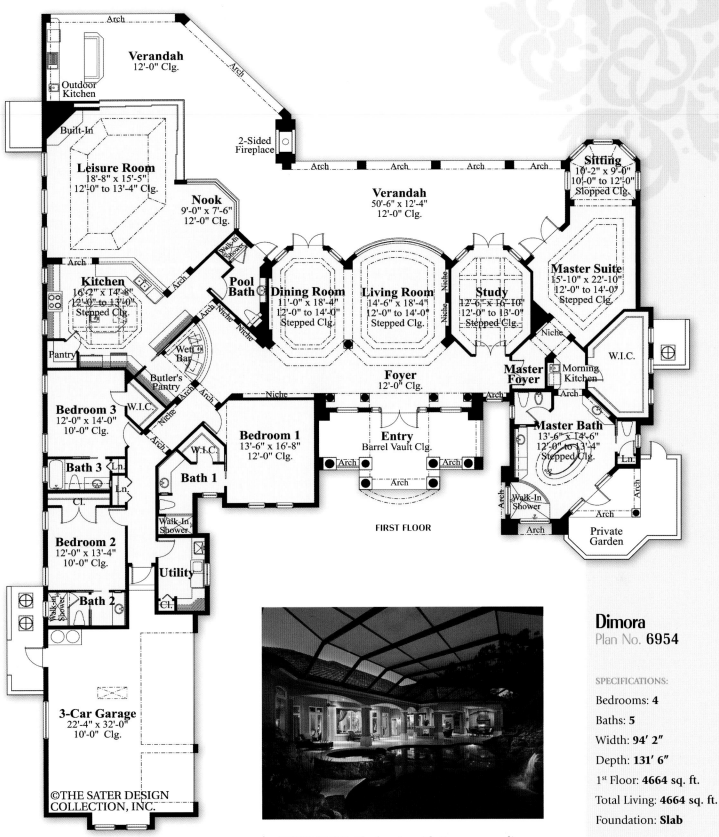

Verandah
12'-0" Clg.

Outdoor Kitchen

Arch

2-Sided Fireplace

Built-In

Leisure Room
18'-8" x 15'-5"
12'-0" to 13'-4" Clg.

Nook
9'-0" x 7'-6"
12'-0" Clg.

Verandah
50'-6" x 12'-4"
12'-0" Clg.

Arch   Arch   Arch   Arch

Sitting
10'-2" x 9'-0"
10'-0" to 12'-0"
Slopped Clg.

Walk-In Shower

Kitchen
16'-2" x 14'-8"
12'-0" to 13'-0"
Stepped Clg.

Pool Bath

Dining Room
11'-0" x 18'-4"
12'-0" to 14'-0"
Stepped Clg.

Living Room
14'-6" x 18'-4"
12'-0" to 14'-0"
Stepped Clg.

Study
12'-6" x 16'-10"
12'-0" to 13'-0"
Stepped Clg.

Master Suite
15'-10" x 22'-10"
12'-0" to 14'-0"
Stepped Clg.

Pantry

Arch

Wet Bar

Niche   Niche

Niche   Niche

Master Foyer

Morning Kitchen

W.I.C.

Butler's Pantry

W.I.C.

Bedroom 3
12'-0" x 14'-0"
10'-0" Clg.

Niche

Foyer
12'-0" Clg.

Niche

Arch

Master Bath
13'-6" x 14'-6"
12'-0" to 13'-4"
Stepped Clg.

Ln.

Bath 3

W.I.C.

Bedroom 1
13'-6" x 16'-8"
12'-0" Clg.

Entry
Barrel Vault Clg.

Arch   Arch

Arch

Cl.

Ln.

Bath 1

Arch

Walk-In Shower

Bedroom 2
12'-0" x 13'-4"
10'-0" Clg.

Walk-In Shower

FIRST FLOOR

Arch

Ln.

Utility

Private Garden

Walk-In Shower

Bath 2

Cl.

3-Car Garage
22'-4" x 32'-0"
10'-0" Clg.

©THE SATER DESIGN COLLECTION, INC.

Dimora
Plan No. **6954**

SPECIFICATIONS:

Bedrooms: **4**

Baths: **5**

Width: **94' 2"**

Depth: **131' 6"**

1st Floor: **4664 sq. ft.**

Total Living: **4664 sq. ft.**

Foundation: **Slab**

PLAN PRICING:

Vellum & PDF - $3032

CAD - $5364

PHOTO ABOVE: The loggia, with its corresponding columns and broadly arched openings, spans from one side of the home to the other, strengthening the transition and connectivity of the indoors to the outdoors through copious window walls and entryways.

Martinique
Plan No. 6932

Front Elevation

© Sater Design Collection, Inc.

A Hint of Sun-Drenched Tuscan Charm

Clearly Mediterranean-inspired, with a barrel-tile roof in terra-cotta hues, lancet arches and Tuscan columns, the sun-drenched façade of this home extends a formal welcome. Crisp, white trim speaks of Spanish influence, and iron detailing adds a hint of sun drenched Tuscan charm.

Past the foyer, an open floor plan emphasizes outdoor living with a seamless transition of indoor and outdoor spaces. Columns, built-ins and ceiling treatments define rooms, while a flowing floor plan creates natural movement.

The formal living room is punctuated by natural light welcomed in by floor-to-ceiling windows. The openness of the leisure room, nook and kitchen create casual gathering areas extended by ample outdoor spaces.

Spacious guest accommodations on both floors assure that visitors stay in comfort. Guests enjoy private or semi-private full baths and private spaces – a garden on the first floor and a loft upstairs.

PHOTO ABOVE: Elegant arches and stunning wood columns define the dining space while giving it a unique connection to the diamond-shaped living room. More wood adds drama to a stepped ceiling, and three dramatic windows provide natural light and an effortless connection to the veranda.

PHOTO LEFT: This extra-large study has it all: a wall of custom cabinetry, another of windows overlooking a front garden, a stepped ceiling and lots of floor space for working and relaxing.

PHOTO LEFT: The handcrafted built-in entertainment center and molded ceiling details provide drama to the spacious leisure room, which opens seamlessly onto the veranda's outdoor kitchen and main entertainment space.

PHOTO FAR LEFT: Well-appointed and well-planned, this kitchen boasts ample storage for tools of the trade and two large islands that add lots of workspace. Ornate woodwork on the cabinetry and soffits adds an exotic flair to this ultra-functional room.

PHOTO RIGHT: Draped floor to ceiling bay picture windows immerse the living room with natural light and open it upon the views beyond. The beamed ceiling gives a rich canopy to this beautiful room.

A stepped ceiling with molding details and elegant lighting crowns a generous master suite. An art niche separates two walk-in closets and provides a visually appealing entry to a fully appointed master bedroom.

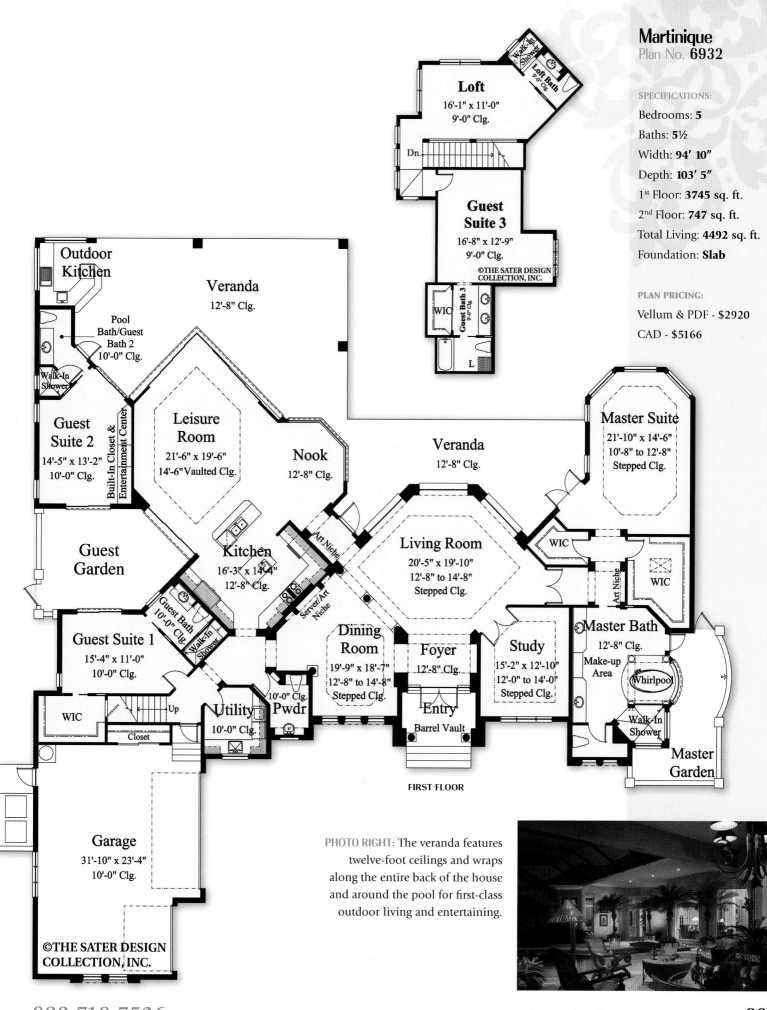

Martinique
Plan No. **6932**

SPECIFICATIONS:

Bedrooms: **5**

Baths: **5½**

Width: **94′ 10″**

Depth: **103′ 5″**

1st Floor: **3745** sq. ft.

2nd Floor: **747** sq. ft.

Total Living: **4492** sq. ft.

Foundation: **Slab**

PLAN PRICING:

Vellum & PDF - $2920

CAD - $5166

Loft
16'-1" x 11'-0"
9'-0" Clg.

Walk-In Shower

Loft Bath
9'-0" Clg.

Dn.

Guest Suite 3
16'-8" x 12'-9"
9'-0" Clg.

©THE SATER DESIGN COLLECTION, INC.

WIC

Guest Bath 3
9'-0" Clg.

L

FIRST FLOOR

Outdoor Kitchen

Veranda
12'-8" Clg.

Pool Bath/Guest Bath 2
10'-0" Clg.

Walk-In Shower

Guest Suite 2
14'-5" x 13'-2"
10'-0" Clg.

Built-In Closet & Entertainment Center

Guest Garden

Leisure Room
21'-6" x 19'-6"
14'-6" Vaulted Clg.

Nook
12'-8" Clg.

Veranda
12'-8" Clg.

Master Suite
21'-10" x 14'-6"
10'-8" to 12'-8"
Stepped Clg.

WIC

Kitchen
16'-3" x 14'4"
12'-8" Clg.

Art Niche

Living Room
20'-5" x 19'-10"
12'-8" to 14'-8"
Stepped Clg.

WIC

Art Niche

WIC

Guest Bath
10'-0" Clg.

Walk-In Shower

Server/Art Niche

Guest Suite 1
15'-4" x 11'-0"
10'-0" Clg.

Dining Room
19'-9" x 18'-7"
12'-8" to 14'-8"
Stepped Clg.

Foyer
12'-8" Clg.

Study
15'-2" x 12'-10"
12'-0" to 14'-0"
Stepped Clg.

Master Bath
12'-8" Clg.

Make-up Area

Whirlpool

WIC

Up

Utility
10'-0" Clg.

Pwdr
10'-0" Clg.

Entry
Barrel Vault

Walk-In Shower

Closet

Garage
31'-10" x 23'-4"
10'-0" Clg.

Master Garden

©THE SATER DESIGN COLLECTION, INC.

PHOTO RIGHT: The veranda features twelve-foot ceilings and wraps along the entire back of the house and around the pool for first-class outdoor living and entertaining.

Palazzo Ripoli
Plan No. 8074

Front Elevation

© Sater Design Collection, Inc.

Innovative Old World Design

The elegant European façade will provide an Old-World flair to any streetscape. Arches line the cloister flowing from the detached guest suite to the barrel-vault entry of this innovative design. Inside, the grand salon welcomes with commanding views past the loggia and a two-sided fireplace shared with the study. A walk-in wet bar adjoins the kitchen and provides a servery to the formal areas. Retreating glass walls open the leisure room to the outside amenities. Multiple connections to the outdoors are present throughout the plan courtesy of French doors, walls of windows, and retreating walls of glass. To the left of the plan the master wing is an indulgent retreat for the owners, particularly with its luxurious his-and-hers amenities located throughout the spacious retreat. Two additional guest suites have ensuite baths and are located on the opposite side of the plan, enhancing privacy for all.

PHOTO ABOVE: Two kitchen islands, one with an eating bar, dual sinks, and plentiful cabinetry come together to make this spacious kitchen spectacular.

PHOTO LEFT: The formal living room greets guests and offers a wall of windows to enjoy views of the pool area. A two-sided fireplace is shared with the study.

PHOTO FAR LEFT: The formal dining room is open, and yet secluded by a distinguished ceiling, with a wet bar providing refreshments. Formal dining occasions are sure to be memorable beneath the elegant stepped ceiling, with a built-in buffet server to ease entertaining.

PHOTO RIGHT: A quiet haven, the sumptuous master suite enjoys access to a private sitting area and a door to the loggia.

PHOTO RIGHT: A luxurious master bath retreat boasts a center tub, walk-in shower, dual vanities and also overlooks a privacy garden complete with a tranquil fountain.

PHOTO LEFT: This beautiful outdoor living area also offers a separate pool bath and an outdoor kitchen area with an eating bar.

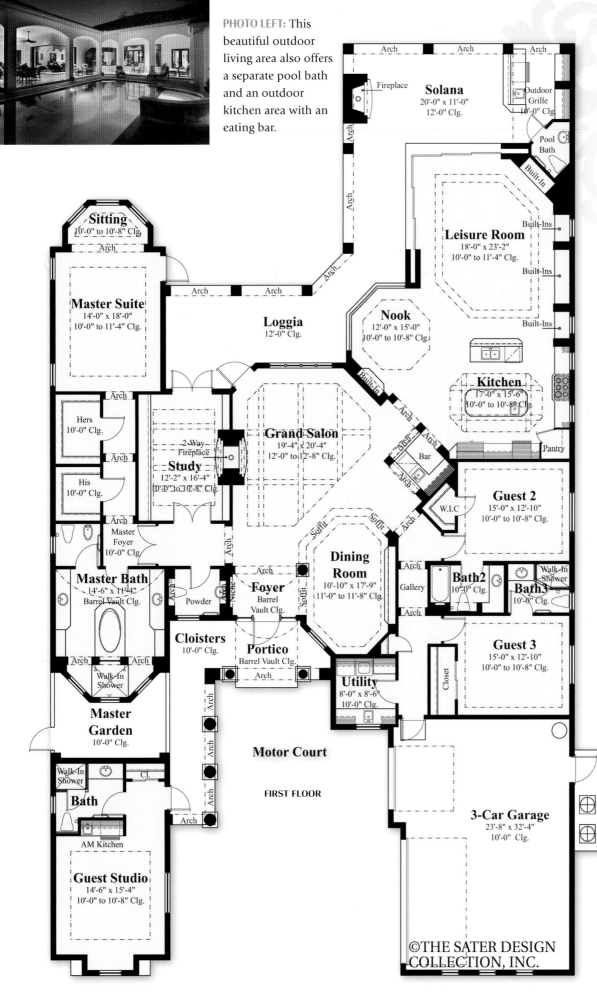

Sitting
10'-0" to 10'-8" Clg.
Arch

Master Suite
14'-0" x 18'-0"
10'-0" to 11'-4" Clg.

Hers
10'-0" Clg.

His
10'-0" Clg.

Arch

Master Foyer
10'-0" Clg.

Master Bath
14'-6" x 11'-4"
Barrel Vault Clg.

Walk-In Shower

Master Garden
10'-0" Clg.

Walk-In Shower
Cl.

Bath

AM Kitchen

Guest Studio
14'-6" x 15'-4"
10'-0" to 10'-8" Clg.

Loggia
12'-0" Clg.
Arch   Arch   Arch

Study
12'-2" x 16'-4"
10'-0" to 10'-8" Clg.

2-Way Fireplace

Grand Salon
19'-4" x 20'-4"
12'-0" to 12'-8" Clg.

Cloisters
10'-0" Clg.

Portico
Barrel Vault Clg.
Arch

Foyer
Barrel Vault Clg.

Powder   Niche

Dining Room
10'-10" x 17'-9"
11'-0" to 11'-8" Clg.

Soffit   Soffit

Motor Court

FIRST FLOOR

Fireplace

Solana
20'-0" x 11'-0"
12'-0" Clg.

Arch   Arch   Arch

Outdoor Grille
10'-0" Clg.

Pool Bath

Leisure Room
18'-0" x 23'-2"
10'-0" to 11'-4" Clg.

Built-In
Built-Ins
Built-Ins
Built-Ins

Nook
12'-0" x 15'-0"
10'-0" to 10'-8" Clg.

Kitchen
17'-0" x 15'-6"
10'-0" to 10'-8" Clg.

Built-In

Bar

W.I.C

Pantry

Guest 2
15'-0" x 12'-10"
10'-0" to 10'-8" Clg.

Gallery

Bath2
10'-0" Clg.

Walk-In Shower

Bath3
10'-0" Clg.

Guest 3
15'-0" x 12'-10"
10'-0" to 10'-8" Clg.

Closet

Utility
8'-0" x 8'-6"
10'-0" Clg.

3-Car Garage
23'-8" x 32'-4"
10'-0" Clg.

©THE SATER DESIGN COLLECTION, INC.

Palazzo Ripoli
Plan No. **8074**

SPECIFICATIONS:

Bedrooms: **4**

Full Baths: **4**

Half Baths: **2**

Width: **69' 10"**

Depth: **120' 0"**

1st Floor: **4266 sq. ft.**

Total Living: **4266 sq. ft.**

Foundation: **Slab**

PLAN PRICING:

Vellum & PDF - **$2773**

CAD - **$4906**

San Filippo
Plan No. 8055

Front Elevation

Spacious and Light-filled

Circular windows echo the curves of the arched transoms and sculpted colonnade of this striking façade. A deeply recessed entry plays counterpoint to two bold turrets that step into the landscape, extending the footprint of the home. Spacious, light-filled rooms allow unencumbered views throughout the interior. The pure geometry of the plan plays raw nature against historic details and 21st century accoutrements. A massive hearth in the living room reinforces the ancient charm of tapered columns along the gallery, while French doors bring in scenery and light. Angled lines melt into the outdoors with walls of retreating glass in the morning nook and kitchen. Guests may step into a side courtyard from a flex room that easily converts into a study. A family valet, conveniently located, provides the perfect place to drop your keys and packages.

From the old-country styling of the central turret to the high ceilings and gracefully arched doorways and windows, San Filippo melds award-winning design with comfortable living. Experience breathtaking vistas immediately upon entering the foyer, where an open floor plan allows views directly into the formal dining and living rooms and out through multiple French doors to the veranda.

Nearby, the open kitchen also affords unobstructed views of the nook and leisure room. Retreating glass doors expand the common living space to the outdoor living areas. Upstairs, French doors open two of the four guest bedrooms to a private deck overlooking the veranda. Enjoying privacy away from the rest of the home, the

master retreat must be seen to be believed. The homeowners will relish the massive bedroom, gorgeously stepped ceiling, veranda access and opulent master bath.

PHOTO ABOVE: Retreating glass doors open the kitchen, nook and leisure room to the veranda where multiple outdoor living areas are found, including a fireplace with built-in entertainment center.

PHOTO LEFT: On the upper level, a guest bedroom was converted into a state-of-the-art media room. Custom built-ins and a spectacular home theater create a gathering place like no other for friends and family.

PHOTO FAR LEFT: The wet bar is one of several modifications that the homeowners inserted in the design. The arched doorways connect multiple open areas nearby, including a butler's pantry and dining nook.

PHOTO LEFT: A perfect combination of function and style, the kitchen includes a stepped ceiling, convenient pantry and work island with prep sink. It's also a very open area affording easy access to a nearby nook and leisure room.

PHOTO FAR LEFT: The grand, two-story barrel-vault ceiling is sure to impress, and the careful attention to detail will not go unnoticed. From the transom-topped glass doors leading to the veranda, to the elegant art niches that flank the soaring fireplace, this living room can be the centerpiece of family gatherings and large-scale entertaining alike.

PHOTO BELOW: The loft balcony creates an elegant overlook to the open living room below, while at the same time creating a dining room area with a lower ceiling for cozy, intimate meals.

PHOTO RIGHT: The master suite is the very picture of quiet, private grace, featuring a stepped ceiling and striking bat window overlooking the pool.

PHOTO RIGHT: Designed to be an indulgent retreat, the master bath offers repose with a whirlpool tub and a generous walk-thru shower framed by a triple set of circular windows and repeating arches.

FIRST FLOOR

Pool Bath

Outdoor Grille

Veranda
29'-9" x 24'-4" Avg.
10'-0" Clg.

Leisure Room
20'-4" x 17'-4"
9'-4" to 10'-0"
Stepped Clg.

Built-In Entertainment

Nook
9'-4" Clg.

Veranda
18'-2" x 8'-8"
14'-2" Clg.

Master Suite
15'-0" x 21'-6"
12'-0" to 13'-0"
Stepped Clg.

Kitchen
13'-8" x 14'-8"
9'-4" to 10'-0"
Stepped Clg.

Courtyard

Pantry

Dining Room
10'-0" x 14'-2"
9'-0" to 10'-0"
Stepped Clg.

Living Room
18'-2" x 14'-2"
Open to Above

Fireplace

WIC

WIC

Study/ Bedroom 5
12'-2" x 13'-8"
10'-0" Clg.

Laundry Chute

Foyer
16'-0" Clg.

Art Niche

Bath 1
10'-0" Clg.

Opt. Closet

Storage

Family Valet

Wine Cellar

Walk-In Shower

Up

Portico
18'-8" x 7'-4"
13'-4" Clg.

Whirlpool

M. Bath
12'-0" to 12'-8"
Stepped Clg.

Coat Closet

Walk-In Shower

Utility
8'-2" x 6'-0"
10'-0" Clg.

Garage
23'-0" x 31'-2"
10'-0" Clg.

©THE SATER DESIGN COLLECTION, INC.

San Filippo
Plan No. 8055

SPECIFICATIONS:

Bedrooms: **6**

Baths: **4½**

Width: **69' 4"**

Depth: **95' 4"**

1st Floor: **2913 sq. ft.**

2nd Floor: **1471 sq. ft.**

Total Living: **4384 sq. ft.**

Foundation: **Slab**

PLAN PRICING:

Vellum & PDF - **$2854**

CAD - **$5050**

SECOND FLOOR

©THE SATER DESIGN COLLECTION, INC.

Deck
35'-1" x 8'-0"

Walk-In Shower

Bedroom 2
14'-0" x 13'-0"
9'-4" Clg.

Bath 2
9'-4" Clg

Bedroom 1
13'-5" x 13'-10"
9'-4" Clg.

WIC

WIC

Bedroom 3
16'-2" x 12'-0"
9'-4" Clg.

Loft
10'-10" x 13'-8"
9'-4" Clg.

Open to Below
18'-4" to 19'-4"
Vaulted Clg.

Bath 3
9'-4" Clg

WIC

Bedroom 4
12'-4" x 14'-0"
9'-4" Clg.

WIC

Laundry Chute

Storage Room

Dn.

Open to Below

PHOTO ABOVE: Allowing boisterous and fun outdoor gatherings to quite late-night contemplations, the indoor and outdoor living spaces provides many different opportunities for family and friends.

Casina Rossa
Plan No. 8071

Front Elevation

© Sater Design Collection, Inc.

Tuscany Inspired Country Estate

Tuscan columns articulate an elegant portico that's merely the beginning of this Old World villa. Rough hewn stone accents the striking tower as well as master bath wall. Inside a beamed ceiling contributes a sense of spaciousness to the heart of the home, while walls of French doors draw the outdoors inside. A repertoire of perennial elements satisfies a singular architectural theme: varied ceiling treatments and sculpted arches define the wide-open interior permitting flexibility as well as great views. The great room is anchored by a massive fireplace flanked by built-in shelves and an entertainment center—visible from the kitchen via an arched pass-through. A private foyer in the master wing links the owners' bedroom and dressing space with a sensational bath that boasts a whirlpool tub and a walk-in shower. Plenty of windows brighten this suite, which provides separate access to the veranda.

PHOTO ABOVE: The stone mantel fireplace with arched built-ins feature ample room for television, storage, pictures and more. Wood beams accentuate the vaulted ceiling and give warmth to the room.

PHOTO LEFT: This beautiful vaulted and beamed great room overlooks the veranda and optional pool beyond via three sets of double French doors. A fireplace with arched built-ins is at one end and is served by the kitchen at the other through an arched serving counter.

PHOTO FAR LEFT: Optional view of great room without fireplace.

PHOTO ABOVE: The rear of home with broad veranda supported via cast stone Tuscan columns creates a warm and elegant appearance. Shown with optional pool and terrace.

PHOTO RIGHT: The spacious master suite features a sitting alcove and stepped tray ceiling with crown moulding as well as views to veranda.

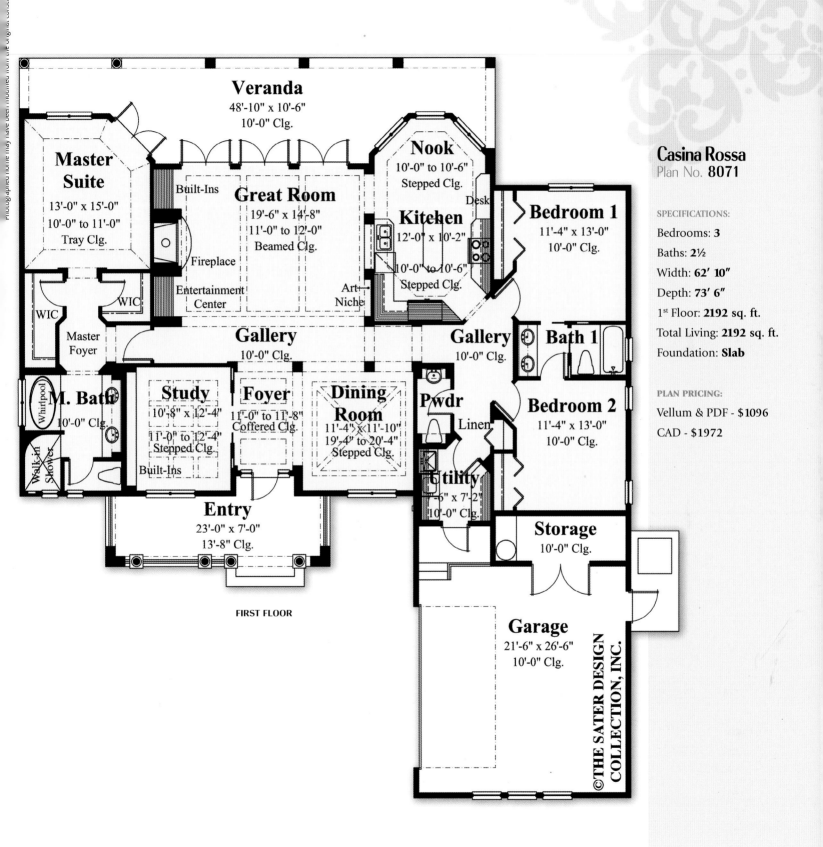

Veranda
48'-10" x 10'-6"
10'-0" Clg.

Master Suite
13'-0" x 15'-0"
10'-0" to 11'-0"
Tray Clg.

Nook
10'-0" to 10'-6"
Stepped Clg.

Built-Ins

Great Room
19'-6" x 14'-8"
11'-0" to 12'-0"
Beamed Clg.

Desk

Kitchen
12'-0" x 10'-2"
10'-0" to 10'-6"
Stepped Clg.

Bedroom 1
11'-4" x 13'-0"
10'-0" Clg.

Fireplace

Entertainment Center

Art Niche

WIC

WIC

Gallery
10'-0" Clg.

Gallery
10'-0" Clg.

Bath 1

Master Foyer

M. Bath
10'-0" Clg.

Whirlpool

Study
10'-8" x 12'-4"
11'-0" to 12'-4"
Stepped Clg.

Built-Ins

Foyer
11'-0" to 11'-8"
Coffered Clg.

Dining Room
11'-4" x 11'-10"
19'-4" to 20'-4"
Stepped Clg.

Pwdr

Linen

Bedroom 2
11'-4" x 13'-0"
10'-0" Clg.

Walk-in Shower

Utility
7'-6" x 7'-2"
10'-0" Clg.

Entry
23'-0" x 7'-0"
13'-8" Clg.

Storage
10'-0" Clg.

FIRST FLOOR

Garage
21'-6" x 26'-6"
10'-0" Clg.

© THE SATER DESIGN COLLECTION, INC.

Casina Rossa
Plan No. **8071**

SPECIFICATIONS:

Bedrooms: **3**

Baths: **2½**

Width: **62' 10"**

Depth: **73' 6"**

1st Floor: **2192 sq. ft.**

Total Living: **2192 sq. ft.**

Foundation: **Slab**

PLAN PRICING:

Vellum & PDF - **$1096**

CAD - **$1972**

La Reina
Plan No. 8046

Impressive Street Presence

Derived from a blend of cultural influences—including Moorish and Renaissance—this clearly Mediterranean elevation creates an impressive, yet not imposing, street presence. Trios of windows bring light to interior spaces, and accentuate rows of decorative tile vents that line the façade. Carved balusters enhance a side balcony that's spacious enough to serve as an outdoor room. The paneled portal opens to a portico and courtyard, which creates a procession to the formal entry of the home. To the front of the courtyard, a casita, or guesthouse, offers space that easily converts to a workshop or home office. The foyer opens directly to the grand room and through an arched opening, to the formal dining room. Glass bayed walls in the central living area and in the study help meld inside and outside spaces, and the dining room leads to a loggia—for open-air meals..

View of entr portico with fountain in foreground.

Centrally located between the formal and informal rooms, the gourmet-caliber kitchen serves both realms with ease. A wraparound eating bar offers "patrons" a place to sit, while the center island with prep sink provides ample counter space for the family "chef".

PHOTO LEFT: Designed for privacy and appointed in elegance, the master suite features a high stepped ceiling and generous views through the suite's multi-paned windows and transoms. French doors provide access to the loggia.

PHOTO FAR LEFT: Soaring two-story ceilings allow for voluminous views and light to stream in through numerous windows that encircle the room. A grand fireplace provides a central gathering area, and a flowing design offers an open avenue to the dining room nearby.

PHOTO LEFT: This master bath opens to the impressive courtyard area and features a whirlpool tub soaked in light from the outdoors, a beautifully stepped ceiling and arches setting off the suite's vanities.

Not only visually stunning, the courtyard is a Zen-like retreat for family and friends to relax and unwind. A mix of retreating glass walls and French doors in the master retreat, dining room, detached guest suite and leisure room integrate the interior with the expansive outdoor living area.

PHOTO LEFT: Light streams in to the bayed breakfast nook through multi-paned windows. A built-in window seat offers storage and a cozy place to sit. Past the archway, the open foyer leads to the grand room.

Photographed home may have been modified from the original construction documents.

©THE SATER DESIGN COLLECTION, INC.

Balcony
10'-12" x 9'-4"

Grand Room
Beamed Clg.
Open to Below

Bedroom 2
10'-11" x 13'-4"
10'-0" Clg.

Open to Below

WIC

Bath 2
10'-0" Clg.

Linen

Dn.

Bath 3
10'-0" Clg.
Walk-In Shower

Balcony
10'-7" x 14'-4"

Bedroom 3
15'-0" x 11'-6"
10'-0" Clg.

WIC

WIC

WIC

Bedroom 4
11'-6" x 16'-8"
10'-0" Clg.

Balcony

SECOND FLOOR

Loggia
26'-10" x 11'-8"
Open to Above

Loggia
15'-6" x 10'-0"
10'-0" Clg.

Master Suite
14'-8" x 22'-4"
12'-0" to 14'-0"
Stepped Clg.

Built-In

Grand Room
19'-0" x 19'-5"
21'-0" to 22'-4"
Open to Above

Dining Room
10'-6" x 13'-4"
10'-0" Clg.

Whirlpool

WIC

Pwdr.
9'-4" Clg.

Foyer

Built-In Server

Utility
6'-8" x 9'
10'-0" Clg.

M. Bath
12'-0" to 14'-0"
Stepped Clg.

WIC

Linen

Up

Study
14'-4" x 15'-0"
12'-0" to 13'-0"
Stepped Clg.

Loggia
10'-0" Clg.

Desk

Walk-In Shower

Kitchen
13'-8" x 15'-4"
10'-0" Clg.

Nook
10'-0" Clg.

Pantry

Fountain

Spa

Optional Pool

Courtyard

Loggia
16'-8" Clg.

Leisure Room
18'-6" x 17'-10"
10'-0" to 14'-6"
Stepped Clg.

Garage
11'-6" x 16'-10"
10'-0" Clg.

Fireplace

Built-In Entertainment

©THE SATER DESIGN COLLECTION, INC.

Loggia
10'-0" Clg.

Outdoor Kitchen

Portico
14'-8" x 14'-4"
Groin Vault

Garage
22'-4" x 25'-6"
10'-0" Clg.

Guest Suite
14'-4" x 13'-5"
10'-0" Clg.

WIC

Pool Bath
10'-0" Clg.

FIRST FLOOR

La Reina
Plan No. **8046**

SPECIFICATIONS:

Bedrooms: **5**

Baths: **4½**

Width: **80' 0"**

Depth: **96' 0"**

1st Floor: **2852 sq. ft.**

2nd Floor: **969 sq. ft.**

Total Living: **4151 sq. ft.**

Foundation: **Slab**

PLAN PRICING:

Vellum & PDF - **$2698**

CAD - **$4774**

Melito
Plan No. 6555

FRONT ELEVATION

© Sater Design Collection, Inc.

Stunning Italian Courtyard Home

This luxury Mediterranean narrow courtyard home creates a private sanctuary to enjoy the outdoors. An airy atmosphere is created because the master suite, great room, dining room, and guest rooms are all open to the porch. The great room and kitchen enjoy coffered ceilings, while the master suite offers a stepped ceiling. The kitchen has plenty of counter space, including a center island. Offering little luxuries, the master suite has his and her closets, a dual vanity, walk-in closet and shower, and a whirlpool tub. The master suite is on the opposite of the house from the guest rooms to offer privacy. The cabana and its private bathroom are disconnected from the house, which makes it a perfect guest retreat. The second floor showcases a generous loft, an extra bedroom and bathroom, and petite deck.

PHOTO ABOVE: Vaulted ceilings with hewn wood beams extend the length of the open kitchen/ great room space. The arched entertainment niche and island kitchen are but, a few of this homes many features.

PHOTO LEFT: The wrap-around loggia overlooks the courtyard and optional pool.

PHOTO FAR LEFT: View of upstairs guest suite balcony and ground floor cabana as seen from courtyard.

PHOTO RIGHT: The spacious master suite with stepped tray ceiling overlooks the loggia and courtyard through large sliding glass doors.

PHOTO RIGHT: The master bath features a double vanity, arched soffit and whirlpool tub for relaxation.

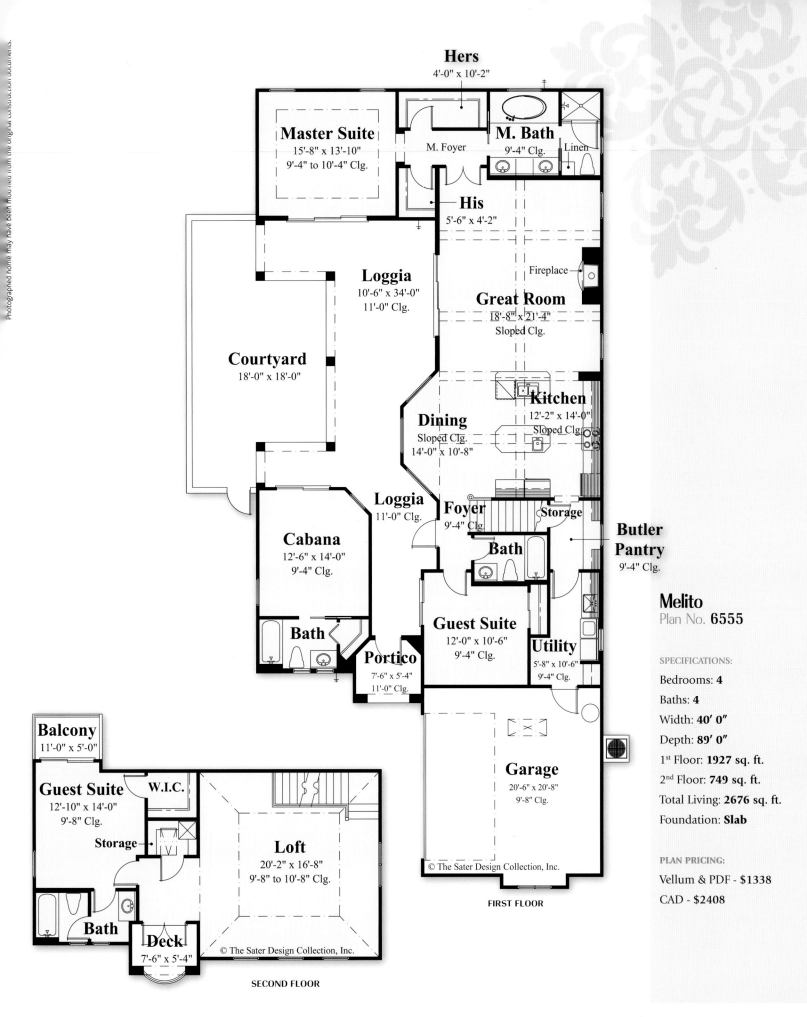

Hers
4'-0" x 10'-2"

Master Suite
15'-8" x 13'-10"
9'-4" to 10'-4" Clg.

M. Bath
9'-4" Clg.

M. Foyer

Linen

His
5'-6" x 4'-2"

Loggia
10'-6" x 34'-0"
11'-0" Clg.

Fireplace

Great Room
18'-8" x 21'-4"
Sloped Clg.

Courtyard
18'-0" x 18'-0"

Kitchen
12'-2" x 14'-0"
Sloped Clg.

Dining
Sloped Clg.
14'-0" x 10'-8"

Loggia
11'-0" Clg.

Foyer
9'-4" Clg.

Storage

Cabana
12'-6" x 14'-0"
9'-4" Clg.

Bath

Butler Pantry
9'-4" Clg.

Bath

Portico
7'-6" x 5'-4"
11'-0" Clg.

Guest Suite
12'-0" x 10'-6"
9'-4" Clg.

Utility
5'-8" x 10'-6"
9'-4" Clg.

Garage
20'-6" x 20'-8"
9'-8" Clg.

© The Sater Design Collection, Inc.

FIRST FLOOR

Balcony
11'-0" x 5'-0"

Guest Suite
12'-10" x 14'-0"
9'-8" Clg.

W.I.C.

Storage

Loft
20'-2" x 16'-8"
9'-8" to 10'-8" Clg.

Bath

Deck
7'-6" x 5'-4"

© The Sater Design Collection, Inc.

SECOND FLOOR

Melito
Plan No. **6555**

SPECIFICATIONS:

Bedrooms: **4**

Baths: **4**

Width: **40' 0"**

Depth: **89' 0"**

1st Floor: **1927 sq. ft.**

2nd Floor: **749 sq. ft.**

Total Living: **2676 sq. ft.**

Foundation: **Slab**

PLAN PRICING:

Vellum & PDF - $1338

CAD - $2408

Porto Velho
Plan No. 6950

Front Elevation

© Sater Design Collection, Inc.

Fabulous Family Living

Spectacular design creates balance and harmony in this outstanding Mediterranean manor. From private guest suites to a wide-open floor plan that melds with a wrapping verandah, the Porto Velho offers infinite charm and function without sacrificing the ultimate in luxury living appointments. The façade invites, with a dramatic, recessed and turreted entry enhanced by multiple arched windows framed with balusters. Inside, the foyer opens to a vaulted great room with views stretching well beyond the retreating glass wall. The master suite is allotted an entire wing and a forward dining room and study, both with octagonal stepped ceilings, provide first-class environments for entertaining and private studies.

A spacious, centralized great room anchors the 4,500 square foot plan. A wall of built-ins is perfect for media components, books and treasures. Another wall is lined with pocketing glass doors, throwing the room open to the verandah and pool area. The gourmet kitchen is accessed through three archways that mimic the Mediterranean windows gracing the front of the home. A breakfast nook, walk-in pantry and powder bath complete the core of the home.

Even the home's small spaces are intimately planned, such as the entry foyer to the master suite. The full-length niche is art in itself, with its elegant wall treatment, soft lighting and tasteful accessories. Every amenity for fabulous family living and memorable entertaining is accentuated inside this highly crafted European flavored home, from wide open rooms that meld with the outdoors to richly detailed private spaces.

PHOTO ABOVE: An elaborately carved center island, hand-rubbed cabinetry and a stunning carved-stone hood add drama to this has-it-all gourmet kitchen. There's even a desk nook through the arched doorway.

PHOTO LEFT: Rustic beams lend texture to the vaulted ceiling of the wide open great room, where glass doors pocket into the walls to extend the room outdoors and elegant arches grant access to the kitchen and its gracious serving counter.

PHOTO FAR LEFT: Tall Tuscan columns and a wooden pergola frame a stunning courtyard. Located near the outdoor kitchen, this plein air living room is idyllic for a lazy Sunday brunch.

PHOTO RIGHT: The molded, stepped ceiling is a dramatic canopy to this regal master bedroom, where floor-to-ceiling windows frame a cozy sitting nook and glass doors disappear to access a private corner of the verandah. Two walk-in closets and a sumptuous bath complete the suite.

PHOTO RIGHT: A center spa tub rests inside gleaming wood and granite, offering an opulent focal point for the master bath. A window-framed, walk-in shower is tucked beneath the curved and wrought iron-adorned wall behind the tub.

Verandah
20'-6" x 35'-8"
12'-0" Clg.

Outdoor Kitchen

Verandah
9'-3" x 40'-7"
12'-0" Clg.

Nook
13'-2" x 13'-2"
Vaulted Clg.

Master Suite
18'-4" x 19'-4"
12'-0"-13'-0"
Stepped Clg.

Guest Suite 2
13'-4" x 16'-0"
12'-0" Clg.

Bath 2
10'-0"

Great Room
23'-3" x 22'-0"
Vaulted Clg.

Stor.

Built-In

Kitchen
16'-0" x 16'-0"
12'-0" Clg.

Bath 1
10'-0" Clg.

WIC

Pantry

Pwdr.

WIC

Gallery

Master Bath
12'-0" Clg.

WIC

Art Niche

Arch

Arch

Arch

Linen

WIC

Guest Suite 1
14'-0" x 13'-2"
12'-0" Clg.

Arch

Desk

Drip Dry

Utility
10'-0" Clg.

Dining Room
13'-2" x 13'-10"
12'-0"-16'-6"
Stepped Clg.

Foyer
12'-0" Clg.

Study
14'-9" x 16'-3"
12'-0"-13'-0"
Stepped Clg.

Built-In

Whirlpool Tub

Storage

Gladiator Workbench

Gladiator Freezerator

Spa Sink

Gallery

Up

Arch

Arch

Entry

Walk-In Shower

Privacy Garden

Garage
24'-8" x 30'-8"
8'-8" Clg.

© THE SATER DESIGN COLLECTION, INC.

FIRST FLOOR

Down

Guest Room
17'-6" x 18'-6"
Vaulted Clg.

TV Niche

© THE SATER DESIGN COLLECTION, INC.

Guest Bath

WIC

SECOND FLOOR

Porto Velho
Plan No. **6950**

SPECIFICATIONS:

Bedrooms: **4**

Baths: **4½**

Width: **105' 9"**

Depth: **100' 9"**

1st Floor: **3947 sq. ft.**

2nd Floor: **545 sq. ft.**

Total Living: **4492 sq. ft.**

Foundation: **Slab**

PLAN PRICING:

Vellum & PDF - **$2920**

CAD - **$5166**

PHOTO LEFT: A beautiful pool with sun shelf and elevated spa glows with reflected light from the striking rear rooms that wrap the verandah.

Mercato
Plan No. 8028

Front Elevation

© Sater Design Collection, Inc.

Italianate Inspired Villa

Spiral columns articulate an elegant arcade that's merely the beginning of this Mediterranean villa. Highlighted by a towering dining room element with cast stone corbels and clerestory arched windows. Inside a beamed ceiling contributes a sense of spaciousness to the heart of the home, while walls of glass draw the outdoors inside. A repertoire of palazzo-sur-mer forms satisfies a singular architectural theme: varied ceiling treatments and sculpted arches define the wide-open interior, permitting flexibility as well as great views. The great room is anchored by a massive fireplace flanked by built-in shelves and an entertainment center—visible from the kitchen via an arched pass-through. A private foyer in the master wing links the owners' bedroom and dressing space with a sensational bath that boasts a whirlpool tub and a walk-in shower. Plenty of windows brighten this suite, which provides separate access to the veranda. ❖

PHOTO ABOVE: The arched built-ins feature ample room for television, storage, pictures and more. Wood beams accentuate this space and give warmth to the room.

PHOTO LEFT: The spacious master suite features a sitting alcove and stepped tray ceiling with crown moulding as well as views to veranda.

PHOTO LEFT: Optional view of great room without fireplace.

PHOTO BELOW: The rear of home with broad veranda supported via cast stone roped columns creates a warm and elegant appearance. Shown with optional pool and terrace.

Veranda
48'-10" x 10'-6"
10'-0" Clg.

Master Suite
13'-0" x 15'-0"
10'-0" to 11'-0"
Tray Clg.

Built-Ins

Great Room
19'-6" x 14'-8"
11'-0" to 12'-0"
Beamed Clg.

Fireplace

Entertainment Center

Nook
10'-0" to 10'-6"
Stepped Clg.

Desk

Kitchen
12'-0" x 10'-2"

10'-0" to 10'-6"
Stepped Clg.

Art Niche

Bedroom 1
11'-4" x 13'-0"
10'-0" Clg.

WIC

WIC

Master Foyer

Gallery
10'-0" Clg.

Gallery
10'-0" Clg.

Bath 1

M. Bath
10'-0" Clg.

Whirlpool

Walk-in Shower

Study
10'-8" x 12'-4"
11'-0" to 12'-4"
Stepped Clg.
Built-Ins

Foyer
11'-0" to 11'-8"
Coffered Clg.

Dining Room
11'-4" x 11'-10"
19'-4" to 20'-4"
Stepped Clg.

Pwdr

Linen

Bedroom 2
11'-4" x 13'-0"
10'-0" Clg.

Utility
5'-6" x 7'-2"
10'-0" Clg.

Entry
23'-0" x 7'-0"
13'-8" Clg.

Storage
10'-0" Clg.

Garage
21'-6" x 26'-6"
10'-0" Clg.

©THE SATER DESIGN COLLECTION, INC.

FIRST FLOOR

Mercato
Plan No. **8028**

SPECIFICATIONS:

Bedrooms: **3**

Baths: **2½**

Width: **62' 10"**

Depth: **73' 6"**

1st Floor: **2192 sq. ft.**

Total Living: **2192 sq. ft.**

Foundation: **Slab**

PLAN PRICING:

Vellum & PDF - **$1096**

CAD - **$1973**

Winthrop
Plan No. 8034

Front Elevation

© Sater Design Collection, Inc.

A Modern Flowing Chateau

Sculpted corbels, slump arches, and parapeted dormers conceal a 21st-century interior tied to its provenance with ornate millwork, chic moulding, cornices and angled arcades. The integrity of the design is further enhanced by coffered and stepped ceiling treatments, and slender, vertical windows with transoms. A highly sophisticated arrangement of public and private rooms, places this plan firmly into tomorrow-like themes. At the center of the home, the living room, dining room and foyer open to one another and when the corner-less glass doors retreat, space extends to the wrapping rear lanai. Convenient for alfresco meals, the leisure room corner-less glass doors here also roll away, blurring the inside/ outside relationship with an outdoor kitchen on the lanai. Authentic detailing plays in harmony with cutting-edge technology throughout the home, particularly in the kitchen, where Euro cabinetry and stainless steel culinary appliances reside together.

PHOTO ABOVE: Centrally located between the public spaces and informal rooms, the gourmet-caliber kitchen is designed to easily serve both. A center prep island, wraparound eating bar, and plenty of storage and counter space meld style with function.

PHOTO LEFT: Flexible spaces that easily adapt to the owners' lifestyles—the kitchen, nook and leisure room—gracefully flow into one common living space. Stepped ceilings provide subtle definition to the rooms.

PHOTO FAR LEFT: The centerpiece of the formal living room is the grand hearth, with its ornately carved mantel supported by decorative corbels. Retreating glass doors bring in views of the outdoors and expand the living space to the lanai.

PHOTO RIGHT: Past the double-door entry, the master suite is a four-star retreat. A morning kitchen, dual walk-in closets, luxe bath, sitting nook and sliding glass doors to the lanai create a haven from the hectic pace of everyday life.

PHOTO RIGHT: Symmetrical arches add grace, serenity and splendor to a master bath complete with an oversized whirlpool tub and walk-in shower. To enhance the spa-like experience, multiple windows bring in views of the private garden.

PHOTO RIGHT: Retreating walls of glass and multiple sets of windows integrate the interior with the expansive outdoor living spaces. An outdoor kitchen ensures easy entertaining for the homeowners, while friends and family enjoy the pool.

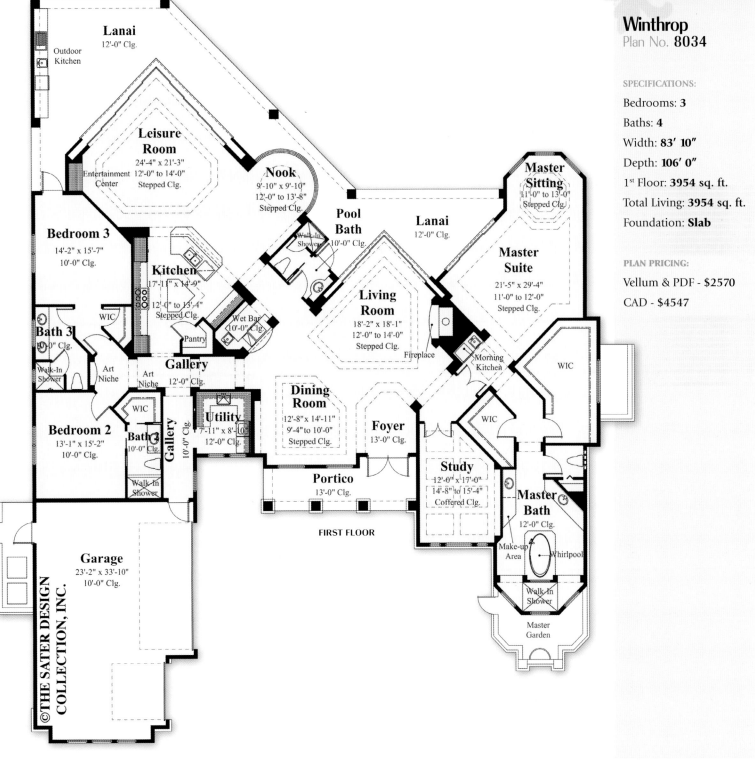

Lanai
12'-0" Clg.

Outdoor Kitchen

Leisure Room
24'-4" x 21'-3"
12'-0" to 14'-0"
Stepped Clg.

Entertainment Center

Nook
9'-10" x 9'-10"
12'-0" to 13'-8"
Stepped Clg.

Bedroom 3
14'-2" x 15'-7"
10'-0" Clg.

Kitchen
17'-11" x 14'-9"
12'-0" to 13'-4"
Stepped Clg.

Pool Bath
10'-0" Clg.

Walk-In Shower

Lanai
12'-0" Clg.

Master Sitting
11'-0" to 13'-0"
Stepped Clg.

WIC

Bath 3
10'-0" Clg.

Walk-In Shower

Art Niche

Wet Bar
10'-0" Clg.

Pantry

Living Room
18'-2" x 18'-1"
12'-0" to 14'-0"
Stepped Clg.

Master Suite
21'-5" x 29'-4"
11'-0" to 12'-0"
Stepped Clg.

Fireplace

Morning Kitchen

WIC

Gallery
12'-0" Clg.

Art Niche

Dining Room
12'-8" x 14'-11"
9'-4" to 10'-0"
Stepped Clg.

WIC

Bedroom 2
13'-1" x 15'-2"
10'-0" Clg.

WIC

Bath
10'-0" Clg.

Walk-In Shower

Utility
7'-11" x 8'-10"
12'-0" Clg.

Gallery
10'-0" Clg.

Foyer
13'-0" Clg.

Study
12'-0" x 17'-0"
14'-8" to 15'-4"
Coffered Clg.

Master Bath
12'-0" Clg.

Portico
13'-0" Clg.

Make-up Area

Whirlpool

FIRST FLOOR

Garage
23'-2" x 33'-10"
10'-0" Clg.

Walk-In Shower

Master Garden

Winthrop
Plan No. **8034**

SPECIFICATIONS:

Bedrooms: **3**

Baths: **4**

Width: **83' 10"**

Depth: **106' 0"**

1st Floor: **3954 sq. ft.**

Total Living: **3954 sq. ft.**

Foundation: **Slab**

PLAN PRICING:

Vellum & PDF - **$2570**

CAD - **$4547**

Wulfert Point
Plan No. 6688

Front Elevation

© Sater Design Collection, Inc.

Roman Flavored Brick Villa

The Wulfert Point draws inspiration from many European styles, represented in the exterior's façade and the rich architectural detailing of this truly unique home. These photos show this client's unique adaptation in brick, but the original plans are detailed in stucco. All about the views, this house positions every common room to at least have a glimpse of, if not be fully oriented toward, its natural surroundings. Fountains, planters and covered porches merge with windows, French doors and an open floor plan to blend indoor and outdoor living. The Charleston inspired side courtyard design fulfills the needs of relaxation and exercise at home.

The second level is reserved for the private bedrooms and bathrooms and includes the master suite and two secondary bedrooms. The master retreat features large walk-in closets and a self-contained master bath. This level boasts its own wraparound covered porch accessible from two bedrooms (including the master) and the hall.

Downstairs, the gourmet kitchen incorporates a step-saving design and services the great room through a pass-thru, while the large central island serves as a prep area as well as a place for quick meals. The bonus room/guest suite performs as a self-sufficient studio apartment or distinctly separate home office. The separate entrance grants it independence from the house proper..

PHOTO ABOVE: The open layout throughout the first floor is centered around a popular hub of activity: the kitchen. Boasting copious counter space as well as a large work island, this kitchen is suitable for cooks of all skill levels.

PHOTO LEFT: Observance of nature is at its finest from the covered porch, inviting you to relish every hour of the day. This space calls for enjoyment of a refreshing or soothing beverage, perhaps coffee in the morning tranquility, ice tea in the afternoon breeze or tea as the moon rises.

PHOTO FAR LEFT: A Tuscan flavor is given to the home's interior, especially with the stone accents in the home's foyer.

The spacious great room interacts easily with both the kitchen and dining room, while providing breathtaking views of the scenery to the rear of the property. Three sets of French doors open onto the covered porch.

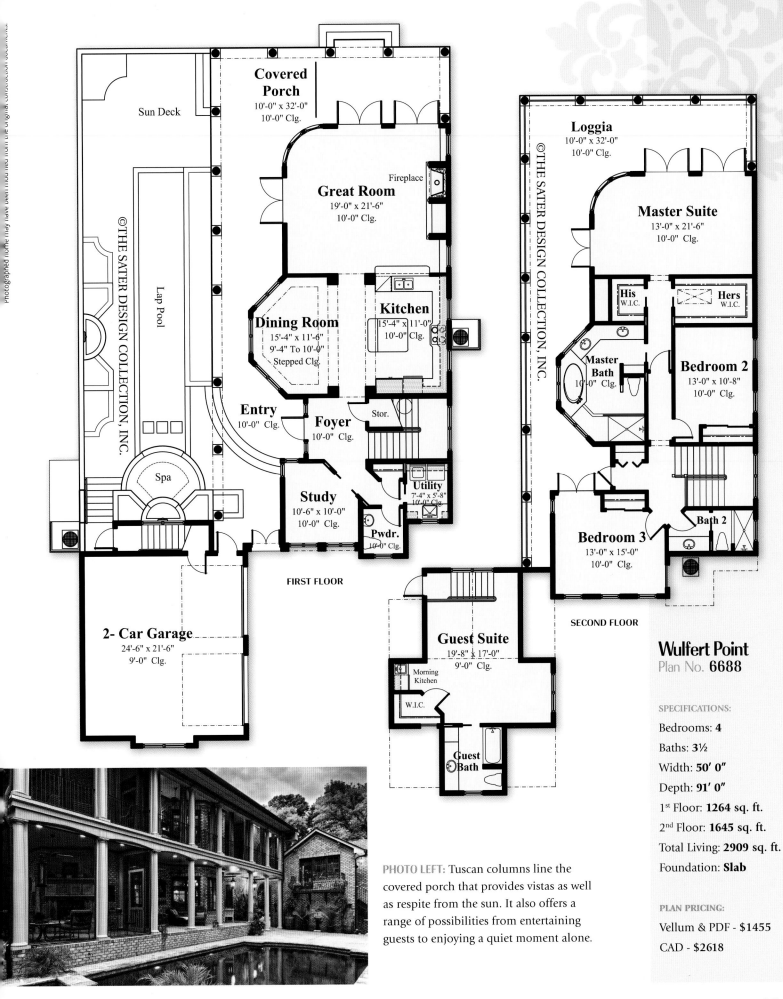

Covered Porch
10'-0" x 32'-0"
10'-0" Clg.

Sun Deck

©THE SATER DESIGN COLLECTION, INC.

Lap Pool

Great Room
19'-0" x 21'-6"
10'-0" Clg.

Fireplace

Kitchen
15'-4" x 11'-0"
10'-0" Clg.

Dining Room
15'-4" x 11'-6"
9'-4" To 10'-0"
Stepped Clg.

Entry
10'-0" Clg.

Foyer
10'-0" Clg.

Stor.

Spa

Study
10'-6" x 10'-0"
10'-0" Clg.

Utility
7'-4" x 5'-8"
10'-0" Clg.

Pwdr.
10'-0" Clg.

FIRST FLOOR

2- Car Garage
24'-6" x 21'-6"
9'-0" Clg.

Loggia
10'-0" x 32'-0"
10'-0" Clg.

©THE SATER DESIGN COLLECTION, INC.

Master Suite
13'-0" x 21'-6"
10'-0" Clg.

His W.I.C.

Hers W.I.C.

Master Bath
10'-0" Clg.

Bedroom 2
13'-0" x 10'-8"
10'-0" Clg.

Bath 2

Bedroom 3
13'-0" x 15'-0"
10'-0" Clg.

SECOND FLOOR

Guest Suite
19'-8" x 17'-0"
9'-0" Clg.

Morning Kitchen

W.I.C.

Guest Bath

Wulfert Point
Plan No. 6688

SPECIFICATIONS:

Bedrooms: **4**

Baths: **3½**

Width: **50' 0"**

Depth: **91' 0"**

1st Floor: **1264 sq. ft.**

2nd Floor: **1645 sq. ft.**

Total Living: **2909 sq. ft.**

Foundation: **Slab**

PLAN PRICING:

Vellum & PDF - $1455

CAD - $2618

PHOTO LEFT: Tuscan columns line the covered porch that provides vistas as well as respite from the sun. It also offers a range of possibilities from entertaining guests to enjoying a quiet moment alone.

Vasari

Plan No. 8025

Front Elevation

© Sater Design Collection, Inc.

Compact Luxury Villa

A stunning window-lined turret, classic columns and repeating arches create a striking façade. An uninhibited spirit prevails within—where a gallery foyer and loft deepen the central living/dining room, allowing a stepped ceiling to soar above open vistas defined only by decorative columns. A two-sided fireplace warms the central area as well as a study that boasts a private porch. A view-oriented leisure room enjoys multiple connections with the outdoors. The openness of the kitchen/nook/leisure room creates a flexible, informal area that is perfect for spending time with friends and family. Above the entry, a sun porch with French doors permits sunlight to invigorate the loft—an inviting space that connects the family's sleeping quarters with a private guest suite. The main level brags a cabana-style guest suite, with access to a compartmented bath and shower from the veranda.

PHOTO ABOVE: The kitchen is no longer just for cooking—it's where everyone gathers and where favorite moments are shared. That means the kitchen must be open unrestrained by walls, free to spill out into other areas just like guests do when you're entertaining or hosting family events.

PHOTO LEFT: Options for comfortable gathering abound throughout the plan's open kitchen area, breakfast nook and leisure room. Arched doorways provide access to the veranda, pool, shore and beyond.

PHOTO FAR LEFT: Overlooking the stairway and landing embraced with an arched bay of windows.

PHOTO ABOVE: *Vasari* has been created with gathering, vacationing and entertaining in mind—but it can also be for escaping. The plan's master retreat includes its own foyer and porch, ideal for seeking impressive, secluded refuge while still remaining under the same roof.

PHOTO RIGHT: The plan's master retreat is rounded out by a master bath—including whirlpool and walk-in shower—also accessed by its own foyer, as well as a massive, two-sided walk-in closet.

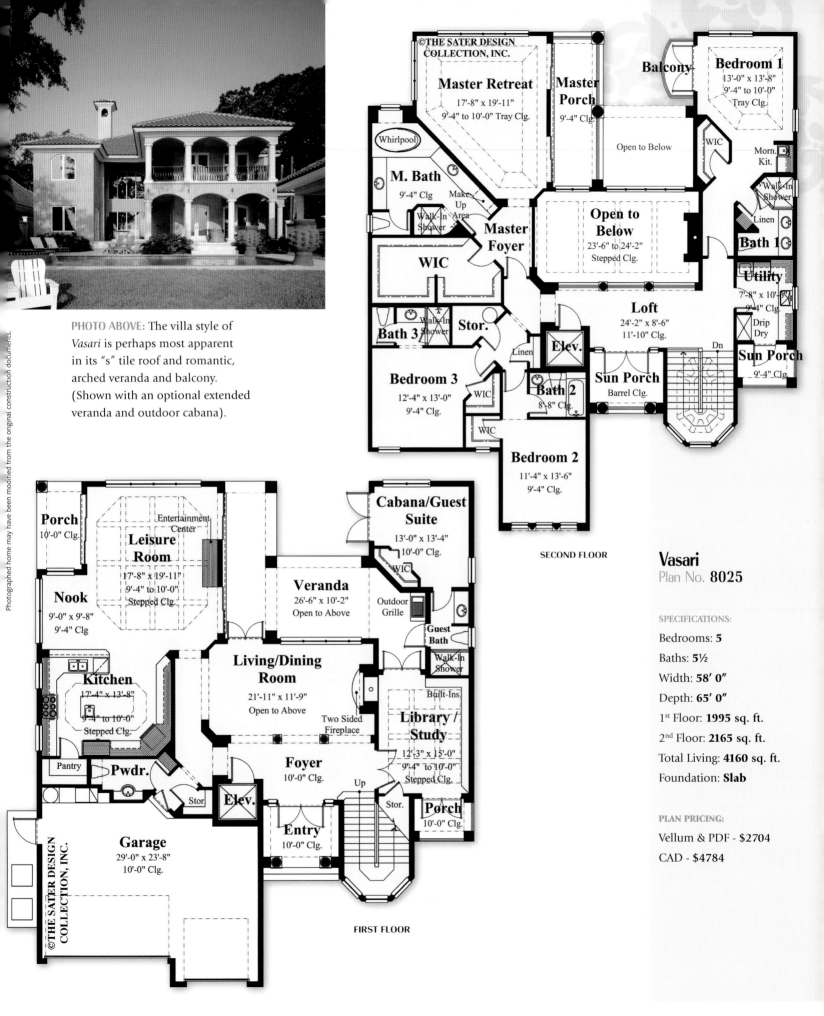

PHOTO ABOVE: The villa style of *Vasari* is perhaps most apparent in its "s" tile roof and romantic, arched veranda and balcony. (Shown with an optional extended veranda and outdoor cabana).

©THE SATER DESIGN COLLECTION, INC.

SECOND FLOOR

Master Retreat 17'-8" x 19'-11" 9'-4" to 10'-0" Tray Clg.

Master Porch 9'-4" Clg.

Balcony

Bedroom 1 13'-0" x 13'-8" 9'-4" to 10'-0" Tray Clg.

Whirlpool

M. Bath 9'-4" Clg.

Make Up Area

Walk-In Shower

Open to Below

WIC

Morn. Kit.

Walk-In Shower

Linen

Bath 1

Master Foyer

WIC

Open to Below 23'-6" to 24'-2" Stepped Clg.

Utility 7'-8" x 10'-7" 9'-4" Clg.

Walk-In Shower

Bath 3

Stor.

Loft 24'-2" x 8'-6" 11'-10" Clg.

Drip Dry

Linen

Elev.

Dn

Bedroom 3 12'-4" x 13'-0" 9'-4" Clg.

WIC

Bath 2 8'-8" Clg.

Sun Porch Barrel Clg.

Sun Porch 9'-4" Clg.

WIC

Bedroom 2 11'-4" x 13'-6" 9'-4" Clg.

FIRST FLOOR

Porch 10'-0" Clg.

Entertainment Center

Leisure Room 17'-8" x 19'-11" 9'-4" to 10'-0" Stepped Clg.

Cabana/Guest Suite 13'-0" x 13'-4" 10'-0" Clg.

WIC

Nook 9'-0" x 9'-8" 9'-4" Clg

Veranda 26'-6" x 10'-2" Open to Above

Outdoor Grille

Kitchen 17'-4" x 13'-8" 9'-4" to 10'-0" Stepped Clg.

Living/Dining Room 21'-11" x 11'-9" Open to Above

Guest Bath

Walk-In Shower

Pantry

Pwdr.

Two Sided Fireplace

Built-Ins

Library / Study 12'-3" x 15'-0" 9'-4" to 10'-0" Stepped Clg.

Foyer 10'-0" Clg.

Stor.

Elev.

Up

Stor.

Porch 10'-0" Clg.

Garage 29'-0" x 23'-8" 10'-0" Clg.

Entry 10'-0" Clg.

©THE SATER DESIGN COLLECTION, INC.

Vasari
Plan No. **8025**

SPECIFICATIONS:

Bedrooms: **5**

Baths: **5½**

Width: **58' 0"**

Depth: **65' 0"**

1st Floor: **1995 sq. ft.**

2nd Floor: **2165 sq. ft.**

Total Living: **4160 sq. ft.**

Foundation: **Slab**

PLAN PRICING:

Vellum & PDF - **$2704**

CAD - **$4784**

English

Old World elegance balances modern sensibilities to create home plans with a strong sense of history and beauty. Combining the very best of formal design with casual comfort, these English-inspired homes offer unique and exciting opportunities for gracious family living. Rugged exterior textures, stately gables and pediments, arches and plentiful windows create a welcoming ambiance reminiscent of the English countryside. Inside, experience the impact of beautifully detailed staircases, vaulted, beamed and stepped ceilings, and copious views of the open rooms and outdoor living areas.

Coach Hill

Plan No. 8013

REAR ELEVATION

SPECIFICATIONS:

Bedrooms: **4**

Baths: **4½**

Width: **70' 0"**

Depth: **100' 0"**

1st Floor: **3030 sq. ft.**

2nd Floor: **1638 sq. ft.**

Total Living: **4668 sq. ft.**

Bonus Room: **290 sq. ft.**

Foundation: **Slab**

PLAN PRICING:

Vellum & PDF - **$3028**

CAD - **$5357**

A striking balcony, bay turret and pediment dormers add curb appeal to this English country design. The foyer surrounds a spiral staircase, enhanced with a dome ceiling and clerestory windows. A stepped ceiling and arched columns define the forward formal room, permitting an unobstructed view of the rear property. Plenty of natural light enters the interior through the two-story bow window in the living room, which shares a two-sided fireplace with the study.

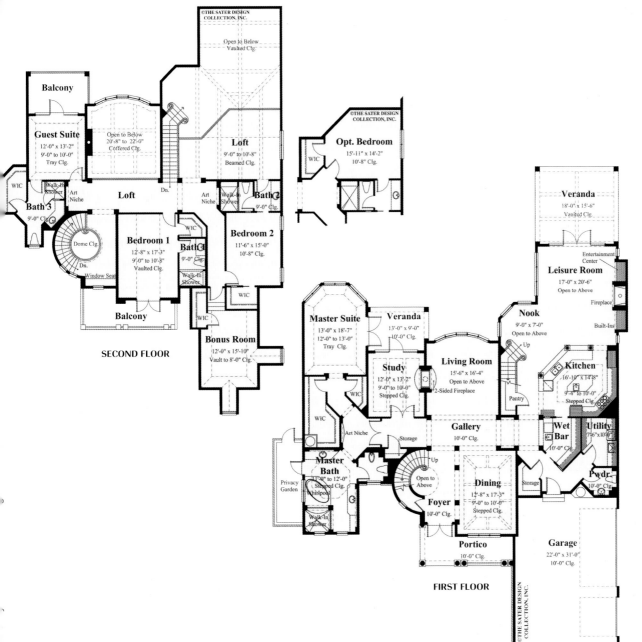

SECOND FLOOR

FIRST FLOOR

Clarissant

Plan No. 8002

REAR ELEVATION

© Sater Design Collection, Inc

SPECIFICATIONS:

Bedrooms: **4**

Baths: **3½**

Width: **85' 0"**

Depth: **76' 8"**

1st Floor: **2829 sq. ft.**

2nd Floor: **1127 sq. ft.**

Total Living: **3956 sq. ft.**

Foundation: **Slab**

PLAN PRICING:

Vellum & PDF - $2571

CAD - $4549

Two-story bays, a renaissance entry and overlapping gables enhance the presentation of this English-inspired manor. Inside, a gallery links the grand foyer with the formal rooms—a study, formal dining room and a palatial living room that flows outdoors. Built-ins and a fireplace anchor the leisure space that also expands to the veranda. A stunning spiral staircase leads to upper-level sleeping quarters that are connected by a balcony hall overlooking the foyer and living room.

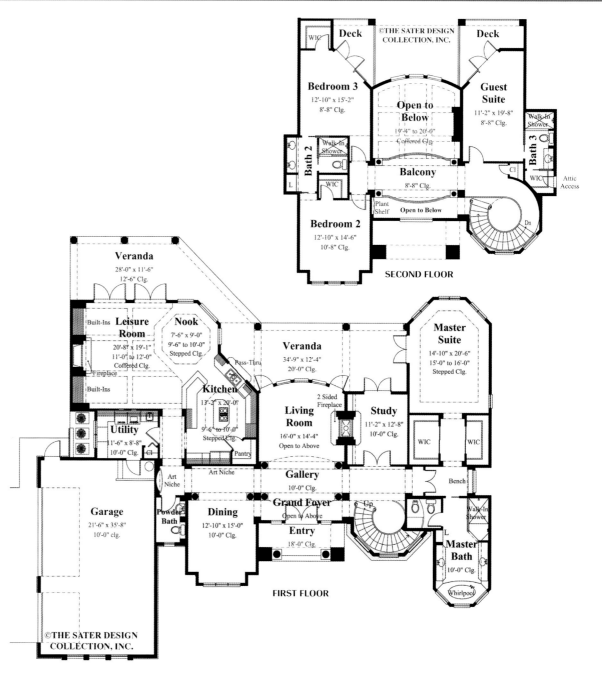

Berkley
Plan No. 8006

REAR ELEVATION

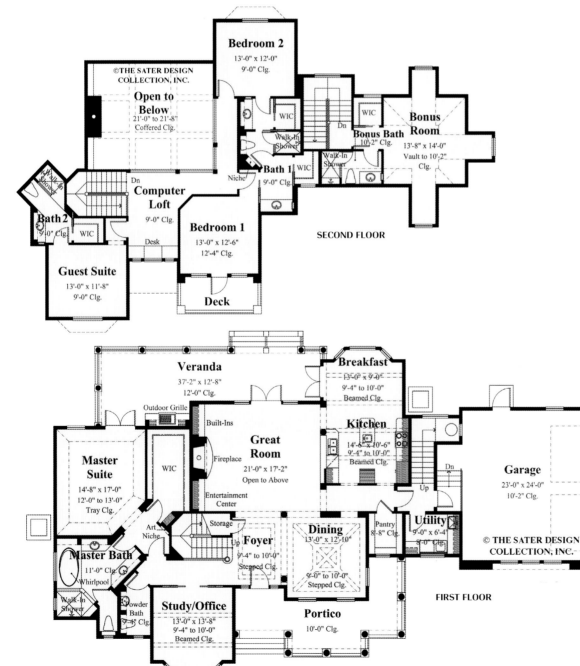

SECOND FLOOR

Bedroom 2
13'-0" x 12'-0"
9'-0" Clg.

©THE SATER DESIGN COLLECTION, INC.

Open to Below
21'-0" to 21'-8"
Coffered Clg.

WIC

WIC

Bonus Room
13'-8" x 14'-0"
Vault to 10'-2" Clg.

Dn

Bonus Bath
10'-2" Clg.

Walk-In Shower

Bath 1
9'-0" Clg.

WIC

Walk-In Shower

Niche

Bath 2
9'-0" Clg.

Walk-In Shower

WIC

Computer Loft
9'-0" Clg.

Dn

Desk

Bedroom 1
13'-0" x 12'-6"
12'-4" Clg.

Guest Suite
13'-0" x 11'-8"
9'-0" Clg.

Deck

FIRST FLOOR

Veranda
37'-2" x 12'-8"
12'-0" Clg.

Outdoor Grille

Breakfast
13'-0" x 9'-0"
9'-4" to 10'-0"
Beamed Clg.

Built-Ins

Great Room
21'-0" x 17'-2"
Open to Above

Kitchen
14'-6" x 10'-6"
9'-4" to 10'-0"
Beamed Clg.

Master Suite
14'-8" x 17'-0"
12'-0" to 13'-0"
Tray Clg.

WIC

Fireplace

Entertainment Center

Dn

Garage
23'-0" x 24'-0"
10'-2" Clg.

Up

Master Bath
11'-0" Clg.

Whirlpool

Art Niche

Storage

Up

Foyer
9'-4" to 10'-0"
Stepped Clg.

Dining
13'-0" x 12'-10"
9'-0" to 10'-0"
Stepped Clg.

Pantry
8'-8" Clg.

Utility
9'-0" x 6'-4"
8'-0" Clg.

© THE SATER DESIGN COLLECTION, INC.

Walk-In Shower

Powder Bath
9'-0" Clg.

Study/Office
13'-0" x 13'-8"
9'-4" to 10'-0"
Beamed Clg.

Portico
10'-0" Clg.

SPECIFICATIONS:

Bedrooms: **4**

Baths: **3½**

Width: **91' 0"**

Depth: **52' 8"**

1st Floor: **2219 sq. ft.**

2nd Floor: **1085 sq. ft.**

Total Living: **3304 sq. ft.**

Bonus Room: **404 sq. ft.**

Foundation: **Slab**

PLAN PRICING:

Vellum & PDF - $1652

CAD - $2974

Pedimented gables, carved balusters and shutters evoke a 19th-century theme, while a wide-open interior emphasizes the benefits of a warm climate. Intentionally informal and cottage-like on the outside, the core of the plan reveals an array of columns, arches and sculpted architectural furnishings. Bay windows punctuate the formal and casual zones, letting in light and the great outdoors. Upstairs, a computer loft overlooks the great room and links three guest bedrooms.

New Abbey

Plan No. **8008**

REAR ELEVATION

© Sater Design Collection, Inc

SPECIFICATIONS:

Bedrooms: **3**

Baths: **3½**

Width: **106′ 4″**

Depth: **102′ 4″**

1st Floor: **3760 sq. ft.**

Total Living: **3760 sq. ft.**

Bonus Room: **111 sq. ft.**

Foundation: **Slab**

PLAN PRICING:

Vellum & PDF - **$2444**

CAD - **$4324**

Stone and stucco create an idyllic presence with this British-inspired design. Inside, the private and public realms are arranged laterally, achieving a natural flow. Specialty ceilings and arched passages unify the central space—three unique rooms that share an orientation to the rear of the plan, allowing great views. The master retreat features retreating walls to the veranda. The opposing side of the plan harbors the informal zone—the kitchen, an inside/outside leisure room and two guest bedrooms.

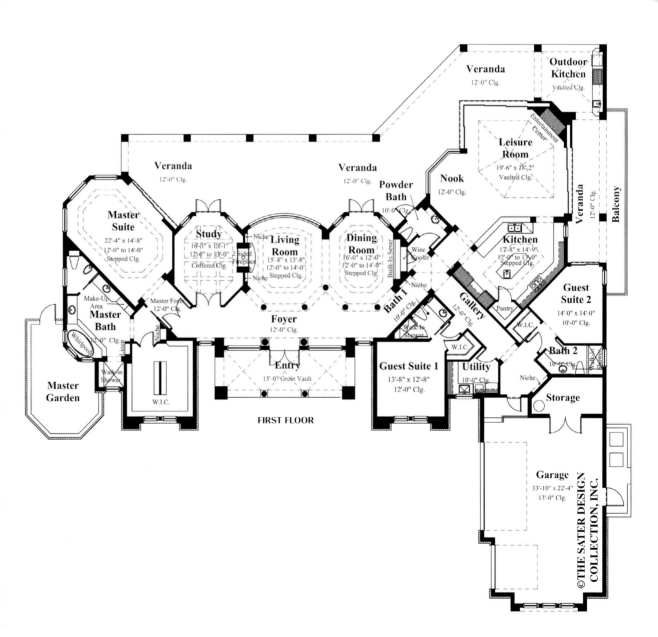

FIRST FLOOR

©THE SATER DESIGN COLLECTION, INC.

Elise
Plan No. 8012

© Sater Design Collection, Inc.

REAR ELEVATION

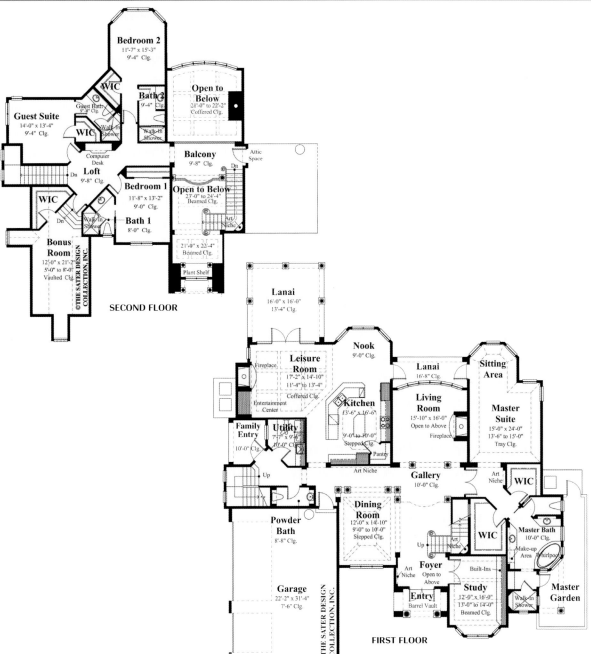

SECOND FLOOR

Bedroom 2
11'-7" x 15'-3"
9'-4" Clg.

WIC

Bath 2
9'-4" Clg.

Guest Bath
9'-4" Clg.

Open to Below
24'-0" to 22'-2"
Coffered Clg.

Walk-In Shower

Guest Suite
14'-0" x 13'-4"
9'-4" Clg.

WIC

Walk-In Shower

Computer Desk

Balcony
9'-8" Clg.

Attic Space

WIC

Loft
9'-8" Clg.

Dn

Dn

Bedroom 1
11'-8" x 13'-2"
9'-0" Clg.

Open to Below
23'-0" to 24'-4"
Beamed Clg.

Walk-In Shower

Bath 1
8'-0" Clg.

Art Niche

Dn

Bonus Room
12'-0" x 21'-2"
5'-0" to 8'-0"
Vaulted Clg.

21'-0" x 22'-4"
Beamed Clg.

Plant Shelf

FIRST FLOOR

Lanai
16'-0" x 16'-0"
13'-4" Clg.

Nook
9'-0" Clg.

Lanai
16'-8" Clg.

Sitting Area

Leisure Room
17'-2" x 14'-10"
11'-4" to 13'-4"
Coffered Clg.

Fireplace

Living Room
15'-10" x 16'-0"
Open to Above
Fireplace

Master Suite
15'-0" x 24'-0"
13'-6" to 15'-0"
Tray Clg.

Kitchen
13'-6" x 16'-6"
9'-0" to 10'-0"
Stepped Clg.

Entertainment Center

Family Entry
10'-0" Clg.

Utility
7'-2" x 9'-0"
10'-0" Clg.

Pantry

Art Niche

Gallery
10'-0" Clg.

Art Niche

WIC

Up

Powder Bath
8'-8" Clg.

Dining Room
12'-0" x 14'-10"
9'-0" to 10'-0"
Stepped Clg.

Up

WIC

Master Bath
10'-0" Clg.

Make-up Area

Whirlpool

Garage
22'-2" x 31'-4"
7'-6" Clg.

Art Niche

Foyer
Open to Above

Entry
Barrel Vault

Built-Ins

Study
12'-0" x 16'-0"
13'-0" to 14'-0"
Beamed Clg.

Walk-In Shower

Master Garden

©THE SATER DESIGN COLLECTION, INC.

SPECIFICATIONS:

Bedrooms: **4**

Baths: **4½**

Width: **71' 6"**

Depth: **82' 2"**

1st Floor: **2866 sq. ft.**

2nd Floor: **1156 sq. ft.**

Total Living: **4022 sq. ft.**

Bonus Room: **371 sq. ft.**

Foundation: **Slab**

PLAN PRICING:

Vellum & PDF - **$2614**

CAD - **$4625**

This English-inspired façade surrounds a sophisticated interior of wide-open spaces and well-defined rooms. Floor-to-ceiling bow and bay windows add natural light to the heart of the home: the living room, gallery, dining room and foyer. Away from the formal realm, an airy indoor/outdoor relationship is also prevalent in the common space shared by the leisure room, nook and kitchen. Upstairs, the balcony links with a computer loft and guest bedrooms.

Aubrey
Plan No. 8016

REAR ELEVATION

© Sater Design Collection, Inc

SPECIFICATIONS:

Bedrooms: **4**

Baths: **3½**

Width: **83' 0"**

Depth: **71' 8"**

1st Floor: **2485 sq. ft.**

2nd Floor: **1127 sq. ft.**

Total Living: **3612 sq. ft.**

Bonus Room: **368 sq. ft.**

Foundation: **Slab**

PLAN PRICING:

Vellum & PDF - $1806

CAD - $3251

Wrought iron balustrades and sculpted masonry define a classic elevation that is anchored by a stunning side turret, twin dormers and Doric columns. Arches and columns frame the foyer and gallery, flanked by well-defined formal rooms. At the heart of the home, a spacious leisure room leads to the lanai and brags a two-sided fireplace shared with a study. The opposing turret harbors a spiral staircase and a loft that links with the balcony and sleeping quarters.

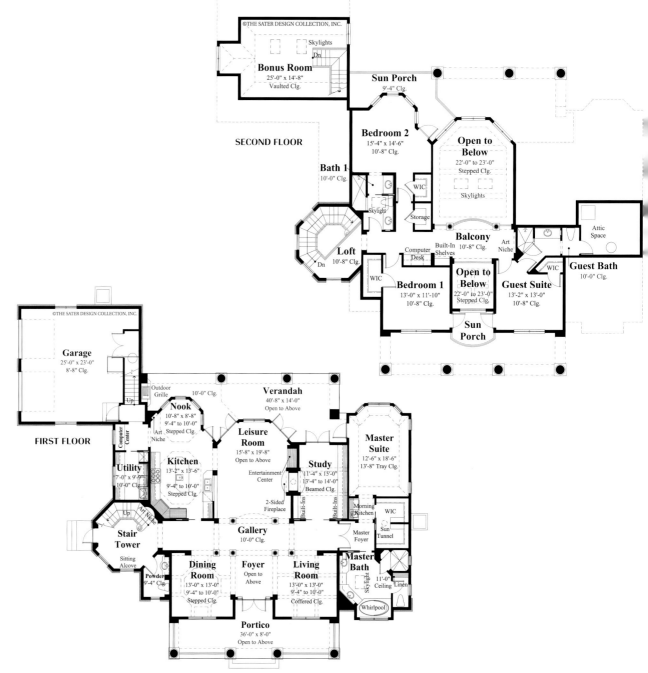

Ascott
Plan No. **8019**

© Sater Design Collection, Inc.

REAR ELEVATION

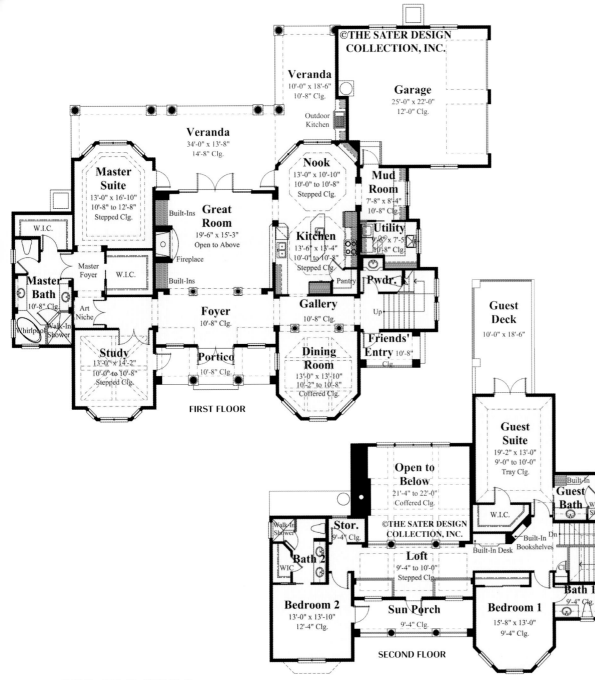

FIRST FLOOR

SECOND FLOOR

©THE SATER DESIGN COLLECTION, INC.

SPECIFICATIONS:

Bedrooms: **4**

Baths: **4½**

Width: **80' 0"**

Depth: **63' 9"**

1st Floor: **2226 sq. ft.**

2nd Floor: **1248 sq. ft.**

Total Living: **3474 sq. ft.**

Foundation: **Slab**

PLAN PRICING:

Vellum & PDF - $1737

CAD - $3127

Vintage lines recall strokes of genius from 19th-century British architecture and marry history with a contemporary sanctuary. French doors and bay windows invite fresh air and panoramic views into the private and public realms, which can flex to suit the changing lifestyles of the owners. A friends' entry and side staircase leads to three upper-level guest quarters. Nearby, the loft overlooks the great room and opens to a sun porch.

Edmonton

Plan No. **8023**

REAR ELEVATION

© Sater Design Collection, Inc

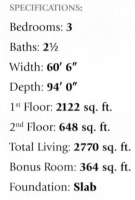

SPECIFICATIONS:

Bedrooms: **3**

Baths: **2½**

Width: **60' 6"**

Depth: **94' 0"**

1st Floor: **2122 sq. ft.**

2nd Floor: **648 sq. ft.**

Total Living: **2770 sq. ft.**

Bonus Room: **364 sq. ft.**

Foundation: **Slab**

PLAN PRICING:

Vellum & PDF - **$1385**

CAD - **$2493**

Arcades and rambling terraces glide into airy, contemporary spaces designed for 21st-century living in this English courtyard home. A massive fireplace anchors the core of the plan—an open arrangement of the foyer and great room that expands to the terrace and courtyard through French doors. Gentle breezes infiltrate the casual zone though the loggia, which boasts an outdoor kitchen and connects to the garage where a spiral staircase leads up to a versatile bonus room.

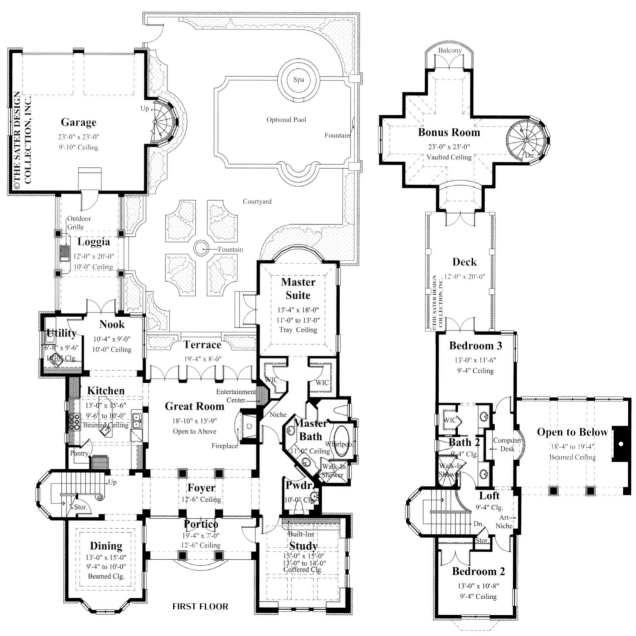

FIRST FLOOR

SECOND FLOOR

© Sater Design Collection, Inc.

Bellamare
Plan No. 8027

REAR ELEVATION

© THE SATER DESIGN COLLECTION, INC.

SECOND FLOOR

Master Retreat 17'-8" x 19'-11" 9'-4" to 10'-0" Tray Clg.

Master Porch 9'-4" Clg.

Whirlpool

M. Bath 9'-4" Clg.

Make-Up Area

Walk-In Shower

WIC Hers His

Bath 3

Walk-In Shower

Stor.

Bedroom 3 12'-4" x 13'-0" 9'-4" Clg.

WIC

Linen

Elev.

Bath 2 8'-8" Clg.

Sun Porch Barrel Clg.

Bedroom 2 11'-4" x 13'-6" 9'-4" Clg.

Balcony

Open to Below

Open to Below 23'-6" to 24'-2" Stepped Clg.

Loft 24'-2" x 8'-6" 11'-0" Clg.

Dn

Bedroom 1 13'-0" x 13'-8" 9'-4" to 10'-0" Tray Clg.

WIC

Morn. Kit.

Walk-In Shower

Bath 1

Linen

Utility 7'-8" x 10'-6" 9'-4" Clg.

Drip Dry

Sun Porch 9'-4" Clg.

FIRST FLOOR

Porch 10'-0" Clg.

Entertainment Center

Leisure Room 17'-8" x 19'-11" 9'-4" to 10'-0" Stepped Clg

Nook 9'-0" x 9'-8" 9'-4" Clg

Kitchen 17'-4" x 13'-8" 9'-4" to 10'-0" Stepped Clg.

Pantry

Pwdr.

Stor.

Elev.

Garage 29'-0" x 23'-8" 10'-0" Clg.

© THE SATER DESIGN COLLECTION, INC.

Living/Dining Room 21'-11" x 11'-9" Open to Above

Two Sided Fireplace

Veranda 26'-6" x 10'-7" Open to Above

Cabana/Guest Suite 13'-0" x 13'-4" 10'-0" Clg.

WIC

Outdoor Grille

Guest Bath Walk-In Shower

Built-Ins

Library / Study 12'-3" x 15'-0" 9'-4" to 10'-0" Stepped Clg.

Foyer 10'-0" Clg.

Up

Stor.

Porch 10'-0" Clg.

Entry 10'-0" Clg.

SPECIFICATIONS:

Bedrooms: **5**

Baths: **5½**

Width: **58' 0"**

Depth: **65' 0"**

1st Floor: **1995 sq. ft.**

2nd Floor: **2184 sq. ft.**

Total Living: **4179 sq. ft.**

Foundation: **Slab**

PLAN PRICING:

Vellum & PDF - **$2716**

CAD - **$4806**

An appealing blend of stone and stucco conveys the charm of the British countryside. Past the foyer, the central living space presents a formal composition designed for planned events and dining, enhanced with a two-sided fireplace shared with the study. To facilitate less formal meals, the common living areas open to a wraparound veranda. An elevator offers an alternative to the spiral staircase that leads to the upper-level bedrooms and loft.

Hamilton
Plan No. **8029**

REAR ELEVATION

SPECIFICATIONS:

Bedrooms: **3**

Baths: **2½**

Width: **62' 10"**

Depth: **73' 6"**

1st Floor: **2192 sq. ft.**

Total Living: **2192 sq. ft.**

Foundation: **Slab**

PLAN PRICING:

Vellum & PDF - **$1096**

CAD - **$1973**

Freely interpreted revival elements empower a country theme with this neo-English manor. With one-story functionality, this deeply comfortable interior easily adapts to the owner's lifestyle. Formal rooms are defined by columns and specialty ceilings. Nearby, the great room enjoys unrestrained access to the veranda through French doors. An extended-hearth fireplace carries warmth to the kitchen and nook area. Guest bedrooms cluster near the casual zone, while a secluded master suite offers repose for the owners.

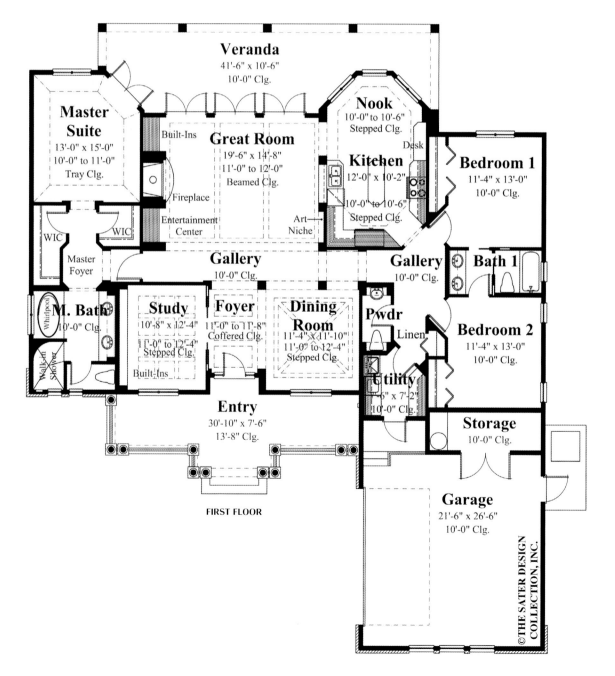

FIRST FLOOR

Gullane
Plan No. **8031**

© Sater Design Collection, Inc.

REAR ELEVATION

SPECIFICATIONS:

Bedrooms: **5**

Baths: **5½**

Width: **58' 0"**

Depth: **65' 0"**

1st Floor: **2164 sq. ft.**

2nd Floor: **2312 sq. ft.**

Total Living: **4476 sq. ft.**

Foundation: **Slab**

PLAN PRICING:

Vellum & PDF - $2909

CAD - $5147

Rows of windows punctuate a stucco façade, which integrates classic lines with an oceanfront attitude. The spirit throughout the house is formal yet extends a sense of welcome to guests. Open, public spaces are framed by columns and beamed ceilings. Floor-to-ceiling windows in the living room offer commanding views. Retreating glass walls integrate the common living space with the loggia. Upstairs, guest bedrooms and the master retreat enjoy repose.

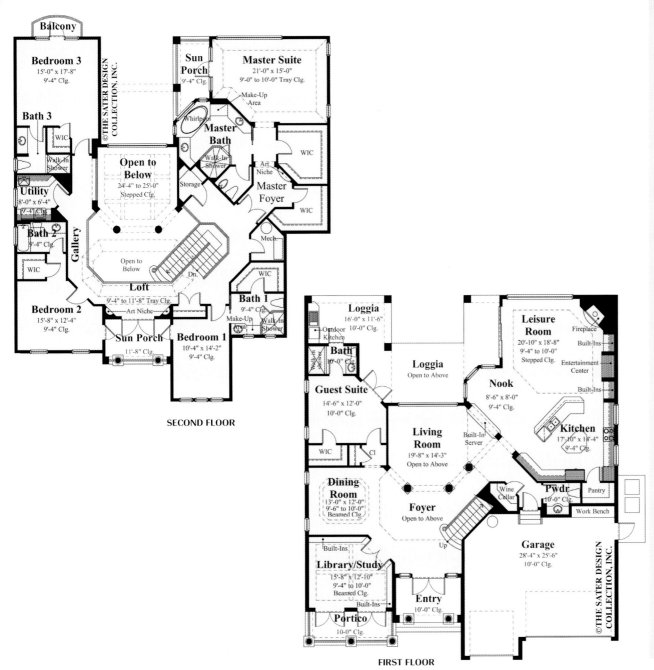

SECOND FLOOR

FIRST FLOOR

Maitena

Plan No. **8036**

REAR ELEVATION

SPECIFICATIONS:

Bedrooms: **3**

Baths: **4**

Width: **83' 10"**

Depth: **106' 0"**

1st Floor: **3954 sq. ft.**

Total Living: **3954 sq. ft.**

Foundation: **Slab**

PLAN PRICING:

Vellum & PDF - $2570

CAD - $4547

Lancet windows with intersecting Gothic tracery, transoms and side panels establish a stunning street presence, evocative of 18th-century England. Past the foyer, stepped ceilings define the formal rooms. Retreating glass walls open the leisure room to the outside amenities and invite a sense of nature into the casual zone. A walk-in wet bar adjoins the kitchen and provides a servery to the formal dining room. To the right of the plan, the master wing enjoys repose.

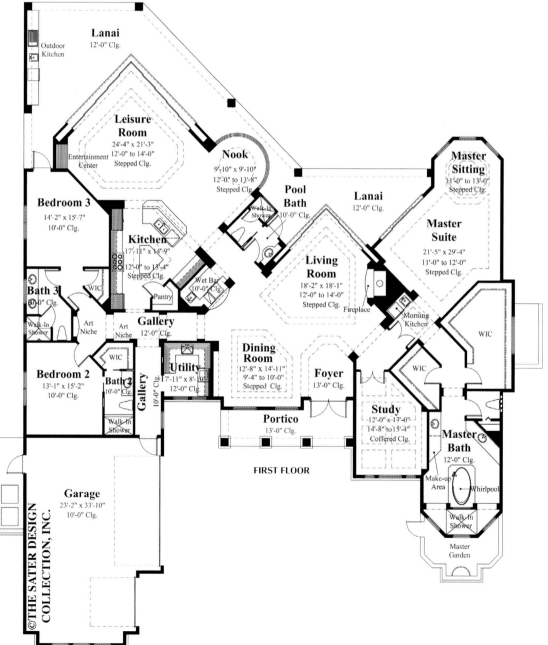

FIRST FLOOR

©THE SATER DESIGN COLLECTION, INC.

Chadwick
Plan No. 8038

REAR ELEVATION

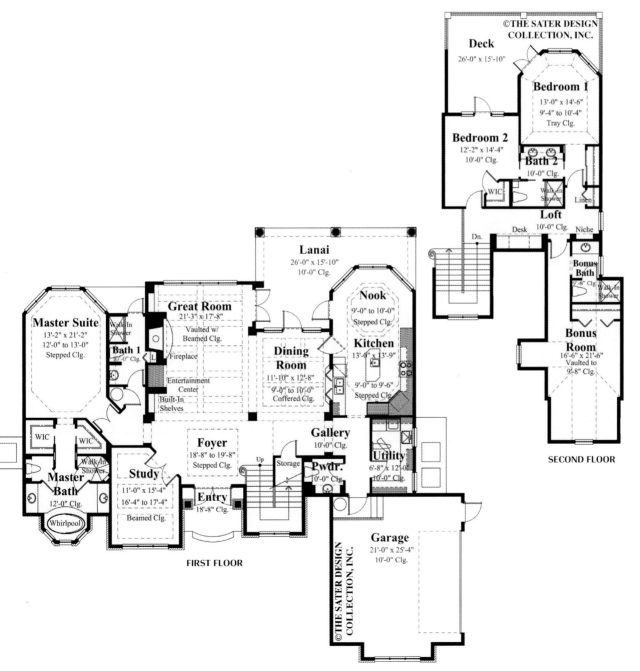

©THE SATER DESIGN COLLECTION, INC.

Deck
26'-0" x 15'-10"

Bedroom 1
13'-0" x 14'-6"
9'-4" to 10'-4"
Tray Clg.

Bedroom 2
12'-2" x 14'-4"
10'-0" Clg.

Bath 2
10'-0" Clg.

WIC

Walk-In Shower

Linen

Loft
10'-0" Clg.

Desk

Niche

Dn.

Bonus Bath
Walk-In Shower

Bonus Room
16'-6" x 21'-6"
Vaulted to 9'-8" Clg.

SECOND FLOOR

Master Suite
13'-2" x 21'-2"
12'-0" to 13'-0"
Stepped Clg.

Walk-In Shower

Bath 1
10'-0" Clg.

Lanai
26'-0" x 15'-10"
10'-0" Clg.

Great Room
21'-3" x 17'-8"
Vaulted w/ Beamed Clg.

Fireplace

Entertainment Center

Built-In Shelves

Dining Room
11'-10" x 12'-8"
9'-0" to 10'-0" Coffered Clg.

Nook
9'-0" to 10'-0"
Stepped Clg.

Kitchen
13'-0" x 12'-9"
9'-0" to 9'-6"
Stepped Clg.

Foyer
18'-8" x 19'-8"
Stepped Clg.

Gallery
10'-0" Clg.

WIC

WIC

Walk-In Shower

Master Bath
12'-0" Clg.

Whirlpool

Study
11'-0" x 15'-4"
16'-4" to 17'-4"
Beamed Clg.

Up

Storage

Pwdr.
0'-0" Clg.

Utility
6'-8" x 12'-0"
10'-0" Clg.

Entry
18'-8" Clg.

Garage
21'-0" x 25'-4"
10'-0" Clg.

FIRST FLOOR

SPECIFICATIONS:

Bedrooms: **3**

Baths: **3½**

Width: **72' 0"**

Depth: **68' 3"**

1st Floor: **2250 sq. ft.**

2nd Floor: **663 sq. ft.**

Total Living: **2913 sq. ft.**

Bonus Room: **351 sq. ft.**

Foundation: **Slab**

PLAN PRICING:

Vellum & PDF - **$1457**

CAD - **$2622**

Vintage lines honor the rural English provenance of this rustic manor. Inside, floor-to-ceiling windows and French doors bring in light and extend the living spaces outward. Ceiling treatments define the open rooms of the central interior. Nearby, a bay window harbors the nook and brings in views shared with the kitchen. The wrapping lanai is accessible from the great room, formal dining room and nook. Upstairs, two guest bedrooms share a sun deck.

Wellington

Plan No. 8041

REAR ELEVATION

© Sater Design Collection, Inc

SPECIFICATIONS:

Bedrooms: **3**

Full Baths: **2**

Half Bath: **2**

Width: **84' 0"**

Depth: **92' 0"**

1st Floor: **3353 sq. ft.**

Total Living: **3353 sq. ft.**

Foundation: **Slab**

PLAN PRICING:

Vellum & PDF - $1677

CAD - $3018

Evocative of early revival homes, this European manor melds a sophisticated brick-and-stucco façade with the kind of livable amenities that endear a home to its owners. A gallery foyer grants vistas that extend to the rear veranda—via an airy living/dining room with a vaulted beamed ceiling. French doors bordering the master and formal wings integrates the interior with the outdoors, while retreating glass doors expand the common living space to the veranda.

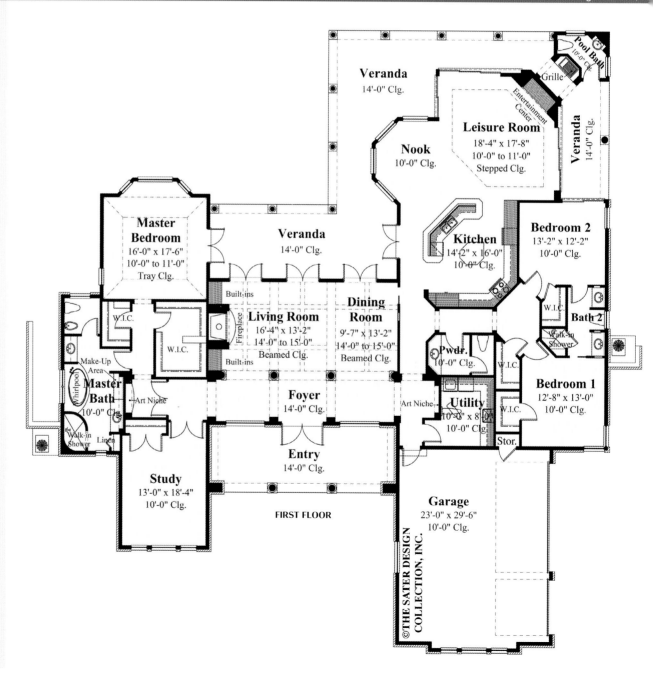

FIRST FLOOR

Demetri
Plan No. 8045

Sater Design Collection, Inc.

REAR ELEVATION

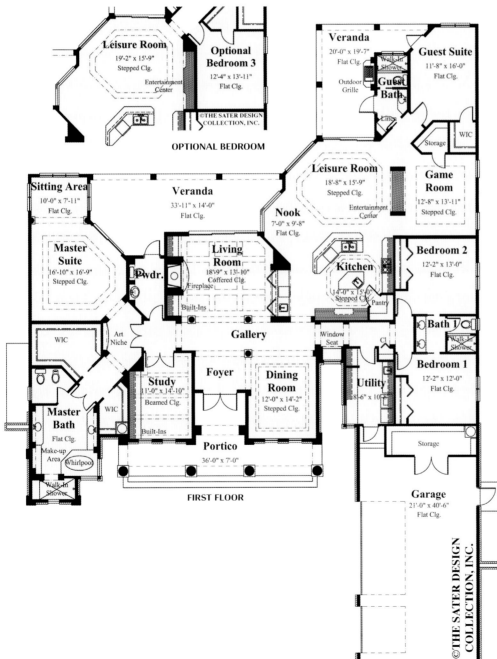

Leisure Room
19'-2" x 15'-9"
Stepped Clg.

Optional Bedroom 3
12'-4" x 13'-11"
Flat Clg.

Entertainment Center

©THE SATER DESIGN COLLECTION, INC.

OPTIONAL BEDROOM

Veranda
20'-0" x 19'-7"
Flat Clg.

Walk In Shower

Outdoor Grille

Guest Suite
11'-8" x 16'-0"
Flat Clg.

Guest Bath

Linen

WIC

Storage

Sitting Area
10'-0" x 7'-11"
Flat Clg.

Veranda
33'-11" x 14'-0"
Flat Clg.

Leisure Room
18'-8" x 15'-9"
Stepped Clg.

Game Room
12'-8" x 13'-11"
Stepped Clg.

Nook
7'-0" x 9'-8"
Flat Clg.

Entertainment Center

Master Suite
16'-10" x 16'-9"
Stepped Clg.

Pwdr.

Living Room
18'-9" x 13'-10"
Coffered Clg.

Fireplace

Built-Ins

Kitchen
14'-0" x 15'-0"
Stepped Clg.

Pantry

Bedroom 2
12'-2" x 13'-0"
Flat Clg.

WIC

Art Niche

Gallery

Window Seat

Cl

Bath 1

Walk In Shower

Bedroom 1
12'-2" x 12'-0"
Flat Clg.

Master Bath
Flat Clg.

WIC

Study
11'-0" x 14'-10"
Beamed Clg.

Foyer

Dining Room
12'-0" x 14'-2"
Stepped Clg.

Utility
8'-6" x 10'-

Make-up Area

Whirlpool

Built-Ins

Storage

Walk-in Shower

Portico
36'-0" x 7'-0"

FIRST FLOOR

Garage
21'-0" x 40'-6"
Flat Clg.

©THE SATER DESIGN COLLECTION, INC.

SPECIFICATIONS:

Bedrooms: **4**

Baths: **3½**

Width: **80' 0"**

Depth: **108' 0"**

1st Floor: **3789 sq. ft.**

Total Living: **3789 sq. ft.**

Foundation: **Slab**

PLAN PRICING:

Vellum & PDF - **$2447**

CAD - **$4329**

Stately Corinthian columns and a trio of pediments set off this revival façade. The interior progresses from the foyer and formal rooms to a central living space that flexes to facilitate planned events as well as cozy family gatherings. As the plan unfolds to the right, halls lead separately to the airy, indoor/ outdoor casual zone and to the guest bedrooms. Secluded to the other side of the home is the generous master retreat.

Kendrick

Plan No. **8050**

REAR ELEVATION

SPECIFICATIONS:

Bedrooms: **5**

Baths: **3½**

Width: **71' 0"**

Depth: **72' 0"**

1st Floor: **2163 sq. ft.**

2nd Floor: **1415 sq. ft.**

Total Living: **3578 sq. ft.**

Foundation: **Slab**

PLAN PRICING:

Vellum & PDF - $1789

CAD - $3220

A triplet of paneled doors leads through the foyer to a spectacular great room with unimpeded views of the rear property. Art niches and a massive hearth define one wall of the great room, and contradict an opposing series of flat soffits that open the space to the kitchen. To the right of the plan, the master wing sports a luxe bath. Upstairs, a balcony loft links four bedrooms and leads to the front deck.

Garnett
Plan No. 8047

REAR ELEVATION

© Sater Design Collection, Inc.

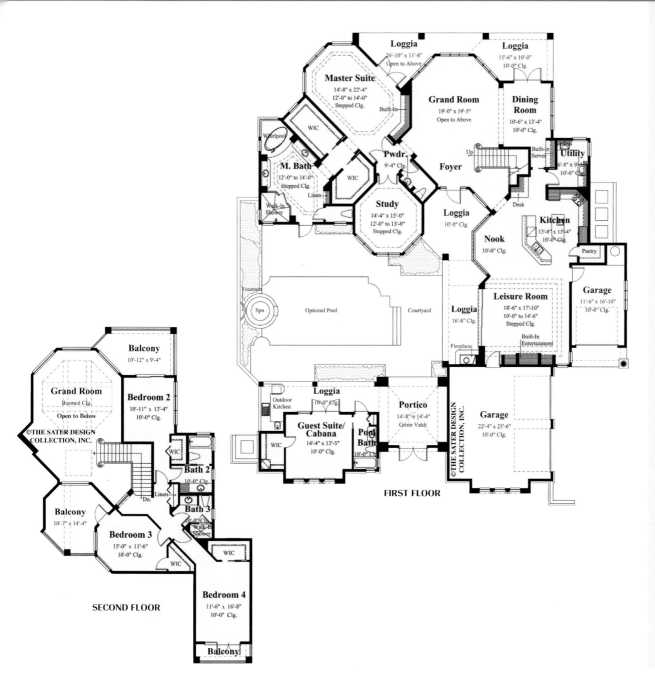

FIRST FLOOR

SECOND FLOOR

Loggia 26'-10" x 11'-8" Open to Above

Loggia 15'-6" x 10'-0" 10'-0" Clg.

Master Suite 14'-8" x 22'-4" 12'-0" to 14'-0" Stepped Clg.

Grand Room 19'-0" x 19'-5" Open to Above

Dining Room 10'-6" x 13'-4" 10'-0" Clg.

Utility 6'-8" x 9'-5" 10'-0" Clg.

WIC

Built-In Server

M. Bath 12'-0" to 14'-0" Stepped Clg.

Pwdr. 9'-4" Clg.

Foyer

WIC

Up

Kitchen 13'-8" x 15'-4" 10'-0" Clg.

Desk

Walk-In Shower

Study 14'-4" x 15'-0" 12'-0" to 13'-0" Stepped Clg.

Loggia 10'-0" Clg.

Nook 10'-0" Clg.

Pantry

Linen

Garage 11'-6" x 16'-10" 10'-0" Clg.

Fountain

Spa

Optional Pool

Courtyard

Loggia 16'-8" Clg.

Leisure Room 18'-6" x 17'-10" 10'-0" to 14'-6" Stepped Clg.

Built-In Entertainment

Fireplace

Balcony 10'-12" x 9'-4"

Grand Room Beamed Clg. Open to Below

Bedroom 2 10'-11" x 13'-4" 10'-0" Clg.

©THE SATER DESIGN COLLECTION, INC.

Bath 2 10'-0" Clg.

Linen

Dn.

Bath 3 10'-0" Clg.

Balcony 10'-7" x 14'-4"

Bedroom 3 15'-0" x 11'-6" 10'-0" Clg.

Walk-In Shower

WIC

WIC

Bedroom 4 11'-6" x 16'-8" 10'-0" Clg.

Balcony

Outdoor Kitchen

Loggia 10'-0" Clg.

WIC

Guest Suite/ Cabana 14'-4" x 13'-5" 10'-0" Clg.

Pool Bath 10'-0" Clg.

Portico 14'-8" x 14'-4" Groin Vault

©THE SATER DESIGN COLLECTION, INC.

Garage 22'-4" x 25'-6" 10'-0" Clg.

SPECIFICATIONS:

Bedrooms: **5**

Baths: **4½**

Width: **80' 0"**

Depth: **96' 0"**

1st Floor: **2852 sq. ft.**

2nd Floor: **969 sq. ft.**

Cabana: **342 sq. ft.**

Total Living: **4163 sq. ft.**

Foundation: **Slab**

PLAN PRICING:

Vellum & PDF - **$2703**

CAD - **$4782**

Varied rooflines and gables command a powerful street presence yet conceal an enchanting courtyard. Beyond a breezy portico and detached guest suite, the courtyard leads to the formal entry. Past the foyer, the grand room features two-story bay windows that extend the footprint of the home. Centrally located, the kitchen easily serves the formal and informal rooms. To the left of the public realm, the master retreat offers repose. Upstairs, guest bedrooms enjoy balcony access.

French

A confident, dignified sense of classic beauty melds seamlessly with state-of-the-art interiors in these award-winning designs. Grand turrets suggest both the permanence of a castle and exude the warmth of a welcoming family home. Elegant balconies, palatial columns and spectacular porticos announce two-story foyers, spacious formal rooms and flexible living spaces. Sunlight streams through open kitchens, verandahs and unparalleled master suites, while views extend through romantic archways and open French doors. Awash in extravagant details, such as art niches, built-ins, pocket doors and double-sided fireplaces, these homes evoke the true beauty, romance and splendor of France.

ROYAL Country Down

Plan No. 8001

© Sater Design Collection, Inc.

REAR ELEVATION

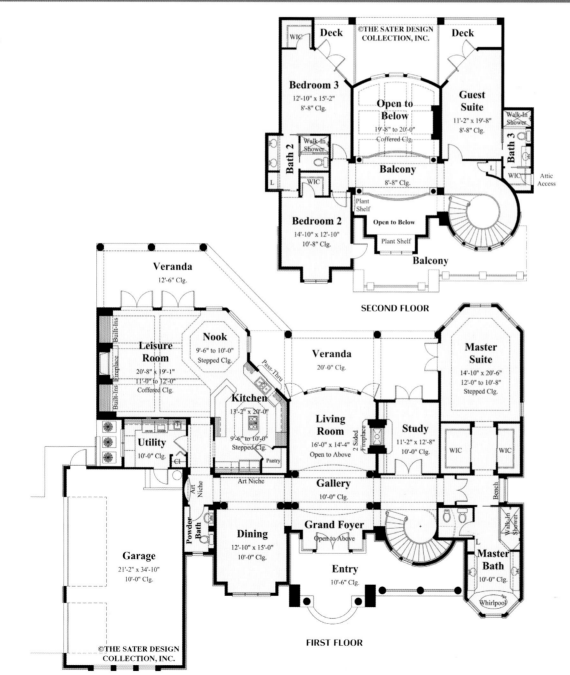

SECOND FLOOR

- WIC
- Deck
- ©THE SATER DESIGN COLLECTION, INC.
- Deck
- Bedroom 3
  12'-10" x 15'-2"
  8'-8" Clg.
- Open to Below
  19'-8" to 20'-0"
  Coffered Clg.
- Guest Suite
  11'-2" x 19'-8"
  8'-8" Clg.
- Walk-In Shower
- Bath 2
- Walk-In Shower
- Bath 3
- WIC
- Balcony
  8'-8" Clg.
- Attic Access
- Plant Shelf
- Bedroom 2
  14'-10" x 12'-10"
  10'-8" Clg.
- Open to Below
- Plant Shelf
- Balcony

FIRST FLOOR

- Veranda
  12'-6" Clg.
- Built-Ins
- Leisure Room
  20'-8" x 19'-1"
  11'-0" to 12'-0"
  Coffered Clg.
- Nook
  9'-6" to 10'-0"
  Stepped Clg.
- Pass-Thru
- Veranda
  20'-0" Clg.
- Master Suite
  14'-10" x 20'-6"
  12'-0" to 10'-8"
  Stepped Clg.
- Kitchen
  13'-2" x 20'-0"
  9'-6" to 10'-0"
  Stepped Clg.
- Living Room
  16'-0" x 14'-4"
  Open to Above
  2 Sided Fireplace
- Study
  11'-2" x 12'-8"
  10'-0" Clg.
- WIC
- WIC
- Utility
  10'-0" Clg.
- Pantry
- Art Niche
- Art Niche
- Gallery
  10'-0" Clg.
- Bench
- Powder Bath
- Dining
  12'-10" x 15'-0"
  10'-0" Clg.
- Grand Foyer
  Open to Above
- Walk-In Shower
- Garage
  21'-2" x 34'-10"
  10'-0" Clg.
- Entry
  10'-6" Clg.
- Master Bath
  10'-0" Clg.
- Whirlpool
- ©THE SATER DESIGN COLLECTION, INC.

SPECIFICATIONS:

Bedrooms: **4**

Baths: **3½**

Width: **85' 0"**

Depth: **76' 8"**

1st Floor: **2829 sq. ft.**

2nd Floor: **1127 sq. ft.**

Total Living: **3956 sq. ft.**

Foundation: **Slab**

PLAN PRICING:

Vellum & PDF - $2571

CAD - $4549

Renaissance details—carved pilasters, rusticated columns and scrolled pediments—highlight the refined spirit of this home, which prevails beyond the grand entry. Formal spaces radiate from a gallery of arches and columns—a deliberate strategy that permits interior vistas past the rear veranda. Built-in shelves frame the fireplace in the leisure room, and anchor an open arrangement of casual space with the nook and kitchen. A spectacular winding staircase leads to the guest quarters on the upper level.

Medoro

Plan No. **8039**

REAR ELEVATION

SPECIFICATIONS:

Bedrooms: **3**

Baths: **3½**

Width: **72' 0"**

Depth: **68' 3"**

1st Floor: **2250 sq. ft.**

2nd Floor: **663 sq. ft.**

Total Living: **2913 sq. ft.**

Bonus Room: **351 sq. ft.**

Foundation: **Slab**

PLAN PRICING:

Vellum & PDF - $1457

CAD - $2622

Stickwork, shutters and bay windows embellish a brick façade influenced by the historic cottages of rural France. The arrangement of interior spaces permits the center of the home to flex from private to public use. Beamed and coffered ceilings enrich the amenities shared by the great room and formal dining room: an entertainment center, built-in shelves and fireplace. French doors connect the main zones with the lanai. Upstairs, guest bedrooms share a spacious deck.

© Sater Design Collection, Inc.

Channing
Plan No. 8005

REAR ELEVATION

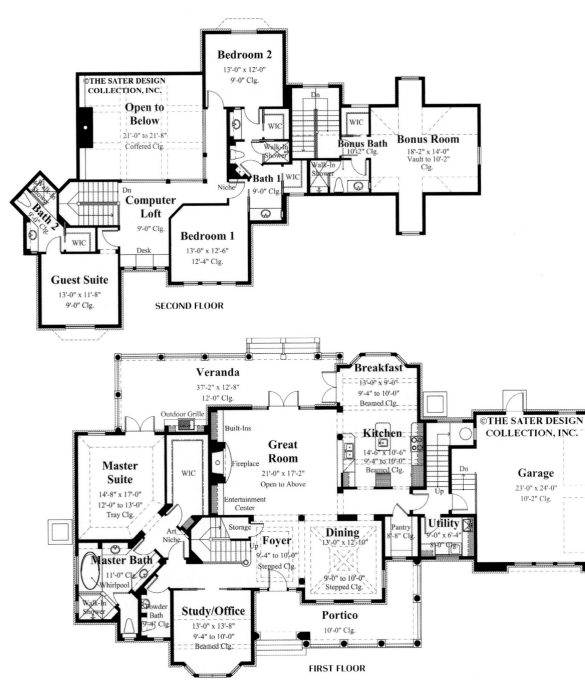

SECOND FLOOR

- ©THE SATER DESIGN COLLECTION, INC.
- **Open to Below** 21'-0" to 21'-8" Coffered Clg.
- **Bedroom 2** 13'-0" x 12'-0" 9'-0" Clg.
- WIC
- **Bonus Bath** 10'-2" Clg.
- **Bonus Room** 18'-2" x 14'-0" Vault to 10'-2" Clg.
- WIC
- Walk-In Shower
- Dn
- **Bath 1** 9'-0" Clg.
- WIC
- Niche
- **Bath 2** 9'-0" Clg.
- Walk-In Shower
- WIC
- Dn
- **Computer Loft** 9'-0" Clg.
- Desk
- **Bedroom 1** 13'-0" x 12'-6" 12'-4" Clg.
- **Guest Suite** 13'-0" x 11'-8" 9'-0" Clg.

FIRST FLOOR

- **Veranda** 37'-2" x 12'-8" 12'-0" Clg.
- Outdoor Grille
- **Breakfast** 13'-0" x 9'-0" 9'-4" to 10'-0" Beamed Clg.
- Built-Ins
- **Great Room** 21'-0" x 17'-2" Open to Above
- Fireplace
- **Kitchen** 14'-6" x 10'-6" 9'-4" to 10'-0" Beamed Clg.
- ©THE SATER DESIGN COLLECTION, INC.
- **Garage** 23'-0" x 24'-0" 10'-2" Clg.
- Entertainment Center
- **Master Suite** 14'-8" x 17'-0" 12'-0" to 13'-0" Tray Clg.
- WIC
- Art Niche
- Storage
- Up
- Dn
- Up
- **Master Bath** 11'-0" Clg. Whirlpool
- Walk-In Shower
- Powder Bath 9'-5" Clg.
- **Foyer** 9'-4" to 10'-0" Stepped Clg.
- **Dining** 13'-0" x 12'-10" 9'-0" to 10'-0" Stepped Clg.
- Pantry 8'-8" Clg.
- **Utility** 9'-0" x 6'-4" 8'-0" Clg.
- **Study/Office** 13'-0" x 13'-8" 9'-4" to 10'-0" Beamed Clg.
- **Portico** 10'-0" Clg.

SPECIFICATIONS:

Bedrooms: **4**

Baths: **3½**

Width: **91' 0"**

Depth: **52' 8"**

1st Floor: **2219 sq. ft.**

2nd Floor: **1085 sq. ft.**

Total Living: **3304 sq. ft.**

Foundation: **Slab**

PLAN PRICING:

Vellum & PDF - $1652

CAD - $2947

State-of-the-art amenities reside together with a spirit of artisanship in this French country home. Inspired spaces flex from private to public, well-defined to wide open. Columns and arches articulate the foyer and formal dining room yet allow the space to mingle with interior vistas granted by the great room. French doors expand the nook, great room and master suite to the veranda. Upstairs, a versatile computer loft connects three guest bedrooms.

Baxter

Plan No. **8009**

REAR ELEVATION

SPECIFICATIONS:

Bedrooms: **3**

Baths: **3½**

Width: **106′ 4″**

Depth: **102′ 4″**

1st Floor: **3760 sq. ft.**

Total Living: **3760 sq. ft.**

Foundation: **Slab**

PLAN PRICING:

Vellum & PDF - **$2444**

CAD - **$4324**

A stunning arcade enhanced with fanlights and French doors leads to a grand interior that is oriented to rear vistas. Retreating walls, glass doors, and bow and bay windows permit plenty of natural light and spectacular views to fill the home. Classic materials and a historic style play well against extraordinary touches, such as a two-way fireplace, stepped ceilings and an angled entertainment center in the leisure room and state-of-the-art appliances in the kitchen.

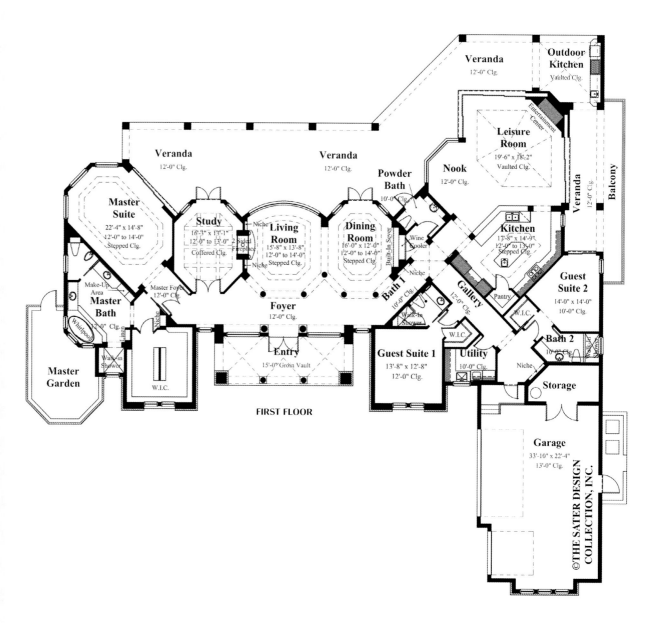

FIRST FLOOR

©THE SATER DESIGN COLLECTION, INC.

© Sater Design Collection, Inc.

REAR ELEVATION

La Riviere
Plan No. **8011**

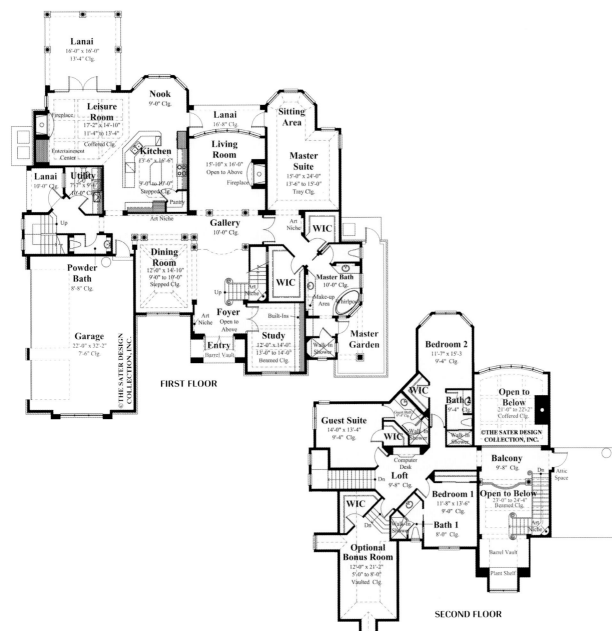

FIRST FLOOR

SECOND FLOOR

SPECIFICATIONS:

Bedrooms: **4**

Baths: **4½**

Width: **71' 6"**

Depth: **83' 0"**

1st Floor: **2830 sq. ft.**

2nd Floor: **1158 sq. ft.**

Total Living: **3988 sq. ft.**

Bonus Room: **371 sq. ft.**

Foundation: **Slab**

PLAN PRICING:

Vellum & PDF - **$2592**

CAD - **$4586**

Arched windows and dormers set off a rich blend of clapboard, stucco and stone with this New World villa. An open arrangement of the public zone secures panoramic views within each of the formal spaces. The living room boasts a sense of nature granted through a two-story bow window, framed by bay windows in the nook and master suite. On the upper level, a computer loft links the guest bedrooms and a step-down bonus room.

Burke House

Plan No. 8015

REAR ELEVATION

SPECIFICATIONS:

Bedrooms: **4**

Baths: **4½**

Width: **70′ 0″**

Depth: **100′ 0″**

1st Floor: **3049 sq. ft.**

2nd Floor: **1871 sq. ft.**

Total Living: **4920 sq. ft.**

Bonus Room: **294 sq. ft.**

Foundation: **Slab**

PLAN PRICING:

Vellum & PDF - **$3936**

CAD - **$7380**

Bold and simply beautiful, this French Country manor promises 21st-century repose combined with Old World architecture. In the center of the plan, a two-story coffered ceiling plays counterpoint to a two-sided fireplace shared by the great room and study. Walls of glass define the rear perimeter, permitting views throughout the home. The kitchen adjoins a wet bar leading to the formal dining room. Upstairs, two lofts connect three guest bedrooms and a bonus room.

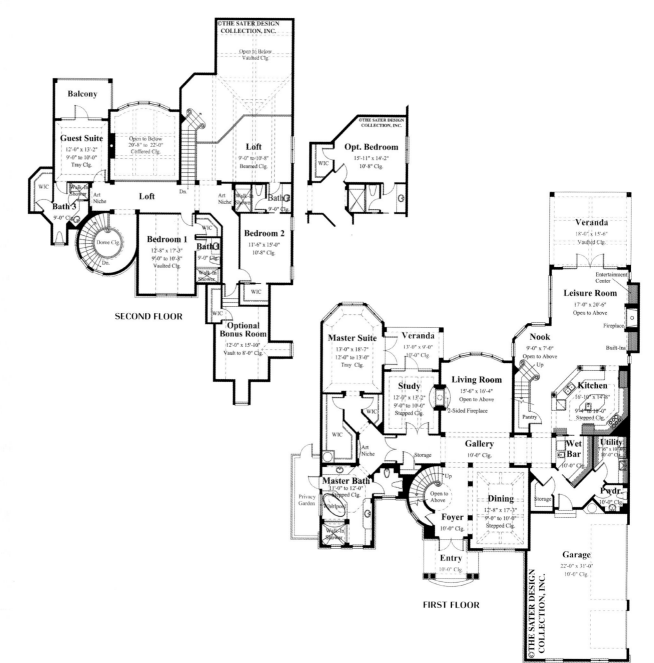

SECOND FLOOR

FIRST FLOOR

Les Tourelles
Plan No. 8017

© Sater Design Collection, Inc.

REAR ELEVATION

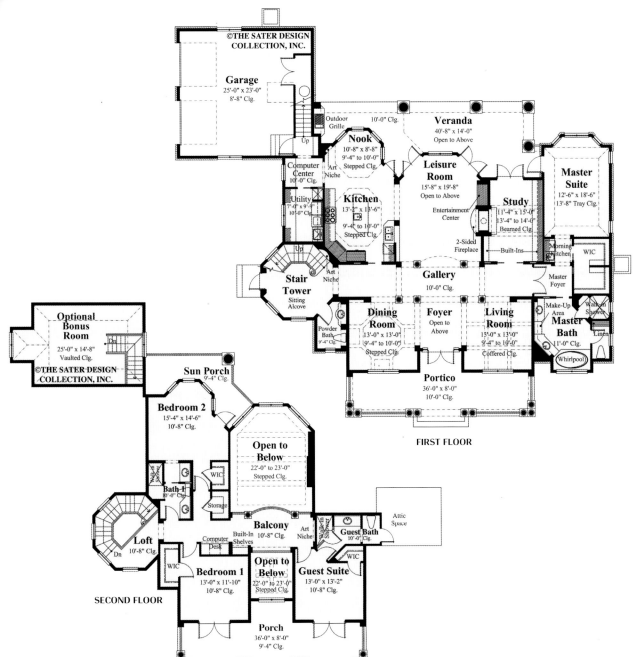

SPECIFICATIONS:

Bedrooms: **4**

Baths: **3½**

Width: **83′ 0″**

Depth: **71′ 8″**

1st Floor: **2485 sq. ft.**

2nd Floor: **1127 sq. ft.**

Total Living: **3612 sq. ft.**

Bonus Room: **368 sq. ft.**

Foundation: **Slab**

PLAN PRICING:

Vellum & PDF - **$1806**

CAD - **$3251**

A steeply pitched roof caps porticos reminiscent of the early French houses of the southeastern coastal regions, while a thoughtfully placed turret reinvents traffic flow within. Formal rooms flank the foyer and open to the gallery. At the center of the plan, great views dominate the two-story leisure room, which leads out to the lanai. Past the study, double doors open to the master suite. On the upper level, three guest bedrooms enjoy deck access.

Bellamy

Plan No. **8018**

REAR ELEVATION

© Sater Design Collection, Inc

SPECIFICATIONS:

Bedrooms: **4**

Baths: **3½**

Width: **83′ 0″**

Depth: **71′ 8″**

1st Floor: **2485 sq. ft.**

2nd Floor: **1127 sq. ft.**

Total Living: **3612 sq. ft.**

Bonus Room: **368 sq. ft.**

Foundation: **Slab**

PLAN PRICING:

Vellum & PDF - $1806

CAD - $3251

Well-crafted millwork, pediments and dormers reinforce a Chateauesque theme with this vernacular design. Transoms and fanlights extend the motif outside and lend texture and natural light to the interior. A sense of French tradition is reiterated in the public realm with an enfilade arrangement of rooms—the living and dining rooms opposite the leisure room and study. Positioned to the side, a winding staircase employs the turret to bring natural light to the main and upper galleries.

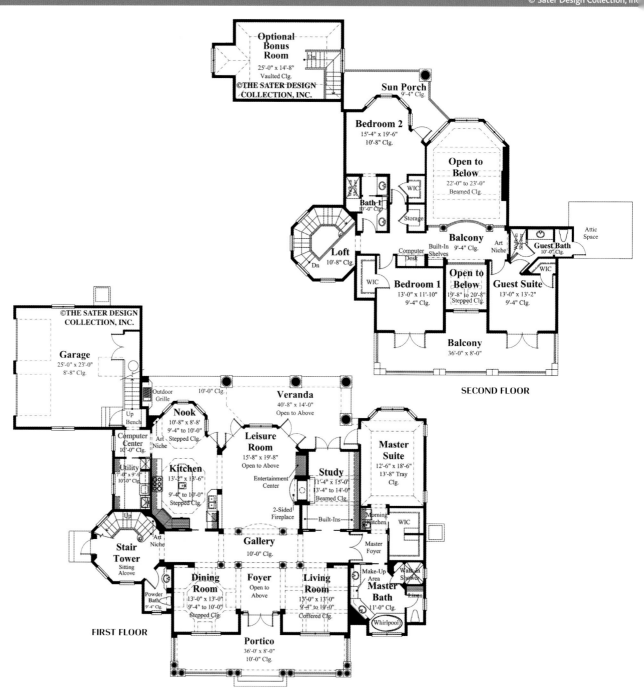

New Brunswick
Plan No. 8021

© Sater Design Collection, Inc.

REAR ELEVATION

FIRST FLOOR

- ©THE SATER DESIGN COLLECTION, INC.
- Veranda 10'-0" x 18'-6" 10'-8" Clg.
- Garage 25'-0" x 22'-0" 12'-0" Clg.
- Outdoor Kitchen
- Veranda 34'-0" x 13'-8" 14'-8" Clg.
- Nook 13'-0" x 10'-10" 10'-0" to 10'-8" Stepped Clg.
- Mud Room 7'-8" x 8'-4" 10'-8" Clg.
- Master Suite 13'-0" x 16'-10" 10'-8" to 12'-8" Stepped Clg.
- Great Room 19'-6" x 15'-3" Open to Above
- Built-Ins
- Fireplace
- Built-Ins
- Kitchen 13'-6" x 15'-4" 10'-0" to 10'-8" Stepped Clg.
- Utility 9'-0" x 7'-5" 10'-8" Clg.
- WIC
- Master Foyer
- WIC
- Master Bath 10'-8" Clg.
- Whirlpool
- Walk-In Shower
- Art Niche
- Pantry
- Pwdr
- Foyer 10'-8" Clg.
- Gallery 10'-8" Clg.
- Up
- Friends' Entry 10'-8" Clg.
- Guest Deck 10'-0" x 18'-6"
- Study 13'-0" x 14'-2" 10'-0" to 10'-8" Stepped Clg.
- Portico 10'-8" Clg.
- Dining Room 13'-0" x 13'-10" 10'-2" to 10'-8" Coffered Clg.

SECOND FLOOR

- Open to Below 21'-4" to 22'-0" Coffered Clg.
- Guest Suite 19'-2" x 13'-0" 9'-0" to 10'-0" Tray Clg.
- Built-In
- Guest Bath
- Walk-In Shower
- W.I.C.
- Walk-In Shower
- Stor. 9'-4" Clg.
- ©THE SATER DESIGN COLLECTION, INC.
- Built-In Bookshelves
- Built-In Desk
- Dn
- Bath 2
- WIC
- Loft 9'-4" to 10'-0" Stepped Clg.
- Bath 1 9'-4" Clg.
- Bedroom 2 13'-0" x 13'-10" 12'-4" Clg.
- Sun Porch 9'-4" Clg.
- Bedroom 1 13'-0" x 13'-10" 9'-4" Clg.

SPECIFICATIONS:

Bedrooms: **4**

Baths: **4½**

Width: **80' 0"**

Depth: **63' 9"**

1st Floor: **2226 sq. ft.**

2nd Floor: **1248 sq. ft.**

Total Living: **3474 sq. ft.**

Foundation: **Slab**

PLAN PRICING:

Vellum & PDF - **$1737**

CAD - **$3127**

Symmetry surrounds a double portico on a distinctly American façade that's rooted in a rich European past. A grand foyer opens to the perfect balance of well-defined formal rooms and inviting casual spaces. The prevalent use of natural light is a primary objective in the design—French doors and bay windows surround the main-level plan, while well-placed windows and access to outdoor places brighten the upper level. A convenient friends' entry leads to the upstairs bedrooms.

Gabriel

Plan No. 8024

REAR ELEVATION

SPECIFICATIONS:

Bedrooms: **3**

Baths: **2½**

Width: **60' 6"**

Depth: **94' 0"**

1st Floor: **2084 sq. ft.**

2nd Floor: **648 sq. ft.**

Total Living: **2732 sq. ft.**

Bonus Room: **364 sq. ft.**

Foundation: **Slab**

PLAN PRICING:

Vellum & PDF - **$1366**

CAD - **$2459**

Arches and stone gables frame an airy arcade in this classic chateaux. The center doors lead to a gallery foyer and great room, anchored by a massive fireplace. French doors open the space to the courtyard. To the left of the plan, a loggia harbors an eating area, which can be accessed from the nook and kitchen. Upstairs, a loft overlooks the great room and links the guest suites. A rear deck leads to a bonus room.

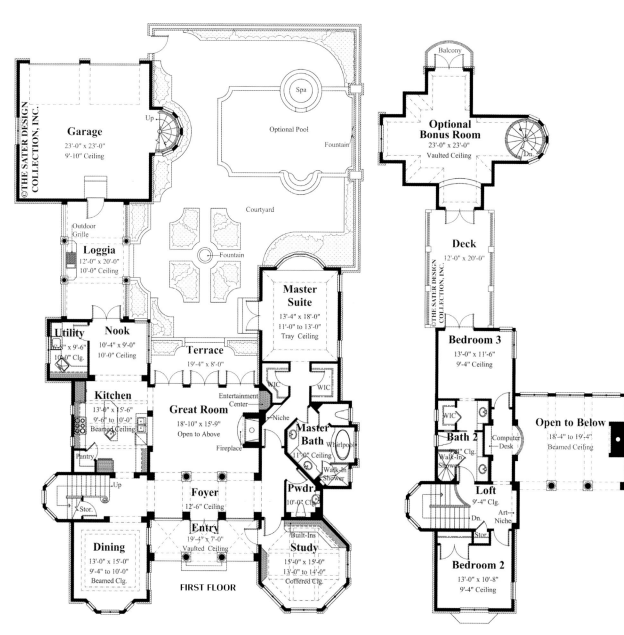

FIRST FLOOR

SECOND FLOOR

Saint-Germain
Plan No. 8026

REAR ELEVATION

© Sater Design Collection, Inc.

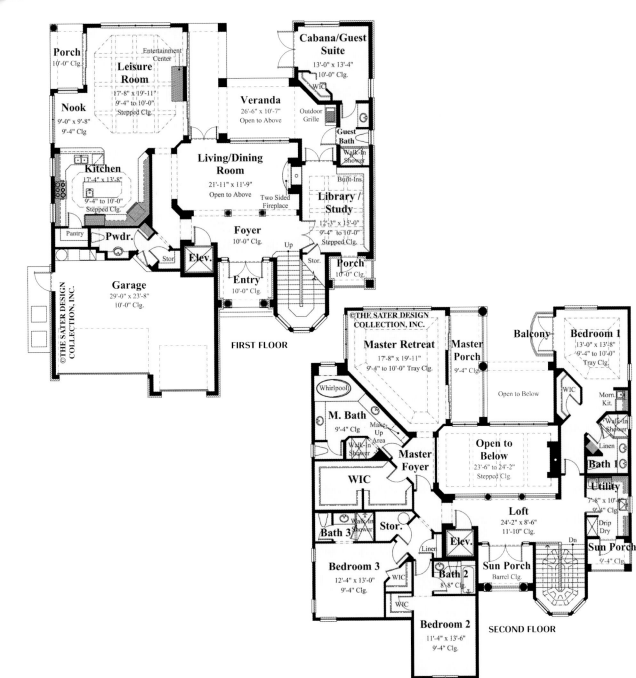

Porch 10'-0" Clg.

Leisure Room 17'-8" x 19'-11" 9'-4" to 10'-0" Stepped Clg.

Entertainment Center

Cabana/Guest Suite 13'-0" x 13'-4" 10'-0" Clg.

WIC

Nook 9'-0" x 9'-8" 9'-4" Clg

Veranda 26'-6" x 10'-7" Open to Above

Outdoor Grille

Guest Bath Walk-In Shower

Kitchen 17'-4" x 13'-8" 9'-4" to 10'-0" Stepped Clg.

Living/Dining Room 21'-11" x 11'-9" Open to Above

Two Sided Fireplace

Built-Ins

Library / Study 12'-3" x 15'-0" 9'-4" to 10'-0" Stepped Clg.

Pantry

Pwdr.

Foyer 10'-0" Clg.

Stor.

Elev.

Up

Stor.

Porch 10'-0" Clg.

Garage 29'-0" x 23'-8" 10'-0" Clg.

Entry 10'-0" Clg.

©THE SATER DESIGN COLLECTION, INC.

FIRST FLOOR

©THE SATER DESIGN COLLECTION, INC.

Master Retreat 17'-8" x 19'-11" 9'-4" to 10'-0" Tray Clg.

Master Porch 9'-4" Clg.

Balcony

Bedroom 1 13'-0" x 13'-8" 9'-4" to 10'-0" Tray Clg.

Whirlpool

M. Bath 9'-4" Clg

Make-Up Area

WIC

Walk-In Shower

Morn. Kit.

Master Foyer

Walk-In Shower

WIC

Open to Below 23'-6" to 24'-2" Stepped Clg.

Linen

Bath 1

Utility 7'-8" x 10'-0" 9'-4" Clg.

Bath 3

Walk-In Shower

Stor.

Elev.

Linen

Loft 24'-2" x 8'-6" 11'-10" Clg.

Drip Dry

Dn

Sun Porch 9'-4" Clg.

Bedroom 3 12'-4" x 13'-0" 9'-4" Clg.

WIC

Bath 2 8'-8" Clg.

Sun Porch Barrel Clg.

Bedroom 2 11'-4" x 13'-6" 9'-4" Clg.

WIC

SECOND FLOOR

SPECIFICATIONS:

Bedrooms: **5**

Baths: **5½**

Width: **58' 0"**

Depth: **65' 0"**

1st Floor: **1995 sq. ft.**

2nd Floor: **2184 sq. ft.**

Total Living: **4179 sq. ft.**

Foundation: **Slab**

PLAN PRICING:

Vellum & PDF - **$2705**

CAD - **$4784**

Sculpted outdoor places lend definition to the elevation, reiterating a highly crafted interior. At the heart of the home, flexible public spaces take on an elegant formality for planned events, yet provide a comfortable retreat for everyday use. Nearby, the library/study features double doors to the veranda. Upstairs, a wraparound loft overlooks the living space and links guest quarters to the owners' retreat. A convenient elevator complements the staircase, which winds upward from the foyer.

Kinsley
Plan No. 8030

REAR ELEVATION

SPECIFICATIONS:

Bedrooms: **3**

Baths: **2½**

Width: **62' 10"**

Depth: **73' 6"**

1st Floor: **2192 sq. ft.**

Total Living: **2192 sq. ft.**

Foundation: **Slab**

PLAN PRICING:

Vellum & PDF - **$1096**

CAD - **$1973**

Natural textures of brick and stone play counterpoint to revival elements, suggesting a neoclassic influence in this French manor. Formal rooms grant a strong visual connection to the outdoors, with the exception of the study, which is secluded by pocket doors. A massive fireplace and beamed ceiling offers an authentic presence in the great room. Drawing on coastal vernaculars, the rear of the home opens to the veranda creating a seamless connection with the outdoors.

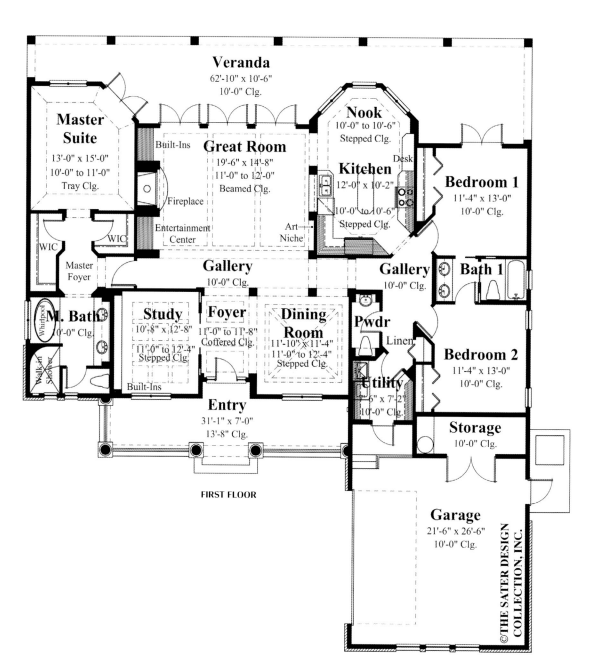

Veranda
62'-10" x 10'-6"
10'-0" Clg.

Master Suite
13'-0" x 15'-0"
10'-0" to 11'-0"
Tray Clg.

Built-Ins

Great Room
19'-6" x 14'-8"
11'-0" to 12'-0"
Beamed Clg.

Nook
10'-0" to 10'-6"
Stepped Clg.

Desk

Kitchen
12'-0" x 10'-2"
10'-0" to 10'-6"
Stepped Clg.

Bedroom 1
11'-4" x 13'-0"
10'-0" Clg.

Fireplace

Entertainment Center

Art Niche

WIC

WIC

Master Foyer

Gallery
10'-0" Clg.

Gallery
10'-0" Clg.

Bath 1

M. Bath
10'-0" Clg.

Whirlpool

Study
10'-8" x 12'-8"
11'-0" to 12'-4"
Stepped Clg.

Foyer
11'-0" x 11'-8"
Coffered Clg.

Dining Room
11'-10" x 11'-4"
11'-0" to 12'-4"
Stepped Clg.

Pwdr

Linen

Bedroom 2
11'-4" x 13'-0"
10'-0" Clg.

Walk-in Shower

Built-Ins

Entry
31'-1" x 7'-0"
13'-8" Clg.

Utility
x 7'-2"
10'-0" Clg.

Storage
10'-0" Clg.

FIRST FLOOR

Garage
21'-6" x 26'-6"
10'-0" Clg.

Stonehaven
Plan No. 8032

REAR ELEVATION

SPECIFICATIONS:

Bedrooms: **5**

Baths: **5½**

Width: **58' 0"**

Depth: **65' 0"**

1st Floor: **2163 sq. ft.**

2nd Floor: **2302 sq. ft.**

Total Living: **4465 sq. ft.**

Foundation: **Slab**

PLAN PRICING:

Vellum & PDF - **$2902**

CAD - **$5135**

Cornice-line brackets and a triple-arch entry set off a grand plan with a host of windows and outdoor living areas. The foyer opens to the heart of the interior—an expansive center of formal and informal rooms, defined only by decorative columns and ceiling treatments. Views and natural light fill the home through a wall of glass to the rear of the plan. Upstairs, a wraparound loft connects the master retreat with three guest suites.

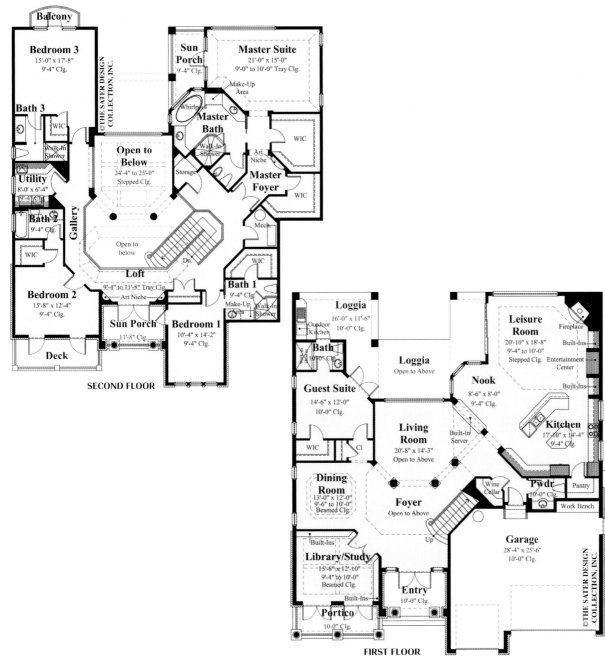

SECOND FLOOR

FIRST FLOOR

Le Marescott

Plan No. 8060

REAR ELEVATION

SPECIFICATIONS:

Bedrooms: **4**

Baths: **3½**

Width: **67′ 0″**

Depth: **90′ 8″**

1st Floor: **3166 sq. ft.**

Total Living: **3166 sq. ft.**

Foundation: **Slab**

PLAN PRICING:

Vellum & PDF - **$1583**

CAD - **$2849**

A flared eave sets a very French tone for this neo-Norman façade. An interior of intimate spaces, angled walls and open rooms melds state-of-the-art technology with a sense of nature. Retreating glass doors expand the living and leisure rooms to the lanai. The kitchen is centrally located between the formal and informal realms, making entertaining easy. The master retreat enjoys privacy away from three guest bedrooms on the opposite side of the home.

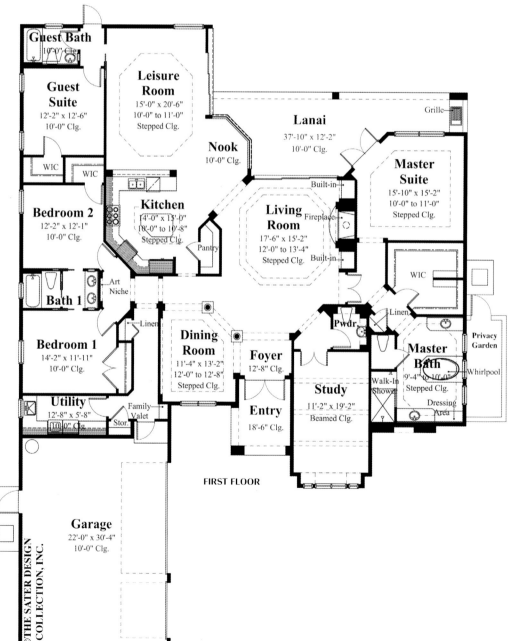

Guest Bath
10'-0" Clg.

Guest Suite
12'-2" x 12'-6"
10'-0" Clg.

Leisure Room
15'-0" x 20'-6"
10'-0" to 11'-0"
Stepped Clg.

WIC

WIC

Bedroom 2
12'-2" x 12'-1"
10'-0" Clg.

Kitchen
14'-0" x 13'-0"
10'-0" to 10'-8"
Stepped Clg.

Nook
10'-0" Clg.

Lanai
37'-10" x 12'-2"
10'-0" Clg.

Grille

Master Suite
15'-10" x 15'-2"
10'-0" to 11'-0"
Stepped Clg.

Built-in

Living Room
17'-6" x 15'-2"
12'-0" to 13'-4"
Stepped Clg.

Fireplace

Built-in

Pantry

Art Niche

Bath 1

Bedroom 1
14'-2" x 11'-11"
10'-0" Clg.

Linen

WIC

Linen

Dining Room
11'-4" x 13'-2"
12'-0" to 12'-8"
Stepped Clg.

Foyer
12'-8" Clg.

Pwdr.

Master Bath
9'-4" to 10'-0"
Stepped Clg.

Privacy Garden

Whirlpool

Entry
18'-6" Clg.

Study
11'-2" x 19'-2"
Beamed Clg.

Walk-In Shower

Dressing Area

Utility
12'-8" x 5'-8"
10'-0" Clg.

Family Valet

Stor.

FIRST FLOOR

Garage
22'-0" x 30'-4"
10'-0" Clg.

©THE SATER DESIGN COLLECTION, INC.

Sater Design Collection, Inc.

Brittany
Plan No. 8040

REAR ELEVATION

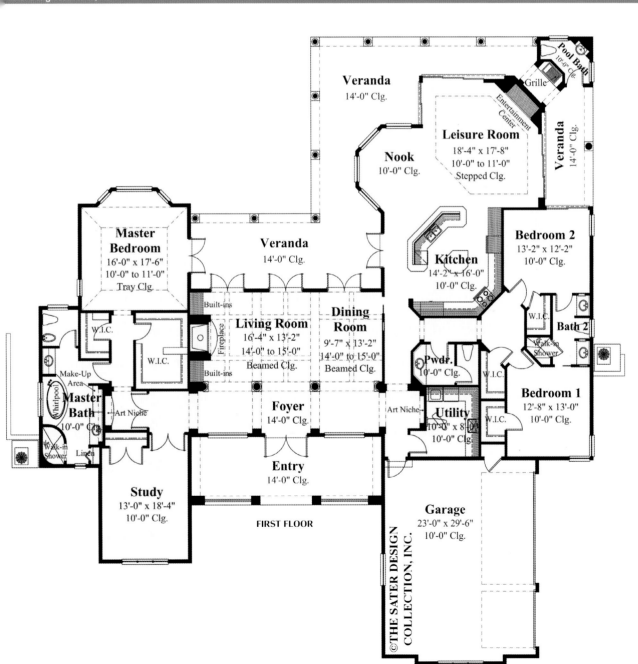

Master Bedroom
16'-0" x 17'-6"
10'-0" to 11'-0"
Tray Clg.

W.I.C.

W.I.C.

Built-ins

Veranda
14'-0" Clg.

Living Room
16'-4" x 13'-2"
14'-0" to 15'-0"
Beamed Clg.

Built-ins

Fireplace

Dining Room
9'-7" x 13'-2"
14'-0" to 15'-0"
Beamed Clg.

Veranda
14'-0" Clg.

Nook
10'-0" Clg.

Leisure Room
18'-4" x 17'-8"
10'-0" to 11'-0"
Stepped Clg.

Entertainment Center

Pool Bath
10'-0" Clg.

Grille

Veranda
14'-0" Clg.

Kitchen
14'-2" x 16'-0"
10'-0" Clg.

Bedroom 2
13'-2" x 12'-2"
10'-0" Clg.

W.I.C.

Bath 2

Walk-in Shower

Make-Up Area

Whirlpool

Master Bath
10'-0" Clg.

Art Niche

Linen

Walk-in Shower

Foyer
14'-0" Clg.

Art Niche

Pwdr.
10'-0" Clg.

Utility
10'-0" x 8'-...
10'-0" Clg.

W.I.C.

Bedroom 1
12'-8" x 13'-0"
10'-0" Clg.

W.I.C.

Study
13'-0" x 18'-4"
10'-0" Clg.

Entry
14'-0" Clg.

FIRST FLOOR

Garage
23'-0" x 29'-6"
10'-0" Clg.

©THE SATER DESIGN COLLECTION, INC.

SPECIFICATIONS:

Bedrooms: **3**

Full Baths: **2**

Half Bath: **2**

Width: **84' 0"**

Depth: **92' 0"**

1st Floor: **3343 sq. ft.**

Total Living: **3343 sq. ft.**

Foundation: **Slab**

PLAN PRICING:

Vellum & PDF - $1672

CAD - $3009

This enchanting villa is more than a home—it's a lifestyle. Centered formal spaces cater to large parties yet easily convert to an intimate gathering spot. French doors extend the living area to the wraparound veranda, which boasts a cabana-style bath and outdoor grille. Away from the public realm, the master retreat enjoys access to the study. On the opposite side of the home, a hall links guest suites with the casual living area and kitchen.

Beauchamp

Plan No. **8044**

REAR ELEVATION

SPECIFICATIONS:

Bedrooms: **4**

Baths: **3½**

Width: **80′ 8″**

Depth: **104′ 8″**

1st Floor: **3790 sq. ft.**

Total Living: **3790 sq. ft.**

Foundation: **Slab**

PLAN PRICING:

Vellum & PDF - $2464

CAD - $4359

Rusticated pilasters, pediments and quoins set off a symmetrical façade that calls up the aristocratic lines of 16th-century French villas. Past the gallery hall, a pass-thru wet bar connects the formal living room with the kitchen, ensuring easy entertaining. An island entertainment center provides definition to the casual zone, separating the game room and the leisure space, which opens to the outdoors. Tucked away on the opposite side of the home, the master suite offers repose.

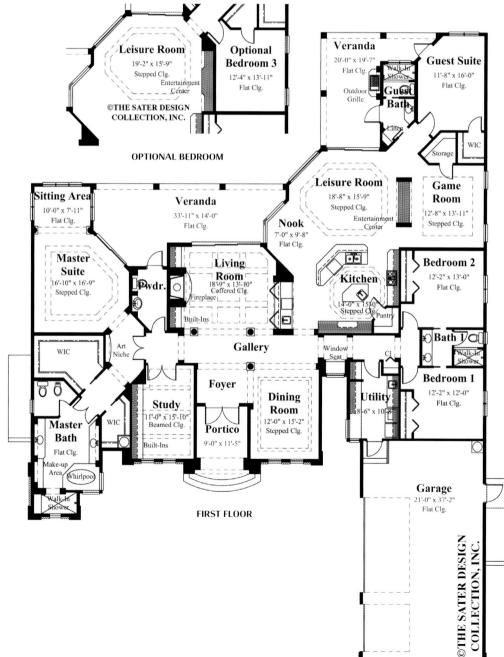

OPTIONAL BEDROOM

FIRST FLOOR

REAR ELEVATION

Solaine
Plan No. 8051

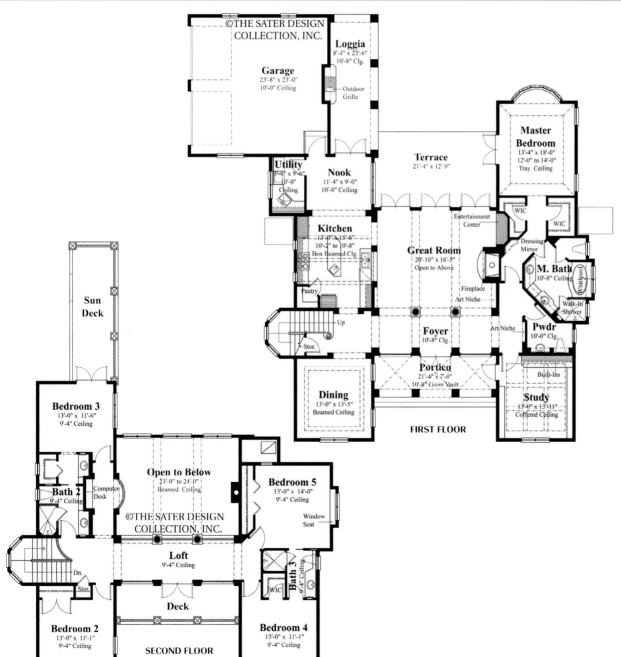

©THE SATER DESIGN COLLECTION, INC.

Loggia
8'-4" x 23'-6"
10'-8" Clg.

Garage
23'-8" x 23'-0"
10'-0" Ceiling

Outdoor Grille

Utility
5'-8" x 9'-6"
10'-0" Ceiling

Nook
11'-4" x 9'-0"
10'-8" Ceiling

Terrace
21'-4" x 12'-9"

Master Bedroom
13'-4" x 18'-0"
12'-0" to 14'-0"
Tray Ceiling

Kitchen
13'-0" x 15'-6"
10'-2" to 10'-8"
Box Beamed Clg.

Entertainment Center

WIC

WIC

Dressing Mirror

Great Room
20'-10" x 16'-5"
Open to Above

Pantry

Fireplace
Art Niche

M. Bath
10'-8" Ceiling

Whirlpool

Walk-In Shower

Up

Stor.

Art Niche

Pwdr
10'-0" Clg.

Foyer
10'-8" Clg.

Dining
13'-0" x 13'-5"
Beamed Ceiling

Portico
21'-4" x 7'-0"
10'-8" Groin Vault

Built-Ins

Study
13'-0" x 13'-11"
Coffered Ceiling

FIRST FLOOR

Sun Deck

Bedroom 3
13'-0" x 11'-6"
9'-4" Ceiling

Bath 2
9'-4" Ceiling

Computer Desk

Open to Below
23'-0" to 24'-0"
Beamed Ceiling

©THE SATER DESIGN COLLECTION, INC.

Bedroom 5
13'-0" x 14'-0"
9'-4" Ceiling

Window Seat

Loft
9'-4" Ceiling

Dn.

Stor.

Deck

WIC

Bath 3
9'-4" Ceiling

Bedroom 2
13'-0" x 11'-1"
9'-4" Ceiling

Bedroom 4
13'-0" x 11'-1"
9'-4" Ceiling

SECOND FLOOR

SPECIFICATIONS:

Bedrooms: **5**

Baths: **3½**

Width: **71' 0"**

Depth: **72' 0"**

1st Floor: **2164 sq. ft.**

2nd Floor: **1342 sq. ft.**

Total Living: **3506 sq. ft.**

Foundation: **Slab**

PLAN PRICING:

Vellum & PDF - **$1753**

CAD - **$3155**

Rusticated columns and a balcony balustrade on this stately elevation suggest early 20th-century influences, yet the interior is purely modern. Well-defined formal rooms flank the gallery leading to the great room. Three sets of French doors link the space to the terrace. Nearby, a loggia boasts an outdoor grille and access to the nook and kitchen. The right wing of the home is dedicated to the owners' retreat. Upstairs, a loft connects four guest bedrooms.

Christabel

Plan No. **8053**

REAR ELEVATION

SPECIFICATIONS:

Bedrooms: **4**

Baths: **3½**

Width: **74′ 8″**

Depth: **118′ 0″**

1st Floor: **3271 sq. ft.**

Total Living: **3271 sq. ft.**

Foundation: **Slab**

PLAN PRICING:

Vellum & PDF - $1636

CAD - $2944

Stacked stone and wood shutters lend rural elements to this urbane design. The spacious interior offers open-air vistas from every room of the house. A refined arrangement of the forward rooms plays counterpoint to the wide-open, state-of-the-art casual zone, which boasts a wall-sized entertainment center. For easy entertaining, the wet bar acts as a pass-thru from the kitchen to the dining room. Retreating walls grant access to the lanai and courtyard warmed by a fireplace.

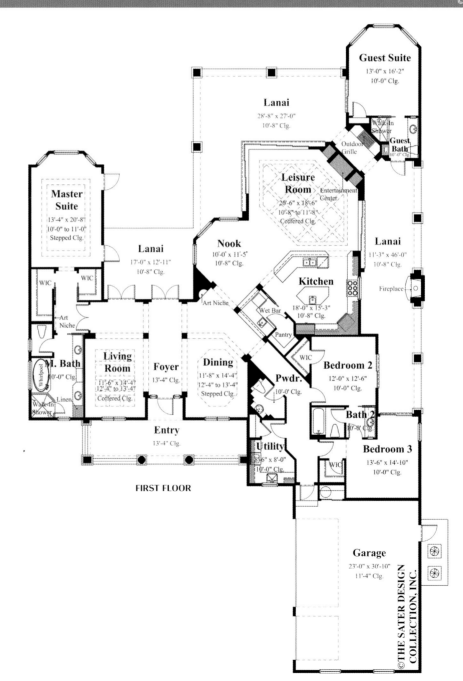

FIRST FLOOR

©THE SATER DESIGN COLLECTION, INC.

Argentellas
Plan No. 8056

© Sater Design Collection, Inc.

REAR ELEVATION

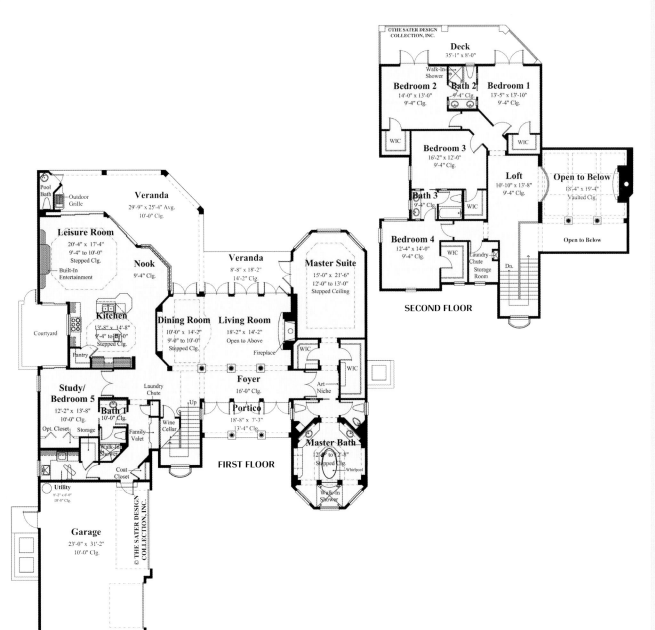

FIRST FLOOR

SECOND FLOOR

SPECIFICATIONS:

Bedrooms: **6**

Baths: **4½**

Width: **69′ 4″**

Depth: **95′ 4″**

1st Floor: **2913 sq. ft.**

2nd Floor: **1471 sq. ft.**

Total Living: **4384 sq. ft.**

Foundation: **Slab**

PLAN PRICING:

Vellum & PDF - $2859

CAD - $5058

Dormers and a graceful colonnade live in harmony with turrets and staggered rooflines on this modern elevation. Surprises prevail throughout the interior with nature intruding on the formal rooms and outdoor areas that beckon from even intimate spaces. A gallery foyer links two private wings and grants panoramic views through the rear of the plan. On the main level, the master wing offers a place of respite. Upstairs, four guest bedrooms and a loft are the perfect retreat for guests.

Italian

Strong, noble homes crafted with a sense of history, art and romance pay homage to the beauty of the Italian countryside. Grand turrets and columns create exhilarating first impressions while alluring porticos offer invitations to enjoy breathtaking courtyards and foyers. Inside, graceful arches and soaring ceilings create a dramatic, Baroque sensation. Large, plentiful windows stream the midday sun and rooms spill freely out to verandahs and captivating outdoor living areas. From stately and luxurious master suites to generous leisure rooms and open kitchens, these Italian homes are created with an abiding commitment to style, comfort and family.

© Sater Design Collection, Inc.

REAR ELEVATION

Brindisi
Plan No. **6963**

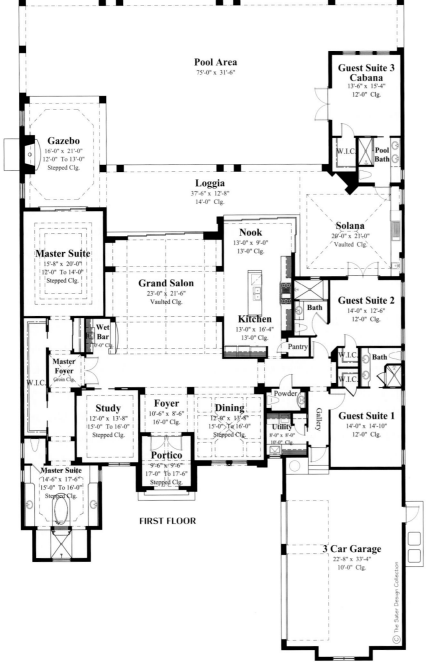

FIRST FLOOR

SPECIFICATIONS:

Bedrooms: **4**

Baths: **4**

Width: **75' 0"**

Depth: **125' 1"**

1st Floor: **3458 sq. ft.**

Cabana: **373 sq. ft.**

Total Living: **3831 sq. ft.**

Foundation: **Slab**

PLAN PRICING:

Vellum & PDF - **$2490**

CAD - **$4406**

A blended influence of Mediterranean and Contemporary architectural styles defines *Brindisi*. This functional plan boasts a multitude of practical amenities throughout the casually elegant living spaces. The result is a plan that lives larger than its square footage. Perfect for hosting friends and family, this home offers three guest suites with private baths.

Della Porta

Plan No. 8007

REAR ELEVATION

SPECIFICATIONS:

Bedrooms: **3**

Baths: **3½**

Width: **106′ 4″**

Depth: **102′ 4″**

1st Floor: **3760 sq. ft.**

Total Living: **3760 sq. ft.**

Foundation: **Slab**

PLAN PRICING:

Vellum & PDF - **$2444**

CAD - **$4324**

Triple arches and stately columns grace the entry of this spacious Italian villa. Designed for 21-st century living, the interior creates flexible spaces that are not formal or self-conscious, but simply comfortable. Defined by arches, columns and magnificent views that extend beyond the veranda, the living room opens to the dining room and shares a two-sided fireplace with the study.

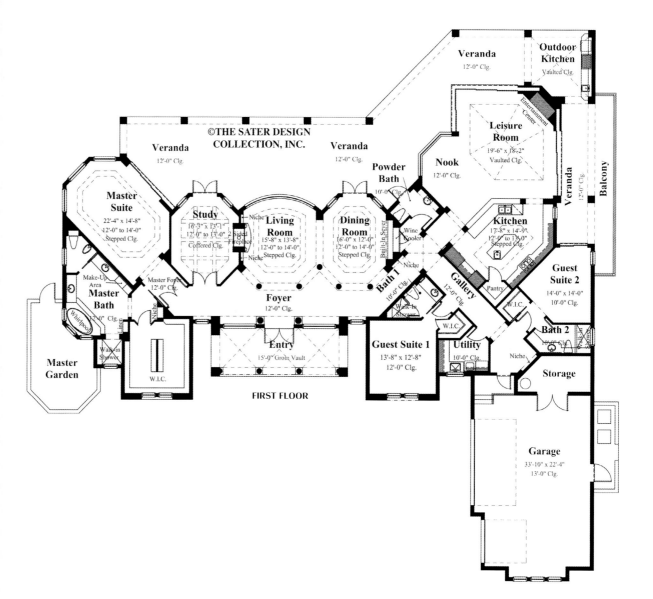

FIRST FLOOR

Maxina
Plan No. 6944

REAR ELEVATION

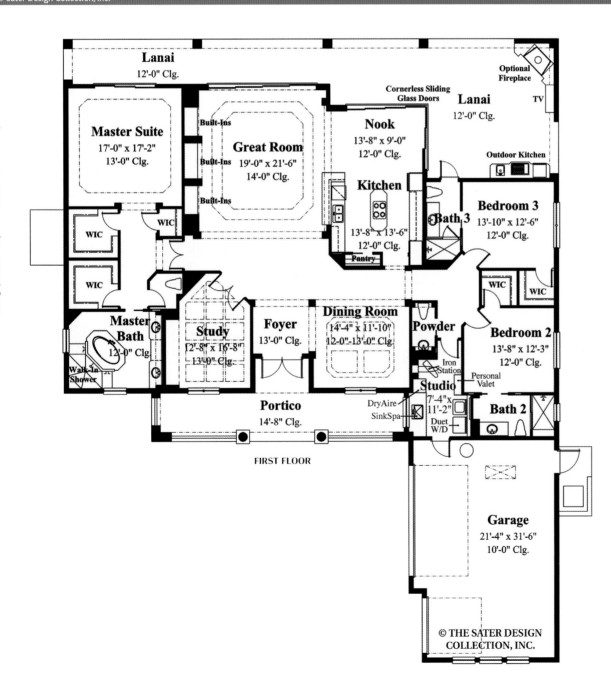

FIRST FLOOR

Lanai 12'-0" Clg.

Master Suite 17'-0" x 17'-2" 13'-0" Clg.

Built-Ins

Great Room 19'-0" x 21'-6" 14'-0" Clg.

Built-Ins

Built-Ins

Nook 13'-8" x 9'-0" 12'-0" Clg.

Cornerless Sliding Glass Doors

Optional Fireplace

Lanai 12'-0" Clg.

TV

Outdoor Kitchen

Kitchen 13'-8" x 13'-6" 12'-0" Clg.

Bath 3

Bedroom 3 13'-10" x 12'-6" 12'-0" Clg.

WIC

WIC

Pantry

WIC

WIC

Master Bath 12'-0" Clg.

Walk-In Shower

Study 12'-8" x 16'-8" 13'-0" Clg.

Foyer 13'-0" Clg.

Dining Room 14'-4" x 11'-10" 12'-0"-13'-0" Clg.

Powder

Iron Station

Personal Valet

Bedroom 2 13'-8" x 12'-3" 12'-0" Clg.

Bath 2

Portico 14'-8" Clg.

DryAire
SinkSpa

Studio 7'-4" x 11'-2"

Duet W/D

Garage 21'-4" x 31'-6" 10'-0" Clg.

© THE SATER DESIGN COLLECTION, INC.

SPECIFICATIONS:

Bedrooms: **3**

Baths: **3½**

Width: **74' 0"**

Depth: **90' 2"**

1st Floor: **3104 sq. ft.**

Total Living: **3104 sq. ft.**

Foundation: **Slab**

PLAN PRICING:

Vellum & PDF - **$1552**

CAD - **$2794**

Enjoy a simple yet elegant floor plan designed for great views, easy entertaining and seamless indoor-outdoor living. Inside, the foyer opens to a spacious great room with retreating glass walls that open to the lanai. Centrally located between the dining and great rooms, the kitchen serves both realms with ease. Away from the public spaces, a split-floor plan places guest bedrooms on one side of the home and the master retreat on the other.

Capucina

Plan No. 8010

REAR ELEVATION

SPECIFICATIONS:

Bedrooms: **4**

Baths: **4½**

Width: **71' 6"**

Depth: **83' 0"**

1st Floor: **2849 sq. ft.**

2nd Floor: **1156 sq. ft.**

Total Living: **4005 sq. ft.**

Bonus Room: **371 sq. ft.**

Foundation: **Slab**

PLAN PRICING:

Vellum & PDF - $2592

CAD - $4586

Stone gables complement the sculpted entry of this romantic, Italian Country manor. An open arrangement of the central living space, gallery and formal dining room permits views of the rear through a two-story bow window. French doors open the leisure room to the outdoors, while the nook grants access to a lanai shared with the master suite's sitting bay. Upstairs, a balcony hall— with views of the living room— connects the family bedrooms and guest quarters.

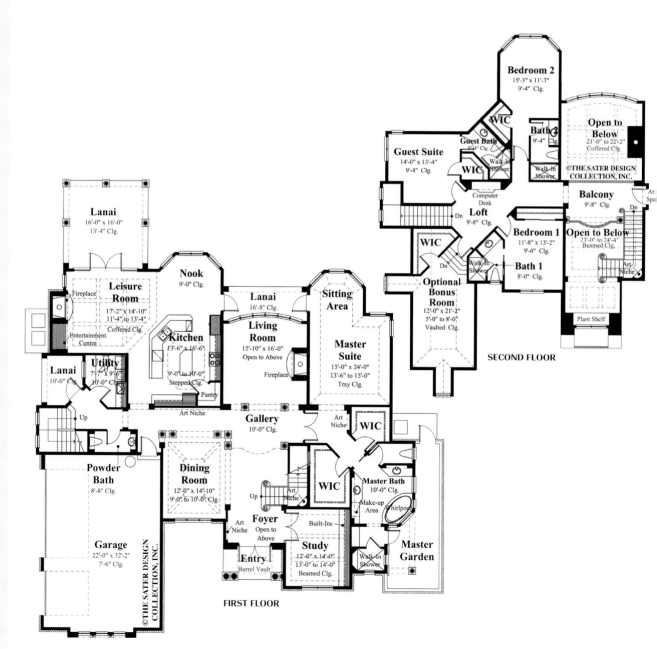

Sater Design Collection, Inc.

Isabella
Plan No. **8033**

REAR ELEVATION

SPECIFICATIONS:

Bedrooms: **5**

Baths: **5½**

Width: **58' 0"**

Depth: **65' 0"**

1st Floor: **2163 sq. ft.**

2nd Floor: **2302 sq. ft.**

Total Living: **4465 sq. ft.**

Foundation: **Slab**

PLAN PRICING:

Vellum & PDF - **$2902**

CAD - **$5135**

Rococo elements frame the double portico, lending contrast to rugged stone accents and a rusticated stucco façade. The paneled entry leads to a two-story foyer that opens to the formal rooms. Private zones frame the rear loggias—a guest suite and the leisure room both open to outdoor spaces. On the upper level, a loft overlooks the living room and accesses a sun porch. To the right, a foyer leads to the private master retreat.

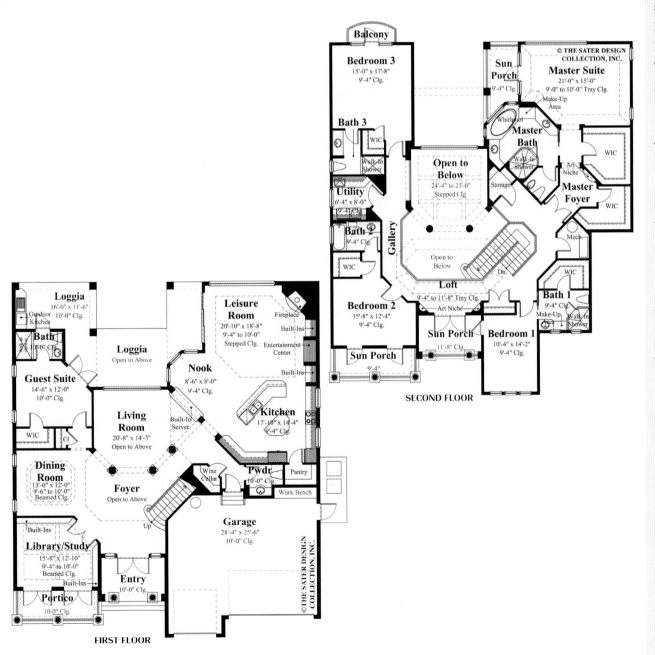

SECOND FLOOR

FIRST FLOOR

© THE SATER DESIGN COLLECTION, INC.

Arezzo
Plan No. 6547

REAR ELEVATION

SPECIFICATIONS:

Bedrooms: **2**

Baths: **2**

Width: **36' 0"**

Depth: **73' 4"**

1st Floor: **1497 sq. ft.**

Total Living: **1497 sq. ft.**

Foundation: **Slab**

PLAN PRICING:

Vellum & PDF - $875

CAD - $1347

This small, luxury Italian home plan provides two bedrooms and two bathrooms, plus a study room. The house plan features the details that count: arched passageways lead from room to room, a spacious kitchen offers a central island, the great room's fireplace warms the dining area as well, and a covered rear veranda offers sheltered outdoor space. The great room has a beautiful vaulted beam ceiling and the master suite showcases a tray ceiling. The master suite offers private veranda access and a bathroom designed for two.

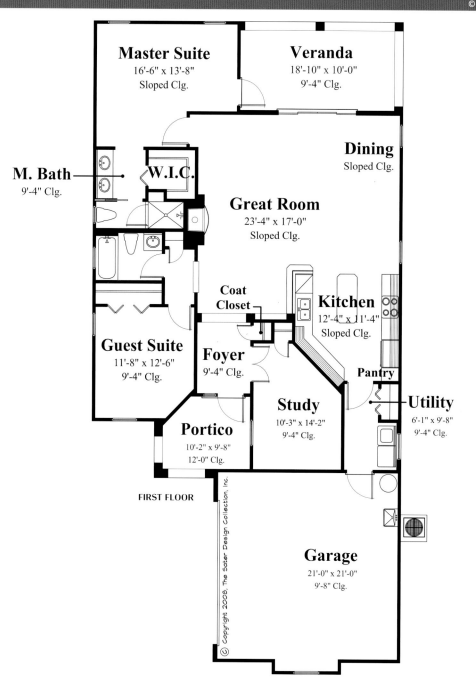

Master Suite
16'-6" x 13'-8"
Sloped Clg.

Veranda
18'-10" x 10'-0"
9'-4" Clg.

Dining
Sloped Clg.

M. Bath
9'-4" Clg.

W.I.C.

Great Room
23'-4" x 17'-0"
Sloped Clg.

Coat Closet

Kitchen
12'-4" x 11'-4"
Sloped Clg.

Guest Suite
11'-8" x 12'-6"
9'-4" Clg.

Foyer
9'-4" Clg.

Pantry

Utility
6'-1" x 9'-8"
9'-4" Clg.

Portico
10'-2" x 9'-8"
12'-0" Clg.

Study
10'-3" x 14'-2"
9'-4" Clg.

FIRST FLOOR

Garage
21'-0" x 21'-0"
9'-8" Clg.

Sater Design Collection, Inc.

Bartolini
Plan No. **8022**

REAR ELEVATION

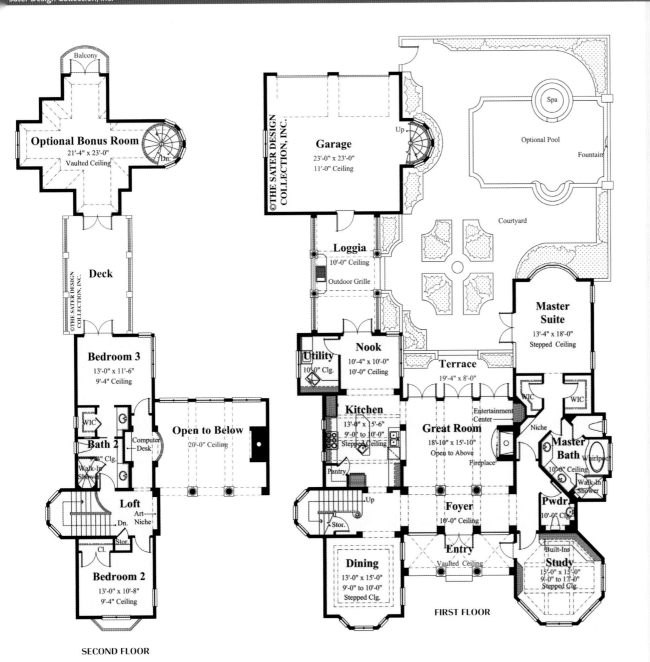

SECOND FLOOR

FIRST FLOOR

SPECIFICATIONS:

Bedrooms: **3**

Baths: **2½**

Width: **60' 6"**

Depth: **94' 0"**

1st Floor: **2084 sq. ft.**

2nd Floor: **648 sq. ft.**

Total Living: **2732 sq. ft.**

Bonus Room: **364 sq. ft.**

Foundation: **Slab**

PLAN PRICING:

Vellum & PDF - **$1366**

CAD - **$2459**

Trefoil windows and a deeply sculpted portico set off a lyrical Italian aesthetic inspired by 15th-century forms and an oceanfront attitude. Inside, three sets of French doors open the great room to the courtyard and terrace. A private wing that includes the kitchen and morning nook also opens to the outdoors. The master suite enjoys ample amounts of space, while the upper level harbors two guest suites, a loft and a bonus room with a bay tower.

Como
Plan No. 6549

SPECIFICATIONS:

Bedrooms: **2**

Baths: **2**

Width: **36' 0"**

Depth: **80' 8"**

1st Floor: **1753 sq. ft.**

Total Living: **1753 sq. ft.**

Foundation: **Slab**

PLAN PRICING:

Vellum & PDF - **$877**

CAD - **$1578**

This small, luxury Italian home plan provides two bedrooms, two bathrooms, and a study/optional bedroom. This compact house plan lives larger than its footprint thanks to an open fusion of living space within. A uniquely shaped kitchen offers an island and eating bar. The great room, with a beautiful coffered ceiling and fireplace, opens to a covered veranda perfect for outdoor entertaining through two sets of sliders. The master suite offers a tray ceiling, dual vanities and a walk-in closet.

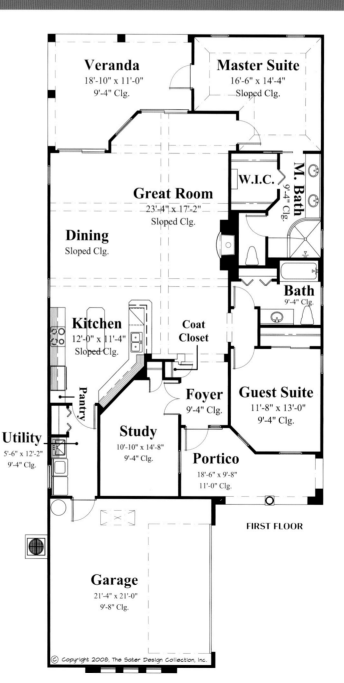

Veranda
18'-10" x 11'-0"
9'-4" Clg.

Master Suite
16'-6" x 14'-4"
Sloped Clg.

W.I.C.

M. Bath
9'-4" Clg.

Great Room
23'-4" x 17'-2"
Sloped Clg.

Dining
Sloped Clg.

Bath
9'-4" Clg.

Kitchen
12'-0" x 11'-4"
Sloped Clg.

Coat Closet

Pantry

Foyer
9'-4" Clg.

Guest Suite
11'-8" x 13'-0"
9'-4" Clg.

Utility
5'-6" x 12'-2"
9'-4" Clg.

Study
10'-10" x 14'-8"
9'-4" Clg.

Portico
18'-6" x 9'-8"
11'-0" Clg.

FIRST FLOOR

Garage
21'-4" x 21'-0"
9'-8" Clg.

© Copyright 2008, The Sater Design Collection, Inc.

Salina
Plan No. 8043

REAR ELEVATION

© Sater Design Collection, Inc.

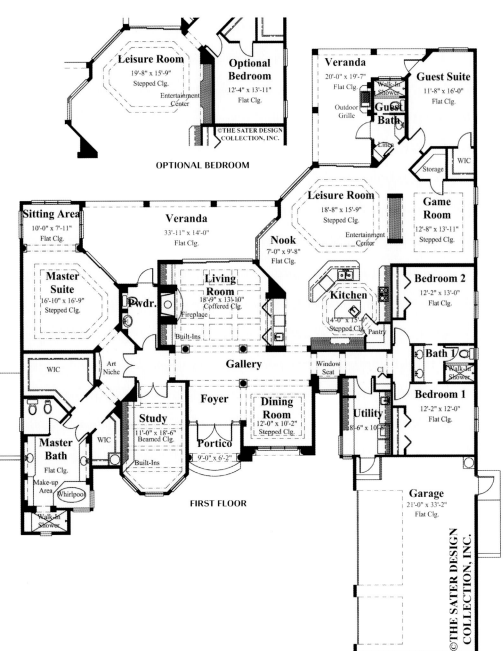

OPTIONAL BEDROOM

Leisure Room 19'-8" x 15'-9" Stepped Clg.

Optional Bedroom 12'-4" x 13'-11" Flat Clg.

Entertainment Center

©THE SATER DESIGN COLLECTION, INC.

Veranda 20'-0" x 19'-7" Flat Clg.

Guest Suite 11'-8" x 16'-0" Flat Clg.

Walk-In Shower

Guest Bath

Outdoor Grille

Linen

Storage

WIC

Leisure Room 18'-8" x 15'-9" Stepped Clg.

Game Room 12'-8" x 13'-11" Stepped Clg.

Entertainment Center

Sitting Area 10'-0" x 7'-11" Flat Clg.

Veranda 33'-11" x 14'-0" Flat Clg.

Nook 7'-0" x 9'-8" Flat Clg.

Master Suite 16'-10" x 16'-9" Stepped Clg.

Pwdr.

Living Room 18'-9" x 13'-10" Coffered Clg.

Fireplace

Built-Ins

Kitchen 14'-0" x 15'-0" Stepped Clg.

Pantry

Bedroom 2 12'-2" x 13'-0" Flat Clg.

WIC

Art Niche

Gallery

Window Seat

Cl

Bath 1

Walk-In Shower

Foyer

Study 11'-0" x 18'-6" Beamed Clg.

Built-Ins

Dining Room 12'-0" x 10'-2" Stepped Clg.

Portico 9'-0" x 6'-2"

WIC

Utility 8'-6" x 10'-2"

Bedroom 1 12'-2" x 12'-0" Flat Clg.

Master Bath Flat Clg.

Make-up Area

Whirlpool

Walk-In Shower

FIRST FLOOR

Garage 21'-0" x 33'-2" Flat Clg.

©THE SATER DESIGN COLLECTION, INC.

SPECIFICATIONS:

Bedrooms: **4**

Baths: **3½**

Width: **80′ 0″**

Depth: **104′ 8″**

1st Floor: **3757 sq. ft.**

Total Living: **3757 sq. ft.**

Foundation: **Slab**

PLAN PRICING:

Vellum & PDF - **$2442**

CAD - **$4321**

Hipped rooflines, carved eave brackets and varied gables evoke a sense of the past, while a blend of old and new prevails inside. Beamed and coffered ceilings juxtapose state-of-the-art amenities—a pass-thru wet bar, cutting-edge appliances in the kitchen, and a standalone media center between the leisure and game rooms. Rounded arches define the transitions between well-appointed rooms and open spaces. Near the rear of the plan, guest quarters and the leisure room open to the veranda.

Bella Mia

Plan No. 6507

REAR ELEVATION

© Sater Design Collection, Inc.

SPECIFICATIONS:

Bedrooms: **3**

Baths: **2**

Width: **42' 8"**

Depth: **63' 4"**

1st Floor: **1404 sq. ft.**

Total Living: **1404 sq. ft.**

Foundation: **Slab**

PLAN PRICING:

Vellum & PDF - $875

CAD - $1264

A turreted breakfast nook sits elegantly aside the entryway, which features a dramatic barrel vault ceiling. Inside, the foyer looks ahead through a disappearing wall of glass that opens the great room to the verandah. The great room and dining room proudly feature step ceiling detail. The master suite and dining room also have sliding doors to the rear living spaces, and a pass-thru bar makes the kitchen user-friendly. This spacious house plan offers a master bathroom with all the trimmings – a double vanity, walk in closet, whirlpool tub, and walk in shower.

FIRST FLOOR

© THE SATER DESIGN COLLECTION, INC.

Laparelli
Plan No. 8035

REAR ELEVATION

SPECIFICATIONS:

Bedrooms: **3**

Baths: **4**

Width: **83' 10"**

Depth: **106' 0"**

1st Floor: **3954 sq. ft.**

Total Living: **3954 sq. ft.**

Foundation: **Slab**

PLAN PRICING:

Vellum & PDF - **$2570**

CAD - **$4547**

Romantic elements reside throughout this Italian villa, melding style and views with a profound level of comfort. Arch-topped windows bring light into the forward formal spaces, while retreating glass walls on the lanai side extend both public and private realms outside. The kitchen serves the formal dining room via a gallery, while a wet bar announces the casual living space. The owners' retreat provides a magnificent bedroom with a morning kitchen and access to the wraparound lanai.

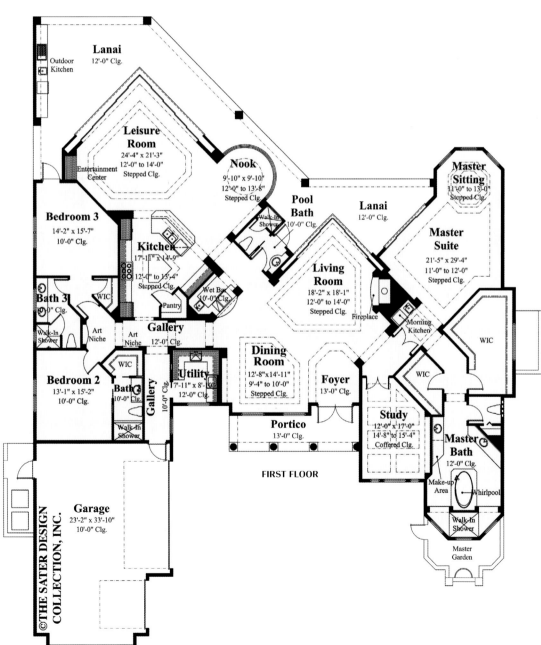

FIRST FLOOR

©THE SATER DESIGN COLLECTION, INC.

Empoli
Plan No. 6551

REAR ELEVATION

SPECIFICATIONS:

Bedrooms: **3**

Baths: **2½**

Width: **38′ 0″**

Depth: **87′ 4″**

1st Floor: **1790 sq. ft.**

Total Living: **1790 sq. ft.**

Foundation: **Slab**

PLAN PRICING:

Vellum & PDF - **$895**

CAD - **$1611**

Its compact floor plan features a courtyard layout, which is perfect for a swimming pool. With an open layout, the great room, dining room, and master suite all have access to the outdoors. The great room showcases a beautiful fireplace and coffered ceilings, while the master suite offers a step ceiling. The master suite and guest suite are on opposite ends of the house to maximize privacy. The kitchen has plenty of counter space, including a center island. The master bathroom has a dual vanity and a walk-in shower and closet.

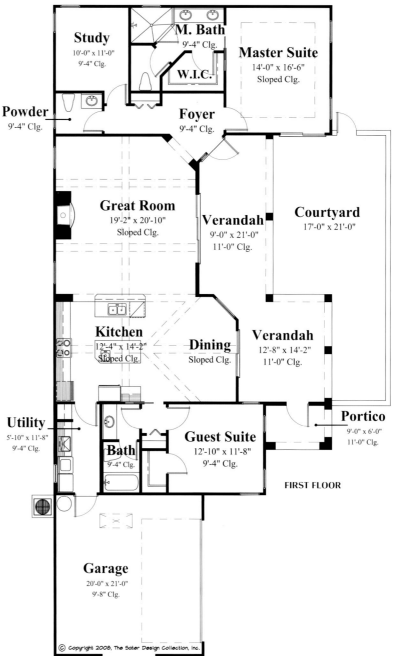

Study
10'-0" x 11'-0"
9'-4" Clg.

M. Bath
9'-4" Clg.

W.I.C.

Master Suite
14'-0" x 16'-6"
Sloped Clg.

Powder
9'-4" Clg.

Foyer
9'-4" Clg.

Great Room
19'-2" x 20'-10"
Sloped Clg.

Verandah
9'-0" x 21'-0"
11'-0" Clg.

Courtyard
17'-0" x 21'-0"

Kitchen
12'-4" x 14'-2"
Sloped Clg.

Dining
Sloped Clg.

Verandah
12'-8" x 14'-2"
11'-0" Clg.

Portico
9'-0" x 6'-0"
11'-0" Clg.

Utility
5'-10" x 11'-8"
9'-4" Clg.

Bath
9'-4" Clg.

Guest Suite
12'-10" x 11'-8"
9'-4" Clg.

FIRST FLOOR

Garage
20'-0" x 21'-0"
9'-8" Clg.

© Copyright 2008, The Sater Design Collection, Inc.

Raphaello
Plan No. 8037

© Sater Design Collection, Inc.

REAR ELEVATION

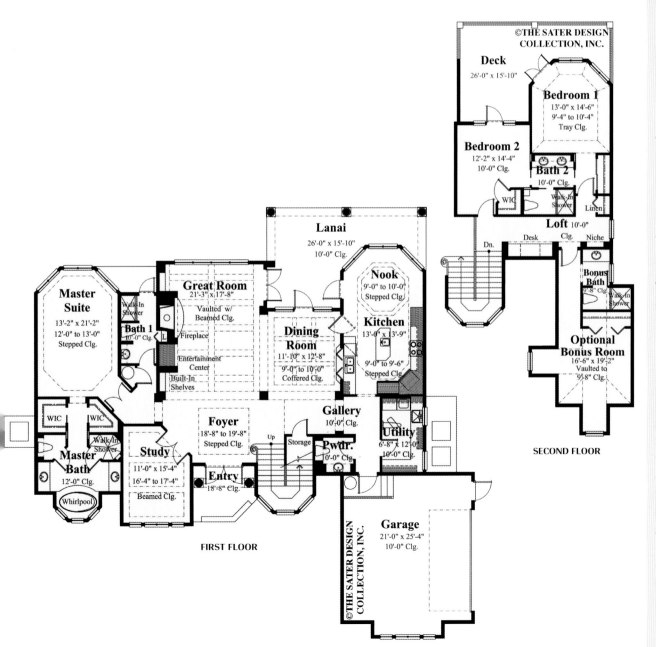

FIRST FLOOR

SECOND FLOOR

©THE SATER DESIGN COLLECTION, INC.

SPECIFICATIONS:

Bedrooms: **3**

Baths: **3½**

Width: **72' 0"**

Depth: **68' 3"**

1st Floor: **2250 sq. ft.**

2nd Floor: **663 sq. ft.**

Total Living: **2913 sq. ft.**

Bonus Room: **351 sq. ft.**

Foundation: **Slab**

PLAN PRICING:

Vellum & PDF - **$1457**

CAD - **$2622**

Turrets integrate the layered elevation, which draws its inspiration from 16th-century forms with symmetry, brackets and pilasters. New-world allocations of space defy tradition throughout the interior, creating a natural flow and easing everyday functions. Living spaces oriented to the rear of the plan take in expansive views through retreating glass walls and access the lanai. On the upper level, guest bedrooms open to a shared deck and a computer loft leads to a spacious bonus room.

Tirano
Plan No. 6509

REAR ELEVATION

© Sater Design Collection, In

SPECIFICATIONS:

Bedrooms: **3**

Baths: **2**

Width: **47' 2"**

Depth: **75' 0"**

1st Floor: **1919 sq. ft.**

Total Living: **1919 sq. ft.**

Foundation: **Slab**

PLAN PRICING:

Vellum & PDF - **$960**

CAD - **$1727**

The interior flows around a large central great room featuring a stepped ceiling. The central living space offers easy access to the master suite and two secondary bedrooms on one side of the home, the dining room and kitchen on the other. The spacious island kitchen has a walk-in pantry. An optional layout changes the dining area into a study or guest room with French doors that open onto the great room. This house plan's master bathroom is full of little luxuries. It has an extensive, double vanity, whirlpool tub, walk in shower, a separate room for the toilet, and disconnected his and her closets.

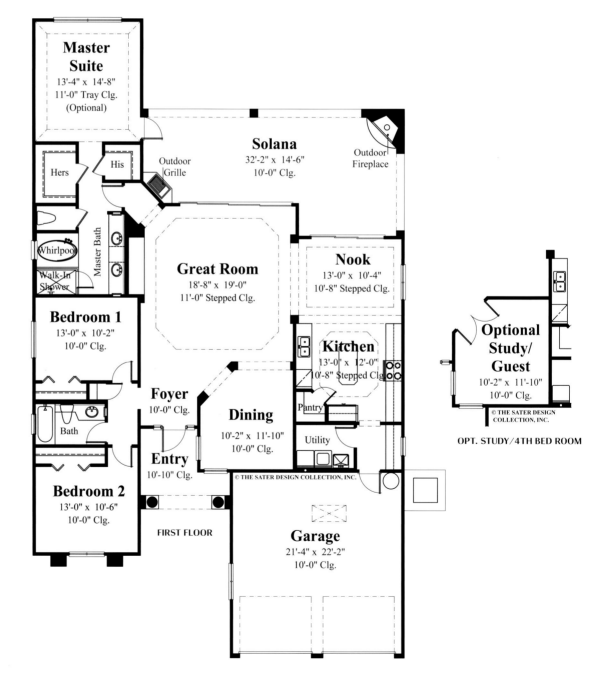

Master Suite
13'-4" x 14'-8"
11'-0" Tray Clg.
(Optional)

Solana
32'-2" x 14'-6"
10'-0" Clg.

Outdoor Grille

Outdoor Fireplace

Hers

His

Master Bath

Whirlpool

Walk-In Shower

Great Room
18'-8" x 19'-0"
11'-0" Stepped Clg.

Nook
13'-0" x 10'-4"
10'-8" Stepped Clg.

Bedroom 1
13'-0" x 10'-2"
10'-0" Clg.

Kitchen
13'-0" x 12'-0"
10'-8" Stepped Clg.

Optional Study/ Guest
10'-2" x 11'-10"
10'-0" Clg.

© THE SATER DESIGN COLLECTION, INC.

OPT. STUDY/4TH BED ROOM

Foyer
10'-0" Clg.

Dining
10'-2" x 11'-10"
10'-0" Clg.

Pantry

Bath

Entry
10'-10" Clg.

Utility

Bedroom 2
13'-0" x 10'-6"
10'-0" Clg.

© THE SATER DESIGN COLLECTION, INC.

FIRST FLOOR

Garage
21'-4" x 22'-2"
10'-0" Clg.

© Sater Design Collection, Inc.

REAR ELEVATION

Bellini

Plan No. **8042**

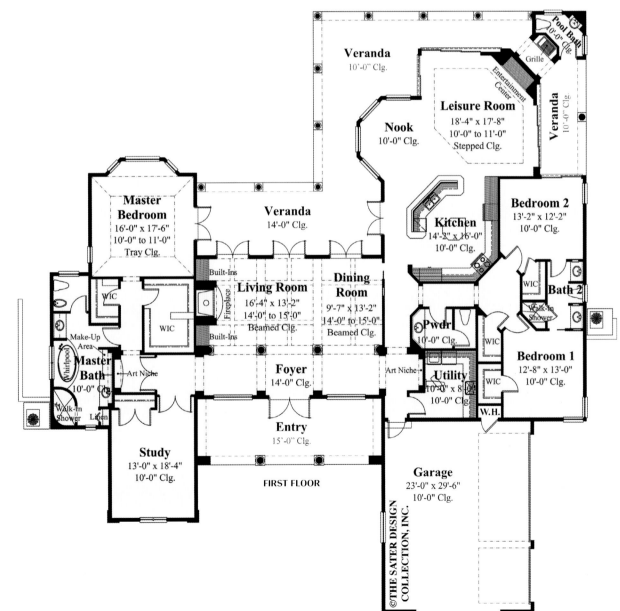

Veranda
10'-0" Clg.

Pool Bath
10'-0" Clg.

Grille

Nook
10'-0" Clg.

Leisure Room
18'-4" x 17'-8"
10'-0" to 11'-0"
Stepped Clg.

Entertainment Center

Veranda
10'-0" Clg.

Master Bedroom
16'-0" x 17'-6"
10'-0" to 11'-0"
Tray Clg.

Veranda
14'-0" Clg.

Kitchen
14'-2" x 16'-0"
10'-0" Clg.

Bedroom 2
13'-2" x 12'-2"
10'-0" Clg.

WIC

Built-Ins

WIC

WIC

Living Room
16'-4" x 13'-2"
14'-0" to 15'-0"
Beamed Clg.

Dining Room
9'-7" x 13'-2"
14'-0" to 15'-0"
Beamed Clg.

Fireplace

Built-Ins

Bath 2
Walk-In Shower

WIC

Make-Up Area

Master Bath
10'-0" Clg.

Whirlpool

Art Niche

Foyer
14'-0" Clg.

Art Niche

Pwdr
10'-0" Clg.

WIC

Bedroom 1
12'-8" x 13'-0"
10'-0" Clg.

Walk-In Shower

Linen

Utility
10'-0" x 8'-0"
10'-0" Clg.

WIC

W.H.

Study
13'-0" x 18'-4"
10'-0" Clg.

Entry
15'-0" Clg.

FIRST FLOOR

Garage
23'-0" x 29'-6"
10'-0" Clg.

© THE SATER DESIGN COLLECTION, INC.

SPECIFICATIONS:

Bedrooms: **3**

Full Baths: **2**

Half Bath: **2**

Width: **84' 0"**

Depth: **92' 2"**

1st Floor: **3343 sq. ft.**

Total Living: **3343 sq. ft.**

Foundation: **Slab**

PLAN PRICING:

Vellum & PDF - $1672

CAD - $3009

Classic architectural lines surround an entry portico inspired by original Italian villas. Ancient and modern elements come together throughout the interior, juxtaposing rusticated beamed ceilings with up-to-the-minute electronics. An open gallery announces the living/dining room—a splendid space anchored by a massive fireplace. A state-of-the-art kitchen overlooks the nook and spacious leisure room. Retreating glass walls open the space to a wraparound veranda that includes an outdoor grille and a secluded area for meals alfresco.

Mezzina

Plan No. **8073**

REAR ELEVATION

SPECIFICATIONS:

Bedrooms: **4**

Baths: **4½**

Width: **69′ 10″**

Depth: **120′ 4″**

1st Floor: **4175 sq. ft.**

Total Living: **4175 sq. ft.**

Foundation: **Slab**

PLAN PRICING:

Vellum & PDF - **$2714**

CAD - **$4801**

This unique villa features private family and guest spaces with open connections to a spacious courtyard area. Past the portico, the foyer opens up to views beyond the grand salon's floor-to-ceiling windows. To the left, the kitchen connects to the formal dining room through a butler's pantry. Nearby, the leisure room opens to the loggia and outdoor kitchen. A gallery leads to two secluded guest suites, while a detached guest suite provides even more privacy.

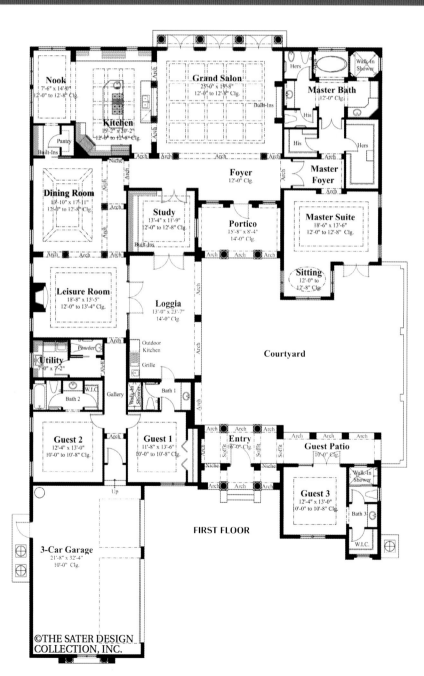

FIRST FLOOR

©THE SATER DESIGN COLLECTION, INC.

Fedora
Plan No. **6513**

REAR ELEVATION

Master Suite
13'-10" x 14'-6"
11'-0" Clg.
Tray Clg.

W.I.C.

W.I.C.

Outdoor Grille

Solana
32'-6" x 13'-10"
10'-0" Clg.

Outdoor Fireplace

Whirlpool

Master Bath

Walk In Shower

Linen

Great Room
18'-10" x 19'-0"
10'-8" Clg.
Stepped Clg.

Dining
13'-4" x 10'-5"
10'-8" Clg.
Stepped Clg.

Bath

Kitchen
13'-4" x 11'-9"
10'-8" Clg.

Bedroom
13'-4" x 11'-2"
10'-0" Clg.

Foyer
10'-0" Clg.

Study/ Guest
11'-2" x 12'-10"
10'-0" Clg.

Entry
10'-0" Clg.

Utility

Garage
20'-2" x 20'-4"
10'-0" Clg.

FIRST FLOOR

© THE SATER DESIGN COLLECTION, INC.

SPECIFICATIONS:

Bedrooms: **3**

Baths: **2**

Width: **47' 0"**

Depth: **74' 0"**

1st Floor: **1727 sq. ft.**

Total Living: **1727 sq. ft.**

Foundation: **Slab**

PLAN PRICING:

Vellum & PDF - **$875**

CAD - **$1554**

Multiple arched windows and varied rooflines add interest to the façade, while a smart floor plan gives style and function to the interior. The centerpiece of this home is the spacious great room that serves as the hub of activity. A kitchen, generous with counter space, is open to the dining room. The master retreat offers his and her walk-in closets and dual vanities to conveniently serve the owners. The master bathroom also provides a walk-in shower and whirlpool bathtub.

Alessandra
Plan No. 8003

REAR ELEVATION

© Sater Design Collection, Inc

SPECIFICATIONS:

Bedrooms: **4**

Baths: **3½**

Width: **85′ 0″**

Depth: **76′ 2″**

1st Floor: **2829 sq. ft.**

2nd Floor: **1127 sq. ft.**

Total Living: **3956 sq. ft.**

Foundation: **Slab**

PLAN PRICING:

Vellum & PDF - $2571

CAD - $4549

Massive square columns frame a spectacular portico and pedimented window above the entry of this romantic villa. Well-defined formal rooms offer both intimacy and grandeur, while the casual zone provides a lose-the-shoes atmosphere. Defined by a series of sculpted arches, the central corridor extends the plan's sight lines to the leisure and the master wings. On the upper level, a balcony hall connects three guest quarters that boast private decks.

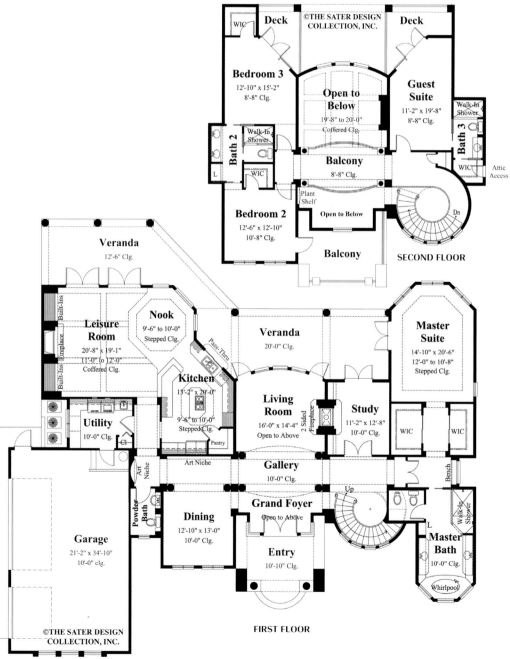

Flagstone Ridge

Plan No. 6765

© Sater Design Collection, Inc.

REAR ELEVATION

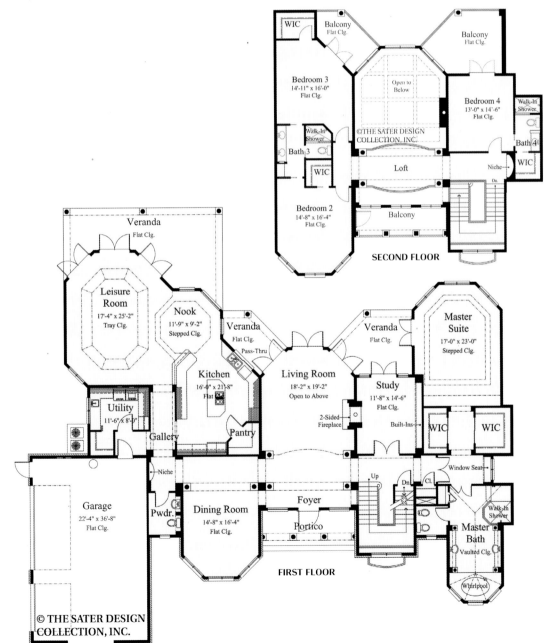

SECOND FLOOR

WIC

Balcony
Flat Clg.

Balcony
Flat Clg.

Bedroom 3
14'-11" x 16'-0"
Flat Clg.

Open to
Below

Bedroom 4
13'-0" x 14'-6"
Flat Clg.

Walk-In
Shower

©THE SATER DESIGN
COLLECTION, INC.

Walk-In
Shower

Bath 3

Bath 4

WIC

Niche

WIC

Loft

Bedroom 2
14'-8" x 16'-4"
Flat Clg.

Balcony

Dn.

FIRST FLOOR

Veranda
Flat Clg.

Leisure
Room
17'-4" x 25'-2"
Tray Clg.

Nook
11'-9" x 9'-2"
Stepped Clg.

Veranda
Flat Clg.

Pass-Thru

Veranda
Flat Clg.

Master
Suite
17'-0" x 23'-0"
Stepped Clg.

Kitchen
16'-0" x 21'-8"
Flat

Living Room
18'-2" x 19'-2"
Open to Above

Study
11'-8" x 14'-6"
Flat Clg.

Utility
11'-6" x 8'-0"

2-Sided
Fireplace

Built-Ins

WIC

WIC

Gallery

Pantry

Niche

Window Seat

Garage
22'-4" x 36'-8"
Flat Clg.

Pwdr.

Dining Room
14'-8" x 16'-4"
Flat Clg.

Foyer

Up

Dn.

Cl.

Walk-In
Shower

Portico

Master
Bath
Vaulted Clg.

Whirlpool

© THE SATER DESIGN
COLLECTION, INC.

SPECIFICATIONS:

Bedrooms: **4**

Baths: **4½**

Width: **95' 0"**

Depth: **84' 8"**

1st Floor: **3556 sq. ft.**

2nd Floor: **1253 sq. ft.**

Total Living: **4809 sq. ft.**

Foundation: **Slab**

PLAN PRICING:

Vellum & PDF - **$4809**

CAD - **$8175**

The dramatic use of stacked stone amidst arch-top windows gives this home a dignified and warm façade. A front portico under triple arches leads to the foyer and living room, where three pairs of French doors open to the veranda and breathtaking views. French doors also lead outside from the study, master suite and oversized leisure room. A second-floor loft views the living room and connects to three upstairs bedrooms.

Spanish

An intoxicating mix of courtyards, arched loggias, turrets and porticos–these Spanish-inspired homes evoke a sense of timeless romanticism. Expansive verandahs, decks and balconies extend the living areas into the outdoors and welcome friends and family to gather, laugh and enjoy. Generous living rooms flow freely into formal dining areas. Gourmet-caliber kitchens open into breakfast nooks and leisure rooms–creating a common living space destined to become a favorite gathering area for friends and family. Bold and simply beautiful, these Mediterranean manors promise 21st-century repose combined with Old-World character and ambiance.

Martelli
Plan No. 8061

© Sater Design Collection, Inc.

REAR ELEVATION

SPECIFICATIONS:

Bedrooms: **4**

Baths: **3½**

Width: **68' 8"**

Depth: **91' 8"**

1st Floor: **3497 sq. ft.**

Total Living: **3497 sq. ft.**

Foundation: **Slab**

PLAN PRICING:

Vellum & PDF - $1749

CAD - $3147

A sculpted, recessed entry defines the finely detailed Spanish eclectic façade, and a quatrefoil window confirms a Moorish influence. Inside, an open arrangement of the foyer and the formal rooms permits natural light to flow freely through the space. Walls of glass to the rear of the plan open the public and private realms to spectacular views, while nearby the gourmet kitchen easily serves planned events both inside and out.

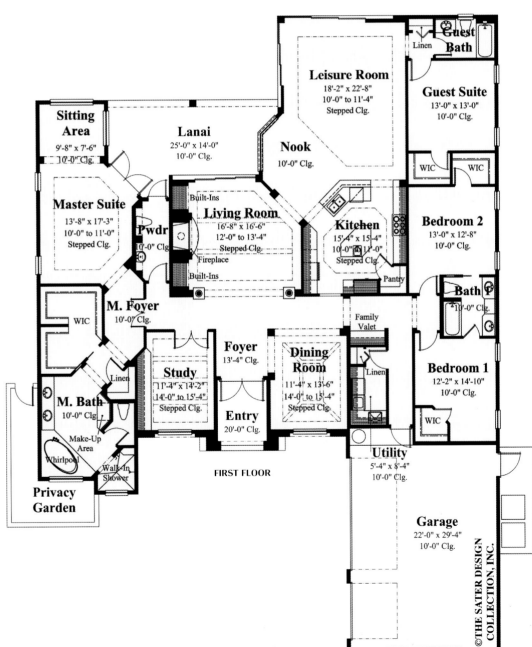

Sitting Area
9'-8" x 7'-6"
10'-0" Clg.

Lanai
25'-0" x 14'-0"
10'-0" Clg.

Leisure Room
18'-2" x 22'-8"
10'-0" to 11'-4"
Stepped Clg.

Guest Bath

Linen

Guest Suite
13'-0" x 13'-0"
10'-0" Clg.

Nook
10'-0" Clg.

Master Suite
13'-8" x 17'-3"
10'-0" to 11'-0"
Stepped Clg.

Built-Ins

Living Room
16'-8" x 16'-6"
12'-0" to 13'-4"
Stepped Clg.

Fireplace

Built-Ins

Pwdr
10'-0" Clg.

Kitchen
15'-4" x 15'-4"
10'-0" to 11'-0"
Stepped Clg.

WIC WIC

Bedroom 2
13'-0" x 12'-8"
10'-0" Clg.

Pantry

Bath
10'-0" Clg.

M. Foyer
10'-0" Clg.

WIC

M. Bath
10'-0" Clg.

Linen

Study
11'-4" x 14'-2"
14'-0" to 15'-4"
Stepped Clg.

Foyer
13'-4" Clg.

Dining Room
11'-4" x 13'-6"
14'-0" to 15'-4"
Stepped Clg.

Entry
20'-0" Clg.

Family Valet

Linen

Bedroom 1
12'-2" x 14'-10"
10'-0" Clg.

WIC

Make-Up Area

Whirlpool

Walk-In Shower

Privacy Garden

FIRST FLOOR

Utility
5'-4" x 8'-4"
10'-0" Clg.

Garage
22'-0" x 29'-4"
10'-0" Clg.

©THE SATER DESIGN COLLECTION, INC.

Gavello
Plan No. **6553**

REAR ELEVATION

© Sater Design Collection, Inc

SPECIFICATIONS:

Bedrooms: **3**

Baths: **3**

Width: **40′ 0″**

Depth: **89′ 0″**

1st Floor: **1629 sq. ft.**

Cabana: **263 sq. ft.**

Total Living: **1892 sq. ft.**

Foundation: **Slab**

PLAN PRICING:

Vellum & PDF - $946

CAD - $1703

With an open layout, the great room, dining room, master suite, and guest rooms all have access to the outdoors. The great room showcases a beautiful fireplace and coffered ceilings, while the master suite offers a step ceiling. The master suite and guest suites are on opposite ends of the house to maximize privacy. The cabana and its private bathroom are disconnected from the house, which makes it perfect as a guest retreat. The kitchen has plenty of counter space, including a center island.

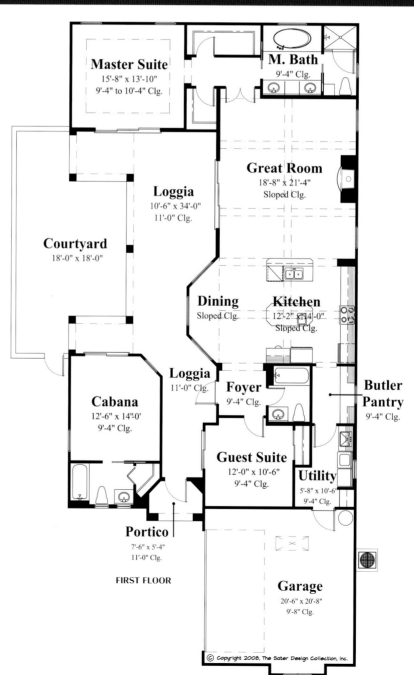

Master Suite
15′-8″ x 13′-10″
9′-4″ to 10′-4″ Clg.

M. Bath
9′-4″ Clg.

Great Room
18′-8″ x 21′-4″
Sloped Clg.

Loggia
10′-6″ x 34′-0″
11′-0″ Clg.

Courtyard
18′-0″ x 18′-0″

Dining
Sloped Clg.

Kitchen
12′-2″ x 14′-0″
Sloped Clg.

Loggia
11′-0″ Clg.

Foyer
9′-4″ Clg.

Butler Pantry
9′-4″ Clg.

Cabana
12′-6″ x 14′-0″
9′-4″ Clg.

Guest Suite
12′-0″ x 10′-6″
9′-4″ Clg.

Utility
5′-8″ x 10′-6″
9′-4″ Clg.

Portico
7′-6″ x 5′-4″
11′-0″ Clg.

FIRST FLOOR

Garage
20′-6″ x 20′-8″
9′-8″ Clg.

© Copyright 2008, The Sater Design Collection, Inc.

Tre Mori
Plan No. 8078

Sater Design Collection, Inc.

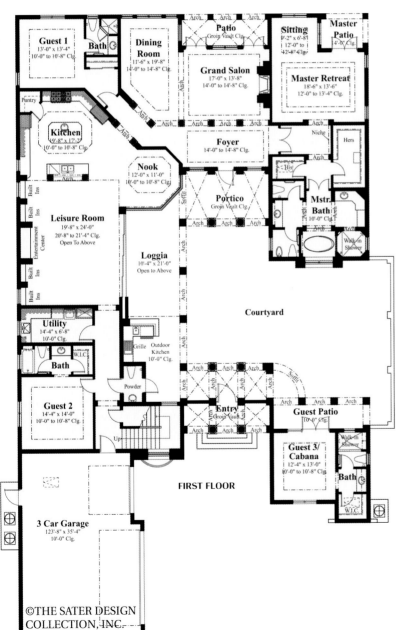

FIRST FLOOR

©THE SATER DESIGN COLLECTION, INC.

Guest 1
13'-0" x 13'-4"
10'-0" to 10'-8" Clg.

Bath

Dining Room
11'-6" x 19'-8"
14'-0" to 14'-8" Clg.

Patio
Groin Vault Clg.

Sitting
9'-2" x 6'-8"
12'-0" to 42'-8" Clg.

Master Patio
4'-0" Clg.

Grand Salon
17'-0" x 13'-8"
14'-0" to 14'-8" Clg.

Master Retreat
18'-6" x 13'-6"
12'-0" to 13'-4" Clg.

Pantry

Kitchen
9'-8" x 17'-2"
10'-0" to 10'-8" Clg.

Nook
12'-0" x 11'-0"
10'-0" to 10'-8" Clg.

Foyer
14'-0" to 14'-8" Clg.

Niche

Hers

His

Built Ins

Leisure Room
19'-8" x 24'-0"
20'-8" to 21'-4" Clg.
Open To Above

Entertainment Center

Portico
Groin Vault Clg.

Mstr. Bath
10'-0" Clg.

Loggia
10'-4" x 21'-0"
Open to Above

Walk-in Shower

Utility
14'-4" x 6'-8"
10'-0" Clg.

Bath

W.I.C.

Powder

Grille Outdoor Kitchen
10'-0" Clg.

Courtyard

Guest 2
14'-4" x 14'-0"
10'-0" to 10'-8" Clg.

Entry
Groin Vault

Guest Patio
10'-0" Clg.

Up

3 Car Garage
123'-8" x 35'-4"
10'-0" Clg.

Guest 3/ Cabana
12'-4" x 13'-0"
10'-0" to 10'-8" Clg.

Walk-in Shower

Bath

W.I.C.

©THE SATER DESIGN COLLECTION, INC.

SECOND FLOOR

©THE SATER DESIGN COLLECTION, INC.

Open to Below

Loggia
Below
21'-4" Clg.

Loft
9'-4" Clg.
Built-Ins

Bath

W.I.C.

Guest Balcony
11'-4" x 15'-3"
9'-4" Clg.

Guest 4
14'-4" x 14'-0"
9'-4" to 10'-0" Clg.

Dn.

SPECIFICATIONS:

Bedrooms: **5**

Baths: **5½**

Width: **69' 10"**

Depth: **120' 0"**

1st Floor: **3683 sq. ft.**

2nd Floor: **563 sq. ft.**

Cabana: **310 sq. ft.**

Total Living: **4556 sq. ft.**

Foundation: **Slab**

PLAN PRICING:

Vellum & PDF - **$2961**

CAD - **$5239**

The classic façade is graced with low-pitched, projecting gables, Palladian-style windows and a triple-arch entry decorated with wrought iron. Past the groin-vaulted entry, an enchanting courtyard greets visitors in this Spanish-inspired villa. Beyond the foyer, the kitchen flows into the nook and leisure room, extending onto the loggia through retreating glass walls. Secluded guest suites include one upstairs with a private balcony and a detached, cabana-style retreat on the main level.

Belizza

Plan No. **6508**

REAR ELEVATION

© Sater Design Collection, In

SPECIFICATIONS:

Bedrooms: **3**

Baths: **2**

Width: **42' 8"**

Depth: **63' 4"**

1st Floor: **1404 sq. ft.**

Total Living: **1404 sq. ft.**

Foundation: **Slab**

PLAN PRICING:

Vellum & PDF - $875

CAD - $1264

A turreted breakfast nook sits elegantly aside the entryway, which features a dramatic barrel vault ceiling. Inside, the foyer looks ahead through a disappearing wall of glass that opens the great room to the verandah. The great room and dining room proudly feature step ceiling detail. The master suite and dining room also have sliding doors to the rear living spaces, and a pass-thru bar makes the kitchen user-friendly. This spacious house plan offers a master bathroom with all the trimmings – a double vanity, walk in closet, whirlpool tub, and walk in shower.

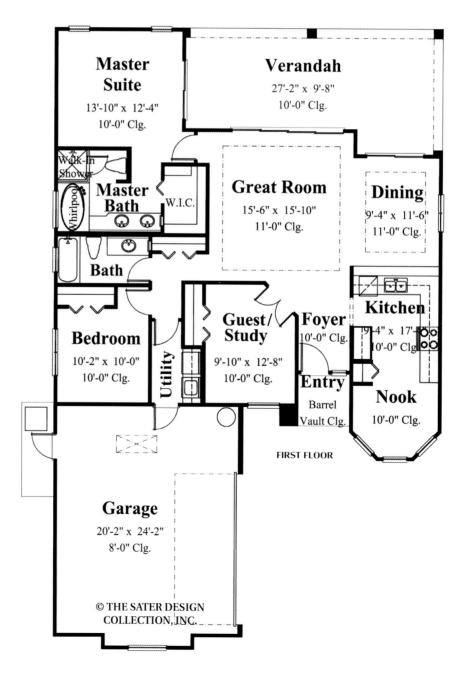

Master Suite
13'-10" x 12'-4"
10'-0" Clg.

Verandah
27'-2" x 9'-8"
10'-0" Clg.

Walk-In Shower

Whirlpool

Master Bath

W.I.C.

Great Room
15'-6" x 15'-10"
11'-0" Clg.

Dining
9'-4" x 11'-6"
11'-0" Clg.

Bath

Kitchen
9'-4" x 17'-
10'-0" Clg

Bedroom
10'-2" x 10'-0"
10'-0" Clg.

Utility

Guest/Study
9'-10" x 12'-8"
10'-0" Clg.

Foyer
10'-0" Clg.

Entry
Barrel Vault Clg.

Nook
10'-0" Clg.

FIRST FLOOR

Garage
20'-2" x 24'-2"
8'-0" Clg.

© THE SATER DESIGN COLLECTION, INC.

Florianne
Plan No. 6514

REAR ELEVATION

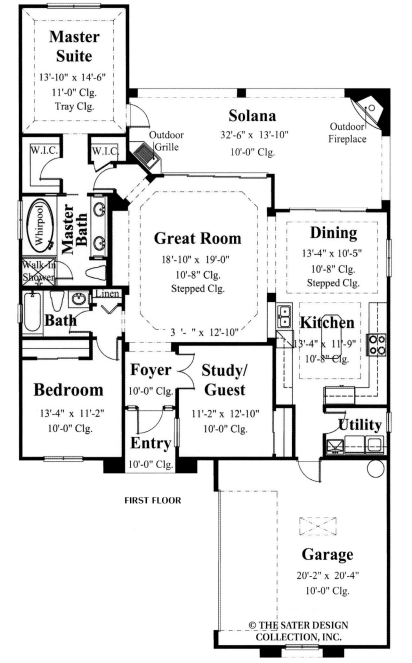

FIRST FLOOR

Master Suite
13'-10" x 14'-6"
11'-0" Clg.
Tray Clg.

W.I.C.

W.I.C.

Solana
32'-6" x 13'-10"
10'-0" Clg.

Outdoor Grille

Outdoor Fireplace

Master Bath

Whirlpool

Walk-In Shower

Linen

Bath

Great Room
18'-10" x 19'-0"
10'-8" Clg.
Stepped Clg.

3'- " x 12'-10"

Dining
13'-4" x 10'-5"
10'-8" Clg.
Stepped Clg.

Kitchen
13'-4" x 11'-9"
10'-8" Clg.

Bedroom
13'-4" x 11'-2"
10'-0" Clg.

Foyer
10'-0" Clg.

Study/Guest
11'-2" x 12'-10"
10'-0" Clg.

Entry
10'-0" Clg.

Utility

Garage
20'-2" x 20'-4"
10'-0" Clg.

© THE SATER DESIGN COLLECTION, INC.

SPECIFICATIONS:

Bedrooms: **3**

Baths: **2**

Width: **47' 0"**

Depth: **74' 0"**

1st Floor: **1727 sq. ft.**

Total Living: **1727 sq. ft.**

Foundation: **Slab**

PLAN PRICING:

Vellum & PDF - $875

CAD - $1554

Multiple arched windows and varied rooflines add interest to the façade, while a smart floor plan gives style and function to the interior. The master suite has a tray ceiling, while the great room, dining room and kitchen have step ceilings. The centerpiece of this house plan is the spacious great room that serves as the hub of activity. A kitchen, generous with counter space, is open to the dining room. The dining room and great room both feature sliding glass walls that, when open, provide a seamless transition to the outdoor living space, which boasts a fireplace and grille.

San Lorenzo
Plan No. 8014

REAR ELEVATION

SPECIFICATIONS:

Bedrooms: **4**

Baths: **4½**

Width: **70' 0"**

Depth: **100' 0"**

1st Floor: **3027 sq. ft.**

2nd Floor: **1952 sq. ft.**

Total Living: **4979 sq. ft.**

Bonus Room: **294 sq. ft.**

Foundation: **Slab**

PLAN PRICING:

Vellum & PDF - $3983

Revival elements—quoins, fractables and sculpted masonry surrounds—recall the beauty of rural Spanish villas. A coffered ceiling and a two-story bow window brighten the core of the plan: the great room, which shares a two-sided fireplace with the study. The foyer and central gallery benefit from the spectacular stairway that winds through the turret, linking with a balcony loft. An open arrangement of the leisure room and kitchen permits breezes to circulate through the entire wing.

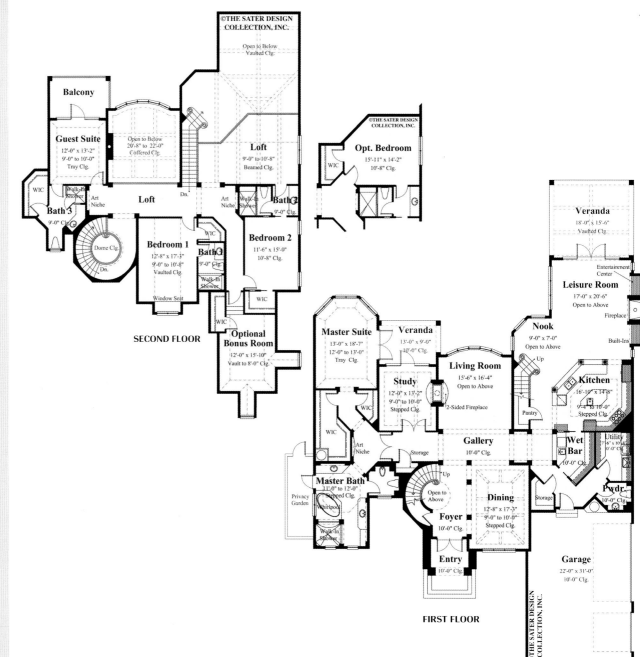

SECOND FLOOR

FIRST FLOOR

Cerafino
Plan No. 6504

© Sater Design Collection, Inc.

REAR ELEVATION

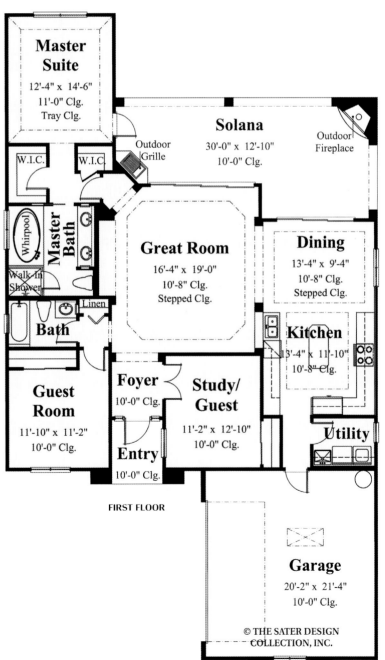

Master Suite
12'-4" x 14'-6"
11'-0" Clg.
Tray Clg.

W.I.C.

W.I.C.

Solana
30'-0" x 12'-10"
10'-0" Clg.

Outdoor Grille

Outdoor Fireplace

Master Bath

Whirlpool

Walk In Shower

Linen

Bath

Great Room
16'-4" x 19'-0"
10'-8" Clg.
Stepped Clg.

Dining
13'-4" x 9'-4"
10'-8" Clg.
Stepped Clg.

Kitchen
13'-4" x 11'-10"
10'-8" Clg.

Guest Room
11'-10" x 11'-2"
10'-0" Clg.

Foyer
10'-0" Clg.

Study/Guest
11'-2" x 12'-10"
10'-0" Clg.

Entry
10'-0" Clg.

Utility

FIRST FLOOR

Garage
20'-2" x 21'-4"
10'-0" Clg.

© THE SATER DESIGN COLLECTION, INC.

SPECIFICATIONS:

Bedrooms: **3**

Baths: **2**

Width: **44' 0"**

Depth: **74' 0"**

1st Floor: **1608 sq. ft.**

Total Living: **1608 sq. ft.**

Foundation: **Slab**

PLAN PRICING:

Vellum & PDF - $875

CAD - $1447

This small, luxury, Spanish Colonial plan boasts step ceilings in the dining room and kitchen, tray ceilings in the master bedroom and octagonal stepped ceilings in the great room. A view-oriented design, this home extends scenic vistas from the master suite, great room and dining room, all of which border a rear solana complete with corner fireplace and outdoor grille. The master suite and guest room are secluded to one side, while the family living space connects easily to the kitchen and a private study.

Caprina
Plan No. **8052**

© Sater Design Collection, In

SPECIFICATIONS:

Bedrooms: **4**

Baths: **3½**

Width: **74′ 8″**

Depth: **118′ 0″**

1st Floor: **3271 sq. ft.**

Total Living: **3271 sq. ft.**

Foundation: **Slab**

PLAN PRICING:

Vellum & PDF - **$1636**

CAD - **$2944**

Evocative of the adobe escapes of the Spanish Colonial vernacular, this exquisite villa integrates the graceful interior with the outdoors. Paneled doors lead to a grand foyer, which defies convention with a no-walls approach to the formal rooms. Coffered ceilings provide spatial separation and a visual link between the private and public realms. Dramatic views further define the interior and a wraparound lanai connects public and private realms with an invitation to enjoy the outdoors.

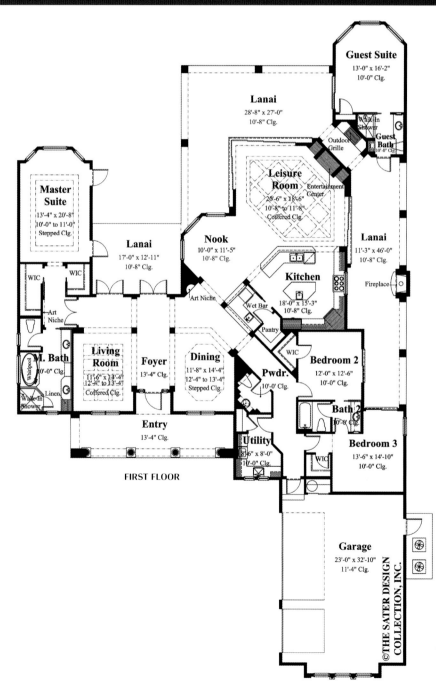

Porta Rosa
Plan No. 8058

Sater Design Collection, Inc.

REAR ELEVATION

SPECIFICATIONS:

Bedrooms: **4**

Baths: **3½**

Width: **67′ 0″**

Depth: **91′ 8″**

1st Floor: **3166 sq. ft.**

Total Living: **3166 sq. ft.**

Foundation: **Slab**

PLAN PRICING:

Vellum & PDF - **$1583**

CAD - **$2849**

Decorative tile vents, spiral pilasters and wrought-iron window treatments achieve a seamless fusion with the powerful, new-century look of this modern revival elevation. Interior vistas mix it up with sunlight and fresh breezes through the plan, with walls of glass that extend living spaces to the outdoors. A high-beamed ceiling, crafted cabinetry and a massive hearth achieve a colonial character that is seamlessly fused with state-of-the art amenities: retreating walls, wide-open rooms, and sleek, do-everything appliances.

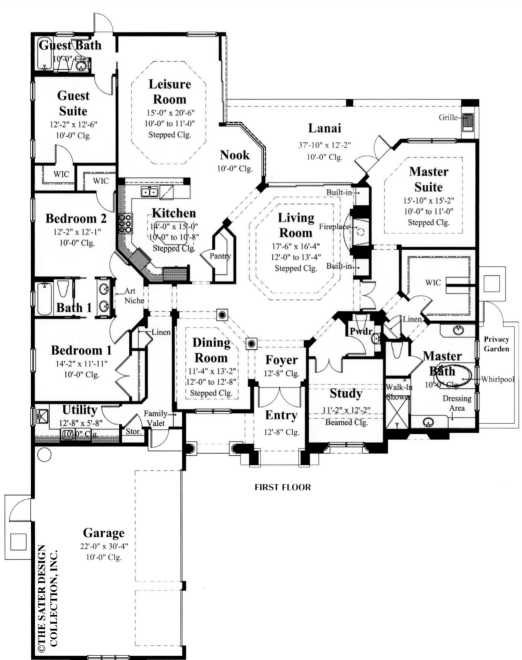

Guest Bath
10'-0" Clg.

Guest Suite
12'-2" x 12'-6"
10'-0" Clg.

Leisure Room
15'-0" x 20'-6"
10'-0" to 11'-0"
Stepped Clg.

WIC

WIC

Bedroom 2
12'-2" x 12'-1"
10'-0" Clg.

Kitchen
14'-0" x 15'-0"
10'-0" to 10'-8"
Stepped Clg.

Nook
10'-0" Clg.

Lanai
37'-10" x 12'-2"
10'-0" Clg.

Grille

Built-in

Master Suite
15'-10" x 15'-2"
10'-0" to 11'-0"
Stepped Clg.

Pantry

Living Room
17'-6" x 16'-4"
12'-0" to 13'-4"
Stepped Clg.

Fireplace

Built-in

WIC

Bath 1

Art Niche

Linen

Linen

Bedroom 1
14'-2" x 11'-11"
10'-0" Clg.

Dining Room
11'-4" x 13'-2"
12'-0" to 12'-8"
Stepped Clg.

Pwdr

Master Bath
10'-0" Clg.

Privacy Garden

Whirlpool

Utility
12'-8" x 5'-8"
10'-0" Clg.

Family Valet

Stor.

Foyer
12'-8" Clg.

Entry
12'-8" Clg.

Study
11'-2" x 12'-2"
Beamed Clg.

Walk-In Shower

Dressing Area

FIRST FLOOR

Garage
22'-0" x 30'-4"
10'-0" Clg.

©THE SATER DESIGN COLLECTION, INC.

Teodora

Plan No. **8066**

REAR ELEVATION

© Sater Design Collection, In

SPECIFICATIONS:

Bedrooms: **5**

Baths: **3½**

Width: **80' 0"**

Depth: **104' 0"**

1st Floor: **3993 sq. ft.**

Total Living: **3993 sq. ft.**

Foundation: **Slab**

PLAN PRICING:

Vellum & PDF - $2595

CAD - $4592

A grand cupola, bay turret and a recessed arch entry adorn this Spanish-inspired home. Inside, rooms are embellished with fine details—built-in cabinetry, fireplaces, art niches and specialty ceilings. The kitchen features an eating bar that connects to the nook and spacious leisure room. Separate verandahs offer intimacy around an outdoor fireplace and a party center around a built-in grille. Three bedrooms plus a guest suite provide quiet spaces for family and friends.

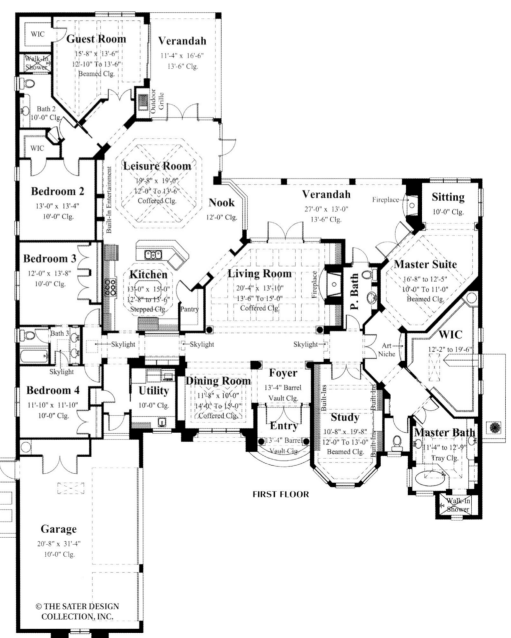

Guest Room
15'-8" x 13'-6"
12'-10" To 13'-6"
Beamed Clg.

Verandah
11'-4" x 16'-6"
13'-6" Clg.

WIC

Walk-In Shower

Bath 2
10'-0" Clg.

WIC

Outdoor Grille

Leisure Room
19'-8" x 19'-0"
12'-0" To 13'-6"
Coffered Clg.

Bedroom 2
13'-0" x 13'-4"
10'-0" Clg.

Built-In Entertainment

Nook
12'-0" Clg.

Verandah
27'-0" x 13'-0"
13'-6" Clg.

Fireplace

Sitting
10'-0" Clg.

Bedroom 3
12'-0" x 13'-8"
10'-0" Clg.

Kitchen
13'-0" x 15'-0"
12'-8" to 13'-6"
Stepped Clg.

Pantry

Living Room
20'-4" x 13'-10"
13'-6" To 15'-0"
Coffered Clg.

Fireplace

P. Bath

Master Suite
16'-8" to 12'-5"
10'-0" To 11'-0"
Beamed Clg.

Bath 3

Skylight

Skylight

Skylight

Art Niche

WIC
12'-2" to 19'-6"

Bedroom 4
11'-10" x 11'-10"
10'-0" Clg.

Utility
10'-0" Clg.

Dining Room
11'-8" x 10'-0"
14'-0" To 15'-0"
Coffered Clg.

Foyer
13'-4" Barrel Vault Clg.

Built-Ins

Built-Ins

Master Bath
11'-4" to 12'-9"
Tray Clg.

Entry
13'-4" Barrel Vault Clg

Study
10'-8" x 19'-8"
12'-0" To 13'-0"
Beamed Clg.

Walk-In Shower

FIRST FLOOR

Garage
20'-8" x 31'-4"
10'-0" Clg.

© THE SATER DESIGN COLLECTION, INC.

© Sater Design Collection, Inc.

Corsini
Plan No. 8049

REAR ELEVATION

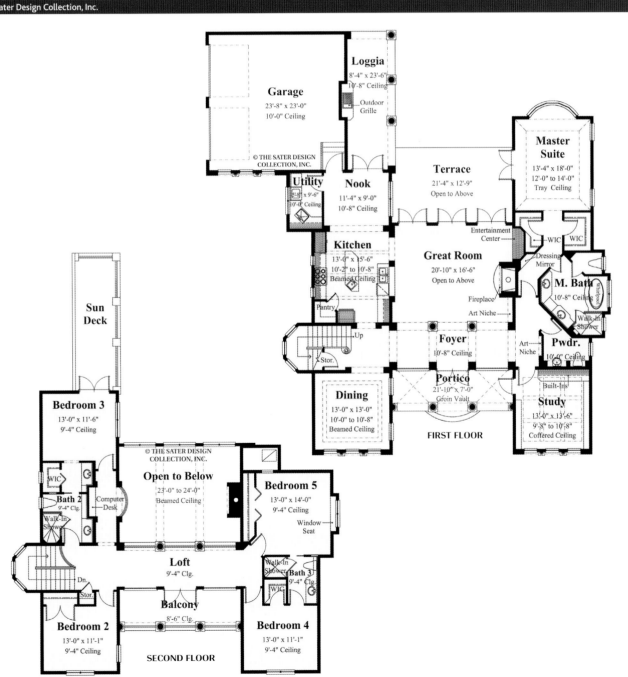

SPECIFICATIONS:

Bedrooms: **5**

Baths: **3½**

Width: **71' 0"**

Depth: **72' 0"**

1st Floor: **2163 sq. ft.**

2nd Floor: **1415 sq. ft.**

Total Living: **3578 sq. ft.**

Foundation: **Slab**

PLAN PRICING:

Vellum & PDF - **$1789**

CAD - **$3220**

Corbels, columns and carved balusters rooted in a timeless Spanish vocabulary establish a striking street presence. Inside, the foyer opens to the great room, an outside-in space that brings in breezes and links with nature. A lateral arrangement of the kitchen, loggia, nook and formal dining room eases entertaining. To the right of the plan, the owners' wing opens to the terrace. The upper-level loft overlooks the great room and connects four guest bedrooms.

Tuscan

Steeped in a profoundly elegant, rich history, Tuscan homes are textured with natural beauty and exude a unique sense of strength and style. Stone, iron and rough-hewn wood join together and envelope you in a Renaissance-like feeling of artistic wonder. The stunning and enduring stone exteriors accented by columns, arches and classic gables give way to generous and handsome rooms of convenience, warmth and comfort. Gourmet kitchens that lead into formal dining rooms and family-style great rooms; secluded master suites that offer peaceful respite in exquisite style; balconies and verandahs that extend outward to reveal fabulous sun decks, terraces and balconies, these are the hallmarks of a Tuscan home's timeless rustic allure.

Salcito
Plan No. 6787

REAR ELEVATION

Mech.
11'-2" x 13'-2"
9'-4 Clg.

Study
15'6" x 13'-0"
9'-4" to 10'-2"
Stepped Clg.

Built-Ins

Deck
8'-6" x 18'-8"

Open To Below

Loft
11'-6" x 17'-10"
9'-4" to 10'-2"
Stepped Clg.

Balcony
20'-0" x 5'-8"
9'-4" Clg.

Bath 2
9'-4" Clg.

Stairwell
10'-4" x 13'-10"
Stepped Clg.

Down

Balconette
9'-4" Clg.

Guest Suite 3
13'-0" x 12'-0"
9'-4" to 10'-2"
Tray Clg.

Guest Suite 2
11'-2" x 14'-0"
9'-4" Clg.

W.I.C.

Bath 3
9'-4" Clg.

Shower

SECOND FLOOR

Lanai
11'-8" x 10'-0"
10'-0" Clg.

Arch

Arch

Built-Ins   Fireplace   Built-Ins

W.I.C.

Walk-In Shower

Master Bath
10'-2" x 15'-0"
10'-0" to 11'-0"
Stepped Clg.

Whirlpool

Living Room
15'-0" x 18'-4"
10'-8" to 12'-0"
Stepped Clg.

Dining
11'-2" x 15'-2"
10'-8" to 12'-0"
Stepped Clg.

Arch

Arch

Desk

Garden

Foyer
15'-0" x 6'-0"
10'-8" Clg.

Arch

Arch

Master Bedroom
16'-6" x 13'-6"
10'-0" to 12'-0"
Tray Clg.

Arch

Kitchen
11'-6" x 13'-6"
11'-4 to 12'-0"
Stepped Clg.

Nook
9'-4" x 13'-0"
11'-4" to 12'-0"
Stepped Clg.

Built-Ins

Leisure Room
17'-2" x 17'-8"

Open to Above

10'-0" Clg.

Loggia
13'-8" x 29'-8"
10'-0" Clg.

Arch

Pool

Fountain

Arch   Arch

Outdoor Grille

Pwdr. Bath

Lin.

Utility Room
10'-0" Clg.

Lin.

Stor.

Up

Portico
6'-6" x 6'-6"
10'-0" Clg.

Cabana/ Guest Suite
13'-0" x 12'-0"
9'-4" to 10'-0"
Tray Clg.

Entry
Barrel Vault Clg.

Bath
9'-4" Clg.

W.I.C.

Walk-In Shower

FIRST FLOOR

Garage
20'-0" x 24'-0"
10'-0" Clg.

SPECIFICATIONS:

Bedrooms: **4**

Baths: **4½**

Width: **45' 0"**

Depth: **94' 0"**

1st Floor: **2087 sq. ft.**

2nd Floor: **1099 sq. ft.**

Cabana: **272 sq. ft.**

Total Living: **3458 sq. ft.**

Foundation: **Slab**

PLAN PRICING:

Vellum & PDF - **$1729**

CAD - **$3112**

This charming Tuscany styled courtyard home features private family and guest spaces filled with Mediterranean design details and open connections to a central loggia with fountain pool. The main-floor leisure room has a two-story boxed-beamed ceiling, a wall of built-ins and retreating glass doors that make it one with the loggia. Nearby, the formal dining and living rooms open to a private lanai. The second-level includes a study, guest bedrooms and multiple decks with courtyard views.

Casoria
Plan No. 6797

SPECIFICATIONS:

Bedrooms: **4**

Baths: **5**

Width: **73′ 2″**

Depth: **118′ 8″**

1st Floor: **2392 sq. ft.**

2nd Floor: **1034 sq. ft.**

Cabana: **351 sq. ft.**

Total Living: **3777 sq. ft.**

Foundation: **Slab**

PLAN PRICING:

Vellum & PDF - $2455

CAD - $4344

This stunning courtyard home features private family and guest spaces filled with Old-World design details and open connections to a central loggia with fountain pool. The great room has a boxed-beamed ceiling, fireplace, built-in cabinetry and retreating glass doors opening to the loggia. The second-level includes a loft, guest bedrooms and decks with courtyard views. The courtyard area is highlighted by an outdoor solana featuring a fireplace and outdoor kitchen.

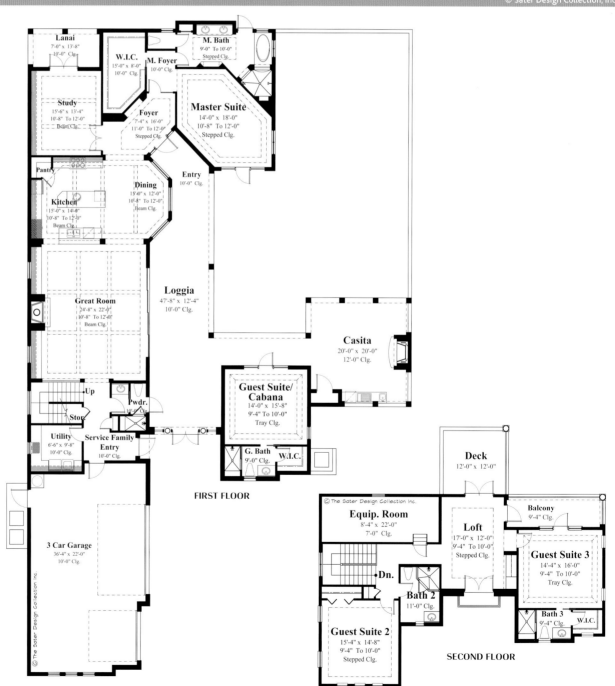

FIRST FLOOR

SECOND FLOOR

Domenico
Plan No. 8069

REAR ELEVATION

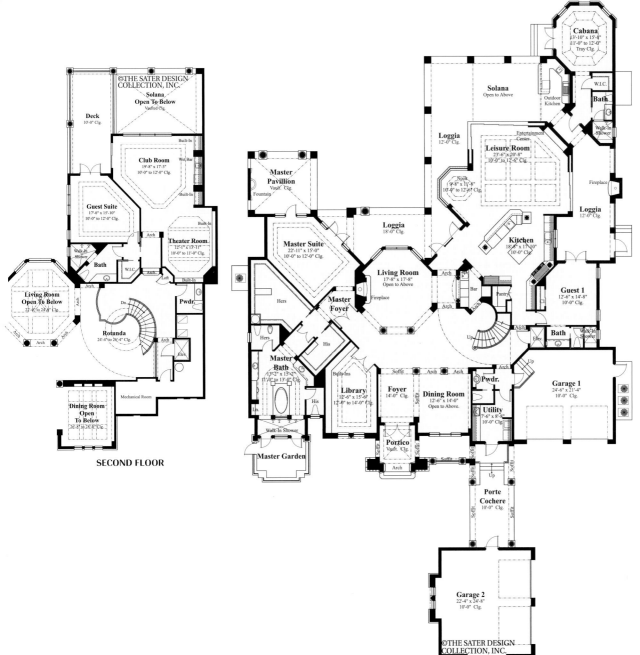

SECOND FLOOR

SPECIFICATIONS:

Bedrooms: **4**

Full Baths: **4**

Half Bath: **2**

Width: **92' 0"**

Depth: **157' 3"**

1st Floor: **4309 sq. ft.**

2nd Floor: **1417 sq. ft.**

Cabana: **400 sq. ft.**

Total Living: **6126 sq. ft.**

Foundation: **Slab**

PLAN PRICING:

Vellum & PDF - **$6126**

CAD - **$10414**

Past the magnificent portico entry, columns and arches define the formal spaces designed for greeting and entertaining guests, with a wet bar providing refreshments. To the rear of the plan, the leisure room flows onto the solana and loggia, with a nearby cabana offering a perfect retreat for guests. On the opposite wing, the master suite opens to a private pavilion. Upstairs, friends and family will enjoy the clubroom, wet bar and state-of-the-art theater room.

Cateena

Plan No. **6503**

REAR ELEVATION

SPECIFICATIONS:

Bedrooms: **3**

Baths: **2**

Width: **44' 0"**

Depth: **74' 0"**

1st Floor: **1608 sq. ft.**

Total Living: **1608 sq. ft.**

Foundation: **Slab**

PLAN PRICING:

Vellum & PDF - $875

CAD - $1447

This small, luxury plan boasts step ceilings in the dining room and kitchen, tray ceilings in the master bedroom, and octagonal stepped ceilings in the great room. Ideal for a view-oriented lot, this home offers scenic vistas from the master suite, great room, and dining room, which border a rear solana complete with corner fireplace and outdoor grille. This floor plan offers a spacious kitchen with a center island. The master bathroom consists of a double vanity, walk in shower, whirlpool bathtub, and separate his and her closets.

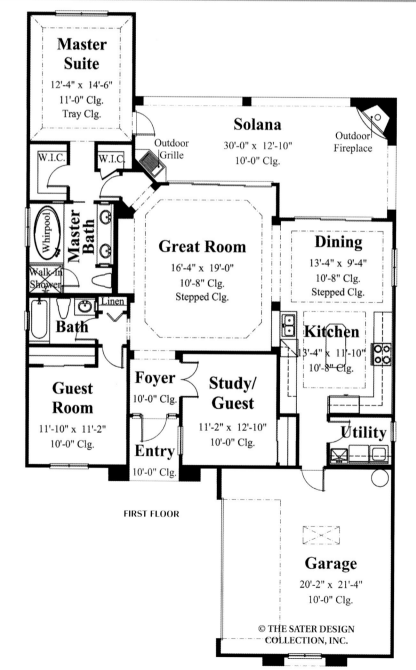

Master Suite
12'-4" x 14'-6"
11'-0" Clg.
Tray Clg.

W.I.C.

W.I.C.

Outdoor Grille

Solana
30'-0" x 12'-10"
10'-0" Clg.

Outdoor Fireplace

Master Bath

Whirlpool

Walk-In Shower

Great Room
16'-4" x 19'-0"
10'-8" Clg.
Stepped Clg.

Dining
13'-4" x 9'-4"
10'-8" Clg.
Stepped Clg.

Linen

Bath

Kitchen
13'-4" x 11'-10"
10'-8" Clg.

Guest Room
11'-10" x 11'-2"
10'-0" Clg.

Foyer
10'-0" Clg.

Study/ Guest
11'-2" x 12'-10"
10'-0" Clg.

Entry
10'-0" Clg.

Utility

FIRST FLOOR

Garage
20'-2" x 21'-4"
10'-0" Clg.

© THE SATER DESIGN COLLECTION, INC.

© Sater Design Collection, Inc.

REAR ELEVATION

Margherita
Plan No. **8075**

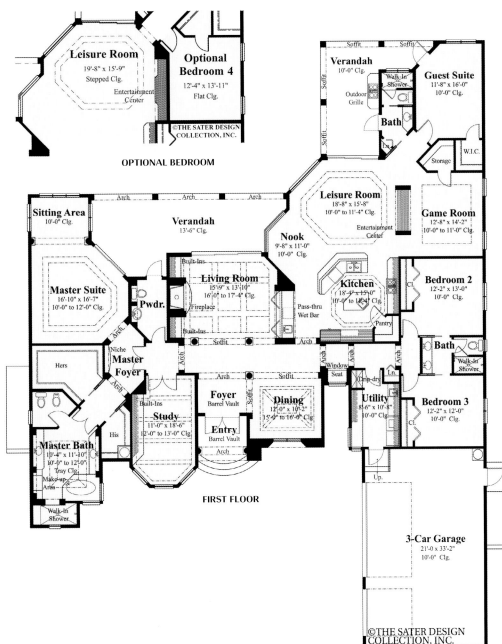

Leisure Room
19'-8" x 15'-9"
Stepped Clg.

Optional Bedroom 4
12'-4" x 13'-11"
Flat Clg.

Entertainment Center

©THE SATER DESIGN COLLECTION, INC.

OPTIONAL BEDROOM

Verandah
10'-0" Clg.

Walk-In Shower

Outdoor Grille

Guest Suite
11'-8" x 16'-0"
10'-0" Clg.

Bath

Ln.

W.I.C.

Storage

Sitting Area
10'-0" Clg.

Verandah
13'-6" Clg.

Nook
9'-8" x 11'-0"
10'-0" Clg.

Leisure Room
18'-8" x 15'-8"
10'-0" to 11'-4" Clg.

Entertainment Center

Game Room
12'-8" x 14'-2"
10'-0" to 11'-0" Clg.

Master Suite
16'-10" x 16'-7"
10'-0" to 12'-0" Clg.

Pwdr.

Living Room
15'-9" x 13'-10"
16'-0" to 17'-0" Clg.

Fireplace

Built-Ins

Pass-thru Wet Bar

Kitchen
18'-9" x 15'-0"
10'-0" to 12'-4" Clg.

Pantry

Cl.

Bedroom 2
12'-2" x 13'-0"
10'-0" Clg.

Niche

Master Foyer

Hers

Arch

Bath

Walk-In Shower

Ln.

Bedroom 3
12'-2" x 12'-0"
10'-0" Clg.

Cl.

Built-Ins

Study
11'-0" x 18'-6"
12'-0" to 13'-0" Clg.

His

Foyer
Barrel Vault

Dining
12'-0" x 10'-2"
15'-0" to 16'-0" Clg.

Window Seat

Drip-dry

Utility
8'-6" x 10'-8"
10'-0" Clg.

Master Bath
10'-4" x 11'-10"
10'-0" to 12'-0" Clg.
Tray Clg.

Make-up Area

Entry
Barrel Vault

Arch

Up.

FIRST FLOOR

Walk-In Shower

3-Car Garage
21'-0" x 33'-2"
10'-0" Clg.

©THE SATER DESIGN COLLECTION, INC.

SPECIFICATIONS:

Bedrooms: **4**

Baths: **3½**

Width: **80' 0"**

Depth: **104' 8"**

1st Floor: **3743 sq. ft.**

Total Living: **3743 sq. ft.**

Foundation: **Slab**

PLAN PRICING:

Vellum & PDF - **$1872**

CAD - **$3369**

A striking center turret resides over the barrel-vault entry of this view-oriented design. Inside, Old World craftsmanship found in built-in cabinetry and beamed and coffered ceilings juxtapose state-of-the-art amenities—a pass-thru wet bar, cutting-edge appliances in the kitchen, and a standalone media center between the leisure and game rooms. Rounded arches define the transitions between well-appointed rooms and open spaces. Near the rear of the plan, the leisure room opens to the veranda.

Chadbryne

Plan No. **8004**

REAR ELEVATION

© Sater Design Collection, Inc

SPECIFICATIONS:

Bedrooms: **4**

Baths: **3½**

Width: **91′ 0″**

Depth: **52′ 8″**

1st Floor: **2219 sq. ft.**

2nd Floor: **1085 sq. ft.**

Total Living: **3304 sq. ft.**

Bonus Room: **404 sq. ft.**

Foundation: **Slab**

PLAN PRICING:

Vellum & PDF - $1652

CAD - $2974

Stacked stone and stucco capture the character of a rural Tuscan manor, influenced by the pastoral forms of Tuscany. Inside, an open foyer is defined by columns and arches, allowing views that extend past the veranda. Architectural details—a coffered ceiling above the two-story great room, an art niche and built-in cabinetry—contribute to the rusticated décor. State-of-the-art appliances in the kitchen and computer loft play counterpoint to rough-hewn ceiling beams and stone accents in the nook and study.

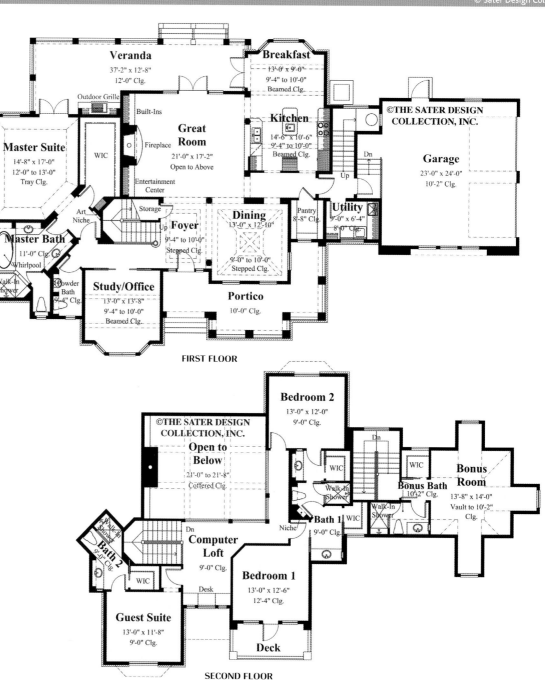

FIRST FLOOR

SECOND FLOOR

Monte Rosa
Plan No. 8077

© Sater Design Collection, Inc.

REAR ELEVATION

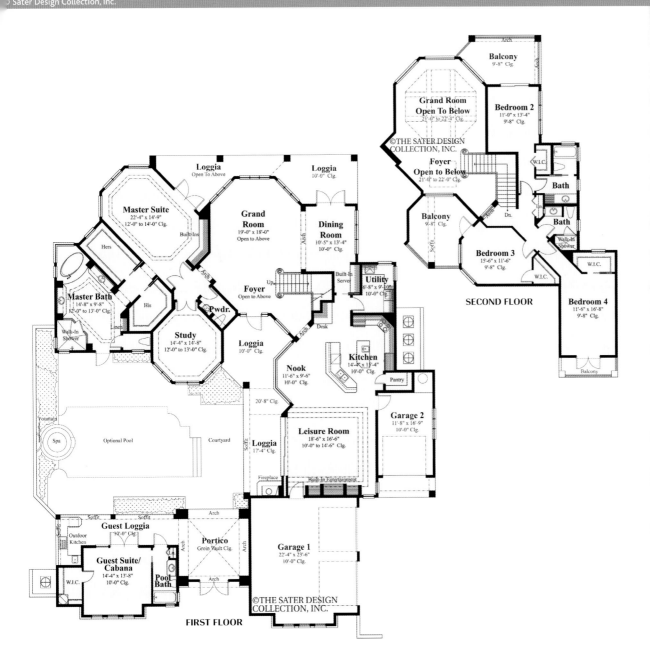

SPECIFICATIONS:

Bedrooms: **5**

Baths: **4½**

Width: **80' 0"**

Depth: **96' 2"**

1st Floor: **2851 sq. ft.**

2nd Floor: **964 sq. ft.**

Cabana: **336 sq. ft.**

Total Living: **4151 sq. ft.**

Foundation: **Slab**

PLAN PRICING:

Vellum & PDF - $2700

The groin-vaulted portico opens to the courtyard and loggia leading to the formal entry of the home. Inside, the foyer opens to the grand room and, through an arched opening, to the formal dining room. Glass bayed walls in the central living area meld interior and outdoor spaces and the dining room leads to a loggia. To the front of the courtyard, a casita offers space that easily converts to a home office.

Vienna

Plan No. **8020**

SPECIFICATIONS:

Bedrooms: **4**

Baths: **4½**

Width: **80′ 0″**

Depth: **63′ 9″**

1st Floor: **2226 sq. ft.**

2nd Floor: **1248 sq. ft.**

Total Living: **3474 sq. ft.**

Foundation: **Slab**

PLAN PRICING:

Vellum & PDF - **$1734**

CAD - **$3121**

A dialogue between tradition and innovation, the Old World elements of this striking façade belie a form-and-function interior packed with new-century amenities. Parallel wings harbor private and public realms, connected by an airy great room and gallery-style foyer. An extended-hearth fireplace shares its beauty with the common living zone—the gourmet kitchen and morning nook. A sun porch on the upper level extends light to the loft, which links two bedroom suites and guest quarters.

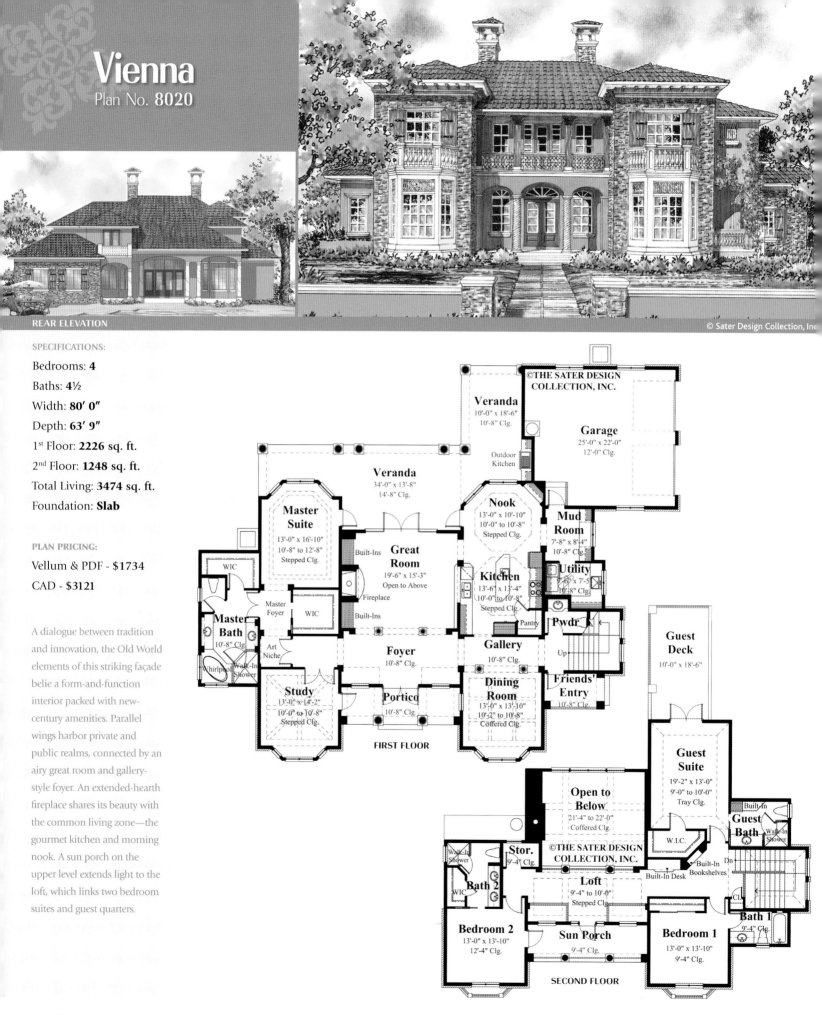

© THE SATER DESIGN COLLECTION, INC.

Veranda
10'-0" x 18'-6"
10'-8" Clg.

Garage
25'-0" x 22'-0"
12'-0" Clg.

Outdoor Kitchen

Veranda
34'-0" x 13'-8"
14'-8" Clg.

Master Suite
13'-0" x 16'-10"
10'-8" to 12'-8"
Stepped Clg.

WIC

Nook
13'-0" x 10'-10"
10'-0" to 10'-8"
Stepped Clg.

Mud Room
7'-8" x 8'-4"
10'-8" Clg.

Built-Ins

Great Room
19'-6" x 15'-3"
Open to Above

Kitchen
13'-6" x 13'-4"
10'-0" to 10'-8"
Stepped Clg.

Utility
9'-0" x 7'-5"
10'-8" Clg.

Master Foyer

Fireplace

WIC

Built-Ins

Pantry

Pwdr

Master Bath
10'-8" Clg.

Art Niche

Whirlpool

Walk-In Shower

Foyer
10'-8" Clg.

Gallery
10'-8" Clg.

Up

Guest Deck
10'-0" x 18'-6"

Study
13'-0" x 14'-2"
10'-0" to 10'-8"
Stepped Clg.

Portico
10'-8" Clg.

Dining Room
13'-0" x 13'-10"
10'-2" to 10'-8"
Coffered Clg.

Friends' Entry
10'-8" Clg.

FIRST FLOOR

Guest Suite
19'-2" x 13'-0"
9'-0" to 10'-0"
Tray Clg.

Open to Below
21'-4" to 22'-0"
Coffered Clg.

Guest Bath

Built-In

Walk-In Shower

W.I.C.

Stor.
9'-4" Clg.

© THE SATER DESIGN COLLECTION, INC.

Built-In Bookshelves

Built-In Desk

Bath 2

WIC

Walk-In Shower

Loft
9'-4" to 10'-0"
Stepped Clg.

Dn

Bath 1
9'-4" Clg.

Bedroom 2
13'-0" x 13'-10"
12'-4" Clg.

Sun Porch
9'-4" Clg.

Bedroom 1
13'-0" x 13'-10"
9'-4" Clg.

SECOND FLOOR

Sater Design Collection, Inc.

Massimo
Plan No. 8057

REAR ELEVATION

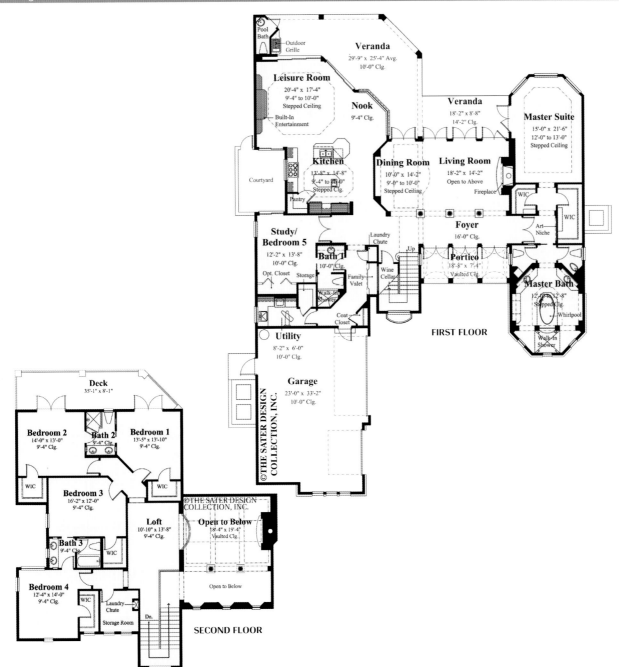

FIRST FLOOR

Pool Bath
Outdoor Grille
Veranda 29'-9" x 25'-4" Avg. 10'-0" Clg.
Leisure Room 20'-4" x 17'-4" 9'-4" to 10'-0" Stepped Ceiling
Built-In Entertainment
Nook 9'-4" Clg.
Veranda 18'-2" x 8'-8" 14'-2" Clg.
Master Suite 15'-0" x 21'-6" 12'-0" to 13'-0" Stepped Ceiling
Kitchen 13'-8" x 14'-8" 9'-4" to 10'-0" Stepped Clg.
Courtyard
Pantry
Dining Room 10'-0" x 14'-2" 9'-0" to 10'-0" Stepped Ceiling
Living Room 18'-2" x 14'-2" Open to Above
Fireplace
WIC
WIC
Study/Bedroom 5 12'-2" x 13'-8" 10'-0" Clg.
Opt. Closet
Storage
Bath 1 10'-0" Clg.
Laundry Chute
Walk-In Shower
Family Valet
Wine Cellar
Foyer 16'-0" Clg.
Up
Portico 18'-8" x 7'-4" Vaulted Clg.
Art Niche
Master Bath 12'-0" x 12'-8" Stepped Clg.
Whirlpool
Walk-In Shower
Coat Closet
Utility 8'-2" x 6'-0" 10'-0" Clg.
Garage 23'-0" x 33'-2" 10'-0" Clg.

©THE SATER DESIGN COLLECTION, INC.

SECOND FLOOR

Deck 35'-1" x 8'-1"
Bedroom 2 14'-0" x 13'-0" 9'-4" Clg.
Bath 2 9'-4" Clg.
Bedroom 1 13'-5" x 13'-10" 9'-4" Clg.
WIC
WIC
Bedroom 3 16'-2" x 12'-0" 9'-4" Clg.
Bath 3 9'-4" Clg.
WIC
Loft 10'-10" x 13'-8" 9'-4" Clg.
Open to Below 18'-4" x 19'-4" Vaulted Clg.
Bedroom 4 12'-4" x 14'-0" 9'-4" Clg.
WIC
Laundry Chute
Storage Room
Dn.
Open to Below

©THE SATER DESIGN COLLECTION, INC.

SPECIFICATIONS:

Bedrooms: **6**

Baths: **4½**

Width: **69' 4"**

Depth: **95' 4"**

1st Floor: **2920 sq. ft.**

2nd Floor: **1474 sq. ft.**

Total Living: **4394 sq. ft.**

Foundation: **Slab**

PLAN PRICING:

Vellum & PDF - **$2856**

CAD - **$5053**

Colonial lines evoke the ancient forms of the houses of Tuscany, yet this grand manor steps boldly into the present. A side courtyard complements a veranda that wraps around the rear of the plan, bordered by walls of glass. French doors open the central living and dining space to the world outside. Upstairs, guest bedrooms open to a shared deck with rear-property views, while a spacious loft overlooks the living room below.

Simone

Plan No. 8059

REAR ELEVATION

SPECIFICATIONS:

Bedrooms: **4**

Baths: **3½**

Width: **67' 0"**

Depth: **91' 8"**

1st Floor: **3231 sq. ft.**

Total Living: **3231 sq. ft.**

Foundation: **Slab**

PLAN PRICING:

Vellum & PDF - $1616

CAD - $2908

Stacked stone gables dramatically define the neighborhood presence of this Tuscan villa. Beyond the entry, the plan offers well-defined rooms and wide-open spaces with views of nature everywhere. Columns define the boundaries of the formal dining room, permitting interior vistas as well as easy service from the kitchen. Retreating glass doors provide views and expand the living and leisure rooms onto the spacious lanai, where guests can enjoy meals al fresco by the built-in grille.

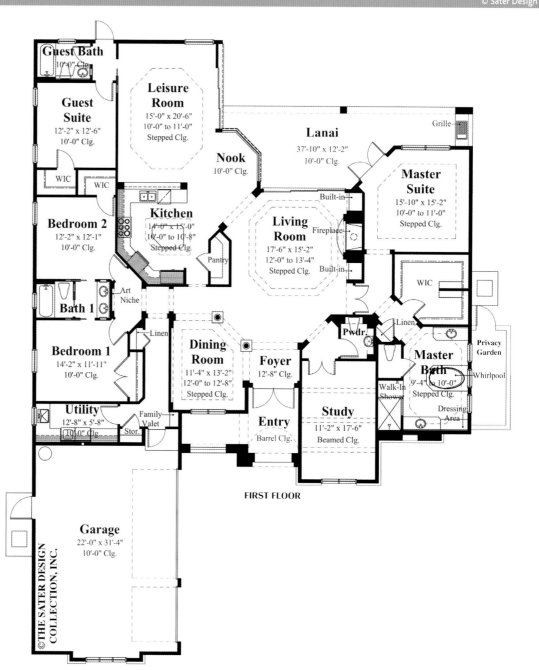

FIRST FLOOR

© THE SATER DESIGN COLLECTION, INC.

Sater Design Collection, Inc.

Santa Trinita
Plan No. 8063

REAR ELEVATION

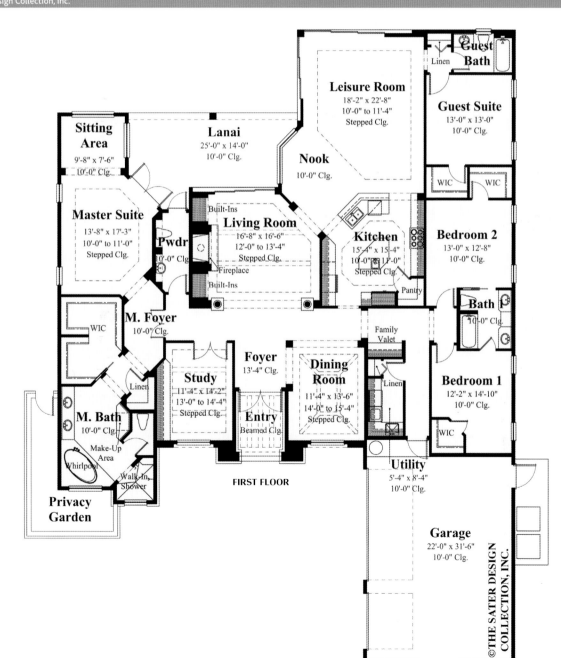

Sitting Area
9'-8" x 7'-6"
10'-0" Clg.

Lanai
25'-0" x 14'-0"
10'-0" Clg.

Leisure Room
18'-2" x 22'-8"
10'-0" to 11'-4"
Stepped Clg.

Guest Bath
Linen

Guest Suite
13'-0" x 13'-0"
10'-0" Clg.

Nook
10'-0" Clg.

WIC   WIC

Master Suite
13'-8" x 17'-3"
10'-0" to 11'-0"
Stepped Clg.

Built-Ins

Pwdr
10'-0" Clg.

Living Room
16'-8" x 16'-6"
12'-0" to 13'-4"
Stepped Clg.

Fireplace

Built-Ins

Kitchen
15'-4" x 15'-4"
10'-0" to 11'-0"
Stepped Clg.

Bedroom 2
13'-0" x 12'-8"
10'-0" Clg.

Pantry

WIC

M. Foyer
10'-0" Clg.

Family Valet

Bath 1
10'-0" Clg.

Linen

Study
11'-4" x 14'-2"
13'-0" to 14'-4"
Stepped Clg.

Foyer
13'-4" Clg.

Dining Room
11'-4" x 13'-6"
14'-0" to 15'-4"
Stepped Clg.

Entry
Beamed Clg.

Bedroom 1
12'-2" x 14'-10"
10'-0" Clg.

Linen

M. Bath
10'-0" Clg.

Make-Up Area

Whirlpool

Walk-In Shower

WIC

Utility
5'-4" x 8'-4"
10'-0" Clg.

FIRST FLOOR

Privacy Garden

Garage
22'-0" x 31'-6"
10'-0" Clg.

©THE SATER DESIGN COLLECTION, INC.

SPECIFICATIONS:

Bedrooms: **4**

Baths: **3½**

Width: **68′ 8″**

Depth: **91′ 8″**

1st Floor: **3497 sq. ft.**

Total Living: **3497 sq. ft.**

Foundation: **Slab**

PLAN PRICING:

Vellum & PDF - **$1749**

CAD - **$3147**

Tuscan charm invites a feeling of home outside and in with floor-to-ceiling windows letting in the sun. The front of the home features formal spaces intended for entertaining with richly textured amenities such as a stone-mantel fireplace, cabinetry and stepped ceilings. To the rear of the plan, the leisure room flows through retreating glass walls onto the lanai. A gallery hall runs the width of the plan, linking three guest bedrooms with the master suite.

Trevi
Plan No. 8065

© Sater Design Collection, In

SPECIFICATIONS:

Bedrooms: **4**

Baths: **3½**

Width: **95′ 0″**

Depth: **84′ 0″**

1st Floor: **3546 sq. ft.**

2nd Floor: **1213 sq. ft.**

Total Living: **4759 sq. ft.**

Foundation: **Basement**

PLAN PRICING:

Vellum & PDF - $4759

CAD - $8090

Turrets frame the entry arcade of this magnificent manor. Inside, a mix of breezy, open spaces creates an at-home feeling that encourages all kinds of gatherings. A two-sided fireplace anchors the living room that extends out to the verandah through French doors. Varied ceiling treatments define rooms that defy their boundaries with walls of glass and unrestrained spaces. Columns whisper the edges of a gallery colonnade that runs nearly the width of the plan.

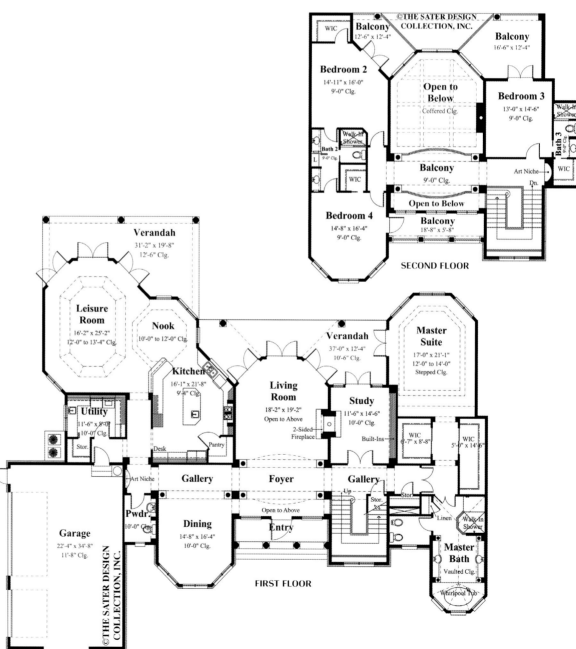

Brescia
Plan No. 6548

REAR ELEVATION

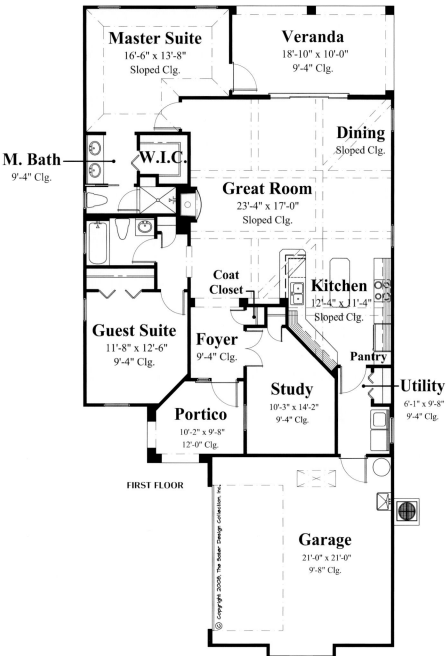

Master Suite
16'-6" x 13'-8"
Sloped Clg.

Veranda
18'-10" x 10'-0"
9'-4" Clg.

Dining
Sloped Clg.

M. Bath
9'-4" Clg.

W.I.C.

Great Room
23'-4" x 17'-0"
Sloped Clg.

Coat Closet

Kitchen
12'-4" x 11'-4"
Sloped Clg.

Guest Suite
11'-8" x 12'-6"
9'-4" Clg.

Foyer
9'-4" Clg.

Pantry

Utility
6'-1" x 9'-8"
9'-4" Clg.

Portico
10'-2" x 9'-8"
12'-0" Clg.

Study
10'-3" x 14'-2"
9'-4" Clg.

FIRST FLOOR

Garage
21'-0" x 21'-0"
9'-8" Clg.

SPECIFICATIONS:

Bedrooms: **2**

Baths: **2**

Width: **36' 0"**

Depth: **73' 4"**

1st Floor: **1497 sq. ft.**

Total Living: **1497 sq. ft.**

Foundation: **Slab**

PLAN PRICING:

Vellum & PDF - **$875**

CAD - **$1347**

This small, luxury Tuscan home plan provides two bedrooms and two bathrooms, plus a study/optional bedroom. The house plan features the details that count: arched passageways lead from room to room, a spacious kitchen offers a central island, the great room's fireplace warms the dining area as well and a covered rear veranda offers sheltered outdoor space. The great room has a beautiful vaulted beam ceiling and the master suite showcases a tray ceiling. The master suite offers private veranda access and a bathroom designed for two.

Lizzano
Plan No. 6554

SPECIFICATIONS:

Bedrooms: **3**

Baths: **3**

Width: **40' 0"**

Depth: **89' 0"**

1st Floor: **1629 sq. ft.**

Cabana: **263 sq. ft.**

Total Living: **1892 sq. ft.**

Foundation: **Slab**

PLAN PRICING:

Vellum & PDF - $946

CAD - $1703

This small, luxury Tuscan home plan has two bedrooms, two bathrooms, and a separate cabana/guest room with a full bath. Its compact floor plan features a courtyard layout, which is perfect for a swimming pool. With an open layout, the great room, dining room, master suite, and guest rooms all have access to the outdoors. The great room showcases a beautiful fireplace and coffered ceilings, while the master suite offers a step ceiling. The master suite and guest suites are on opposite ends of the house to maximize privacy.

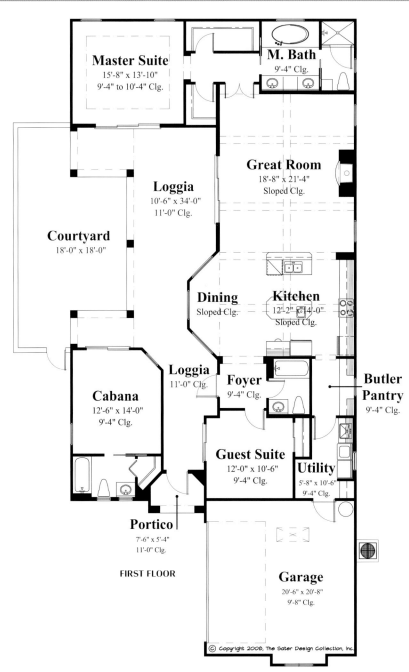

REAR ELEVATION

Dentro
Plan No. 6550

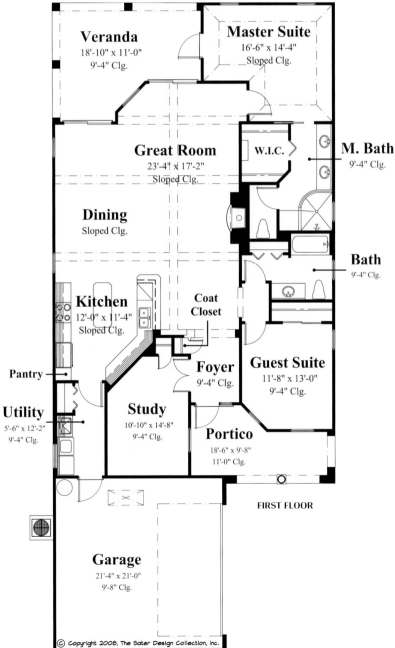

FIRST FLOOR

Veranda
18'-10" x 11'-0"
9'-4" Clg.

Master Suite
16'-6" x 14'-4"
Sloped Clg.

Great Room
23'-4" x 17'-2"
Sloped Clg.

W.I.C.

M. Bath
9'-4" Clg.

Dining
Sloped Clg.

Kitchen
12'-0" x 11'-4"
Sloped Clg.

Coat Closet

Bath
9'-4" Clg.

Pantry

Foyer
9'-4" Clg.

Guest Suite
11'-8" x 13'-0"
9'-4" Clg.

Utility
5'-6" x 12'-2"
9'-4" Clg.

Study
10'-10" x 14'-8"
9'-4" Clg.

Portico
18'-6" x 9'-8"
11'-0" Clg.

Garage
21'-4" x 21'-0"
9'-8" Clg.

SPECIFICATIONS:

Bedrooms: **2**

Baths: **2**

Width: **36' 0"**

Depth: **80' 8"**

1st Floor: **1753 sq. ft.**

Total Living: **1753 sq. ft.**

Foundation: **Slab**

PLAN PRICING:

Vellum & PDF - $877

CAD - $1578

This small, luxury Tuscan compact house plan lives larger than its footprint thanks to an open fusion of living space within. A uniquely shaped kitchen offers an island and eating bar. The great room, with a beautiful coffered ceiling and fireplace, opens to a covered veranda perfect for outdoor entertaining through two sets of sliders. The master suite offers a tray ceiling, dual vanities and a walk-in closet.

Bianca

Plan No. **6506**

SPECIFICATIONS:

Bedrooms: **3**

Baths: **2**

Width: **42' 8"**

Depth: **63' 4"**

1st Floor: **1404 sq. ft.**

Total Living: **1404 sq. ft.**

Foundation: **Slab**

PLAN PRICING:

Vellum & PDF - $875

CAD - $1264

A turreted breakfast nook sits elegantly aside the entryway, which features a dramatic barrel vault ceiling. Inside, the foyer looks ahead through a disappearing wall of glass that opens the great room to the verandah. The great room and dining room proudly feature step ceiling detail. The master suite and dining room also have sliding doors to the rear living spaces, and a pass-thru bar makes the kitchen user-friendly. This spacious house plan offers a master bathroom with all the trimmings – a double vanity, walk in closet, whirlpool tub, and walk in shower.

Master Suite
13'-10" x 12'-4"
10'-0" Clg.

Verandah
27'-2" x 9'-8"
10'-0" Clg.

Walk-In Shower

Master Bath

W.I.C.

Great Room
15'-6" x 15'-10"
11'-0" Clg.

Dining
9'-4" x 11'-6"
11'-0" Clg.

Whirlpool

Bath

Kitchen
9'-4" x 17'-4"
10'-0" Clg.

Bedroom
10'-2" x 10'-0"
10'-0" Clg.

Utility

Study/Guest
9'-10" x 12'-8"
10'-0" Clg.

Foyer
10'-0" Clg.

Entry
Barrel Vault Clg.

Nook
10'-0" Clg.

FIRST FLOOR

Garage
20'-2" x 24'-2"
8'-0" Clg.

© THE SATER DESIGN COLLECTION, INC.

Florenze
Plan No. 6552

REAR ELEVATION

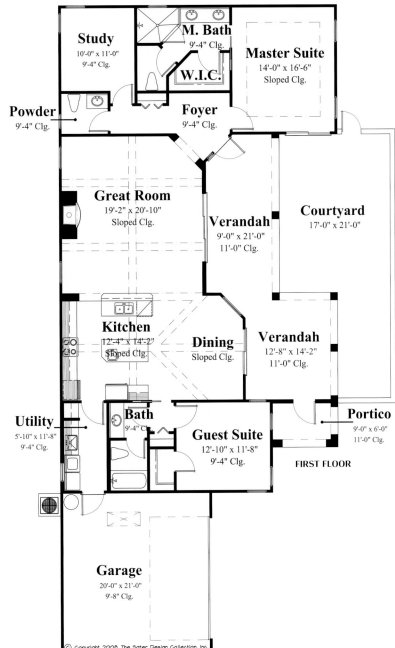

Study
10'-0" x 11'-0"
9'-4" Clg.

M. Bath
9'-4" Clg.

W.I.C.

Master Suite
14'-0" x 16'-6"
Sloped Clg.

Powder
9'-4" Clg.

Foyer
9'-4" Clg.

Great Room
19'-2" x 20'-10"
Sloped Clg.

Verandah
9'-0" x 21'-0"
11'-0" Clg.

Courtyard
17'-0" x 21'-0"

Kitchen
12'-4" x 14'-2"
Sloped Clg.

Dining
Sloped Clg.

Verandah
12'-8" x 14'-2"
11'-0" Clg.

Utility
5'-10" x 11'-8"
9'-4" Clg.

Bath
9'-4" Clg.

Guest Suite
12'-10" x 11'-8"
9'-4" Clg.

Portico
9'-0" x 6'-0"
11'-0" Clg.

FIRST FLOOR

Garage
20'-0" x 21'-0"
9'-8" Clg.

SPECIFICATIONS:

Bedrooms: **3**

Baths: **2½**

Width: **38' 0"**

Depth: **87' 4"**

1st Floor: **1790 sq. ft.**

Total Living: **1790 sq. ft.**

Foundation: **Slab**

PLAN PRICING:

Vellum & PDF - **$895**

CAD - **$1611**

This small, luxury Tuscan style floor plan features a courtyard layout, which is perfect for a swimming pool. With an open layout, the great room, dining room, and master suite all have access to the outdoors. The great room showcases a beautiful fireplace and coffered ceilings, while the master suite offers a step ceiling. The master suite and guest suite are on opposite ends of the house to maximize privacy. The kitchen has plenty of counter space, including a center island. The master bathroom has a dual vanity, a walk-in shower and closet.

Del Rosa

Plan No. 6510

REAR ELEVATION

SPECIFICATIONS:

Bedrooms: **3**

Baths: **2**

Width: **47' 2"**

Depth: **78' 0"**

1st Floor: **1919 sq. ft.**

Total Living: **1919 sq. ft.**

Foundation: **Slab**

PLAN PRICING:

Vellum & PDF - **$960**

CAD - **$1727**

The turreted, recessed entry grants elegance to the façade of this Tuscan charmer. The interior flows around a large central great room featuring a stepped ceiling. The spacious island kitchen has a walk-in pantry. An optional layout changes the dining area into a study or guest room with French doors that open onto the great room. The nook boasts a step ceiling and the great room and kitchen have an octagonal stepped ceiling, while the master bedroom exhibits tray ceilings. This house plan's master bathroom is full of little luxuries.

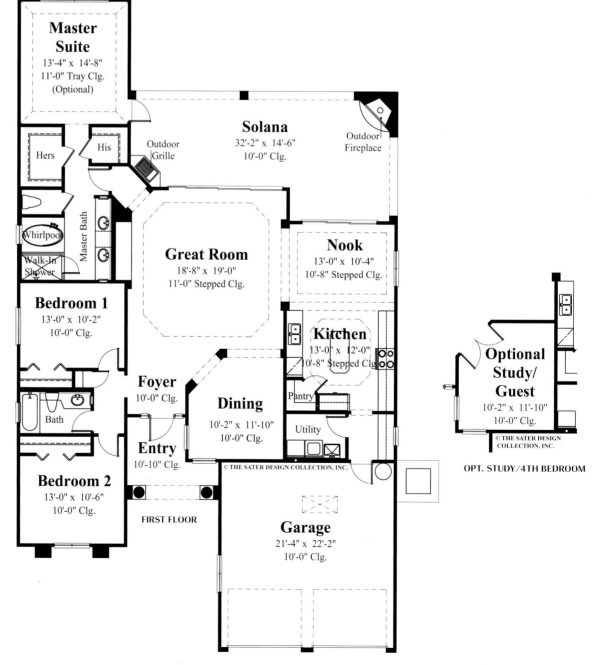

Master Suite
13'-4" x 14'-8"
11'-0" Tray Clg.
(Optional)

Hers His

Master Bath

Whirlpool

Walk-In Shower

Outdoor Grille

Solana
32'-2" x 14'-6"
10'-0" Clg.

Outdoor Fireplace

Great Room
18'-8" x 19'-0"
11'-0" Stepped Clg.

Nook
13'-0" x 10'-4"
10'-8" Stepped Clg.

Bedroom 1
13'-0" x 10'-2"
10'-0" Clg.

Kitchen
13'-0" x 12'-0"
10'-8" Stepped Clg.

Foyer
10'-0" Clg.

Pantry

Dining
10'-2" x 11'-10"
10'-0" Clg.

Utility

Bath

Entry
10'-10" Clg.

© THE SATER DESIGN COLLECTION, INC.

Bedroom 2
13'-0" x 10'-6"
10'-0" Clg.

FIRST FLOOR

Garage
21'-4" x 22'-2"
10'-0" Clg.

Optional Study/ Guest
10'-2" x 11'-10"
10'-0" Clg.

© THE SATER DESIGN COLLECTION, INC.

OPT. STUDY/4TH BEDROOM

© Sater Design Collection, Inc.

REAR ELEVATION

Pelago
Plan No. 6556

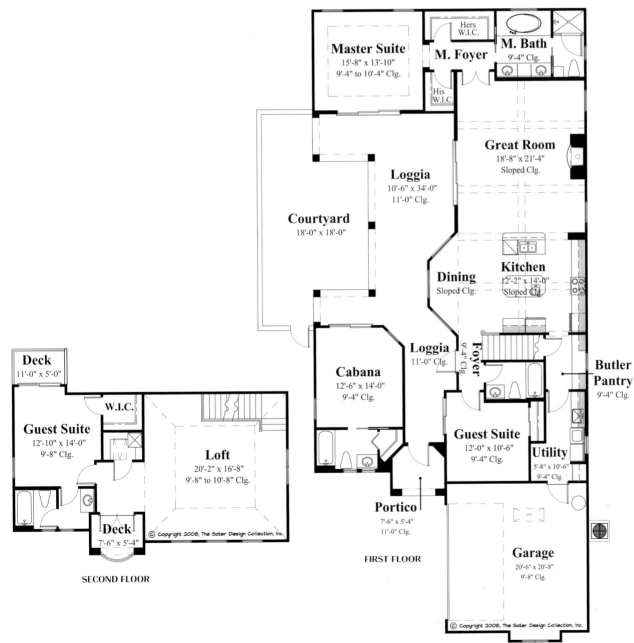

Master Suite
15'-8" x 13'-10"
9'-4" to 10'-4" Clg.

M. Foyer

Hers W.I.C.

His W.I.C.

M. Bath
9'-4" Clg.

Great Room
18'-8" x 21'-4"
Sloped Clg.

Loggia
10'-6" x 34'-0"
11'-0" Clg.

Courtyard
18'-0" x 18'-0"

Kitchen
12'-2" x 14'-0"
Sloped Clg.

Dining
Sloped Clg.

Loggia
11'-0" Clg.

Foyer
9'-4" Clg.

Butler Pantry
9'-4" Clg.

Cabana
12'-6" x 14'-0"
9'-4" Clg.

Guest Suite
12'-0" x 10'-6"
9'-4" Clg.

Utility
5'-8" x 10'-6"
9'-4" Clg.

Portico
7'-6" x 5'-4"
11'-0" Clg.

Garage
20'-6" x 20'-8"
9'-8" Clg.

© Copyright 2008, The Sater Design Collection, Inc.

FIRST FLOOR

Deck
11'-0" x 5'-0"

Guest Suite
12'-10" x 14'-0"
9'-8" Clg.

W.I.C.

Loft
20'-2" x 16'-8"
9'-8" to 10'-8" Clg.

Deck
7'-6" x 5'-4"

© Copyright 2008, The Sater Design Collection, Inc.

SECOND FLOOR

SPECIFICATIONS:

Bedrooms: **3**

Baths: **4**

Width: **40' 0"**

Depth: **89' 0"**

1st Floor: **1664 sq. ft.**

2nd Floor: **749 sq. ft.**

Cabana: **263 sq. ft.**

Total Living: **2676 sq. ft.**

Foundation: **Slab**

PLAN PRICING:

Vellum & PDF - **$1338**

CAD - **$2408**

This luxury, Tuscan courtyard home creates a private sanctuary to enjoy the outdoors. An airy atmosphere is created because the master suite, great room, dining room and guest rooms are all open to the porch. The great room and kitchen enjoy coffered ceilings, while the master suite offers a step ceiling. The kitchen has plenty of counter space, including a center island. Offering little luxuries, the master suite has his and her closets, a dual vanity, walk-in closet and shower, and a whirlpool tub.

index

from Sater Design Collection, Inc.

1-800-718-7526
www.saterdesign.com

index
Plans listed by square
footage largest to smallest.

WHAT'S IN A SET OF *plans?*

A set of plans is a collection of drawings that show the important structural components and how the home should be built. Architectural and construction terms are complex. If you have further questions about these terms, ask your builder or visit our glossary online at www.saterdesign.com.

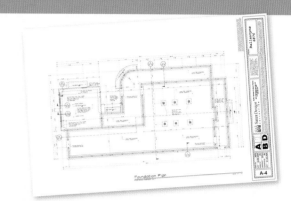

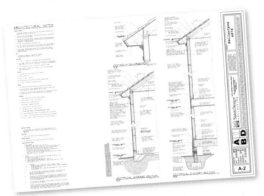

COVER SHEET, INDEX & SITE PLAN — The cover sheet features an elevation of the exterior of the house that shows approximately how the home will look when built. The index lists the order of the drawings included, with page numbers for easy reference. The site plan is a scaled footprint of the house to help determine how the home will be placed on the building site.

WALL SECTION & NOTES — This section shows section cuts of the exterior wall from the roof down through the foundation. These wall sections specify the home's construction and building materials. They also show the number of stories, type of foundation and the construction of the walls. Roofing materials, insulation, floor framing, wall finishes and elevation heights are all shown and referenced.

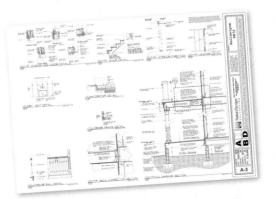

TYPICAL DETAILS & NOTES — This section addresses all the facets and details you will want to include in your home, with the exception of local building code requirements. Architectural and structural elements are detailed, including: window and door components, railings, balusters, wood stairs and headers, interior walls, interior partitions, concrete steps and footings (if applicable).

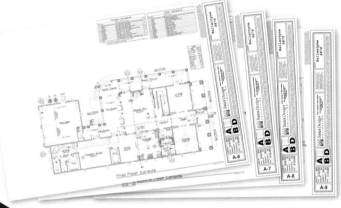

FOUNDATION PLAN — This sheet provides a fully dimensioned and noted foundation layout, including references to footings, pads, and support walls. For plans with a basement, additional walls and columns may be shown. Basement plans come with a floor framing layout which may be included in this section or the floor framing section, depending on the plan.

DETAILED FLOOR PLAN — This section provides detailed drawings and descriptions of all the elements that will be included on each floor of the home. The home's exterior footprint, openings and interior rooms are carefully dimensioned. Important features are noted including built-ins, niches and appliances. All doors and windows are identified. Typically this section also includes the square footage information.

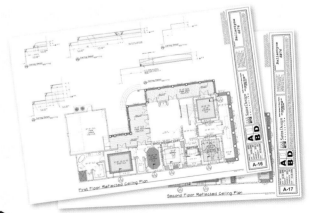

REFLECTED CEILING PLAN — One of Sater home's most distinguishable features is the highly detailed ceiling treatments. This section shows ceiling heights and treatments. It also shows the details, profiles and finishes of the ceiling treatments. Arches and soffits are also specified in this section.

bonus:

electronic plans:

Our plans are also available in an electronic format, supplied on a CD-ROM. All of the features explained below are included on this disk.

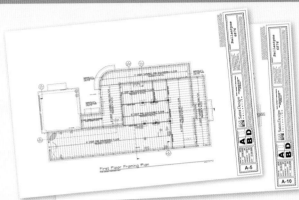

FLOOR FRAMING PLANS — Homes with a basement or crawl space will have a floor framing plan for the first floor. Multi-story homes will have floor framing plans for upper floors as well. The floor framing plans provide structural information such as the joist location, spacing and direction, as well as the floor heights and stair openings.

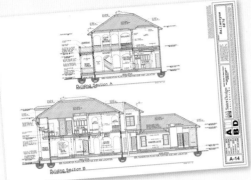

CROSS SECTION & DETAILS — This section will illustrate the important changes in the floor, ceiling and roof heights or the relationship of different floors to one another. Interior elements of rooms and areas, such as columns, arches, headers and soffits, are also discernible and easier to visualize in a cross section.

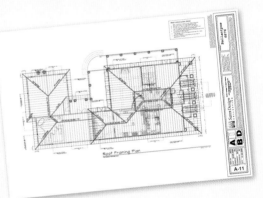

ROOF PLAN — The overall layout and necessary details for roof design are provided in this section. If trusses are used, we suggest using a local truss manufacturer to design your roof trusses to comply with your local codes and regulations.

INTERIOR ELEVATIONS — These elevations show the specific details and design of the kitchen, bathrooms, utility rooms, fireplaces, bookcases, built-in units and other special interior features. The interior elevations vary based on the complexity of the home.

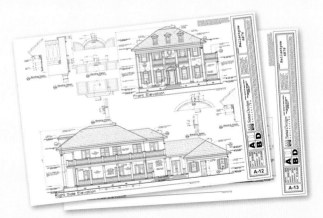

EXTERIOR ELEVATIONS — Elevations are drawings that show how the finished home will approximately look. In this section, elevations of the front, rear and left and right sides of the home are shown. Exterior materials, details and heights are noted on these drawings.

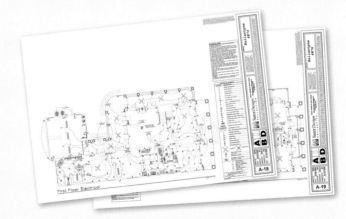

ELECTRICAL PLAN — This section shows an electrical plan that will enhance functionality and highlight the unique architectural features of the home.

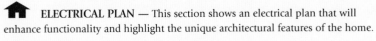

QUICK TURNAROUND

If you place your order before 3:00 P.M. eastern time, we can usually have your plans to you the next business day. Some restrictions may apply. We cannot ship to a post office box, so please be prepared to supply us with a physical street address.

OUR EXCHANGE POLICY

We do not accept returns because each set of plans or disk is generated just for you at the time of your order. However, if you should find that the plan you purchased does not meet your needs, we do permit exchanges requested within sixty days of the date of purchase. At the time of exchange, you will be charged a processing fee of 20% of the total of your original order plus the difference in price between the plans (if applicable) and the cost to ship the new plans to you.

WHAT FORMAT OF PLANS SHOULD I GET?

Our plans are available in three formats: PDF plan sets, a reproducible vellum set and an electronic version on a disk. Most people select a format based on the changes they will make to their plan.

PDF plan sets are the fastest, most convenient way to get going. With a PDF file you can obtain the necessary copies (up to twenty) at your local print shop. This saves you shipping costs and time.

Vellum is a special type of paper that can be erased for small changes, such as moving kitchen appliances, or enlarging a shower. You will receive one set of plans on the special paper with permission to make up to twenty copies for the construction process.

Most customers, and engineers, prefer the electronic version of the plans. The AutoCAD file facilitates major modifications and dimensional changes. You will receive one disk with permission to make up to twenty copies for the construction process.

LOCAL BUILDING CODES AND ZONING REQUIREMENTS

Our plans are designed to meet or exceed the International Residential Code. Because of the great differences in geography and climate, each state, county and municipality has its own building codes and zoning requirements. Your plan may need to be modified to comply with local requirements regarding snow loads, energy codes, soil and seismic conditions and a wide range of other matters. Prior to using plans ordered from us, we strongly advise that you consult a local building official.

ARCHITECTURAL AND/OR ENGINEERING REVIEW

Some cities and states require a licensed architect or engineer to review and approve any set of building documents prior to permitting. These cities and states want to ensure that the proposed new home will be code compliant, zoning compliant, safe, and structurally sound. Often, this architect or engineer will have to create additional structural drawings to be submitted for permitting. You can learn if this will be necessary in your area from a local building official.

DISCLAIMER

We have put substantial care and effort into the creation of our house plans. We authorize the use of our plans on the express condition that you strictly comply with all local building codes, zoning requirements and other applicable laws, regulations and ordinances. However, because we cannot provide on-site consultation, supervision or control over the actual construction and because of the great variance in local building requirements, building practices and soil, seismic, weather and other conditions, WE CANNOT MAKE ANY WARRANTY, EXPRESS OR IMPLIED, WITH RESPECT TO THE CONTENT OR USE OF OUR PLANS, INCLUDING, BUT IS NOT LIMITED TO, ANY WARRANTY OF MARKETABILITY OR OF FITNESS FOR A PARTICULAR PURPOSE. Please note that floor plans included in this magazine are not construction documents and are subject to change. Renderings are an artist's concept only.

IGNORING COPYRIGHT LAWS CAN BE A
$150,000 mistake!

Recent changes in Federal Copyright Laws allow for statutory penalties of up to $150,000 per incident for copyright infringement involving any of the copyrighted plans found in this publication. The law can be confusing. So, for your own protection, take the time to understand what you cannot do when it comes to home plans.

WHAT YOU CAN'T DO:

- **YOU CANNOT BUILD A HOME WITHOUT BUYING A LICENSE.**

- **YOU CANNOT DUPLICATE HOME PLANS WITHOUT PERMISSION.**

- **YOU CANNOT COPY ANY PART OF A HOME PLAN TO CREATE ANOTHER.**

- **YOU MUST OBTAIN A SEPARATE LICENSE EACH TIME YOU BUILD A HOME.**

from Sater Design Collection, Inc.

1-800-718-7526
www.saterdesign.com

what is a license?

**CONSIDERATIONS IN ORDERING
A SATER DESIGN PLAN.**

PRINT LICENSE

This license is issued in the form of a single vellum set of plan prints. The licensee is entitled to customize and build one time only.

ELECTRONIC LICENSE

This license is issued in the form of an electronic (AutoCAD or PDF) files. The licensee is entitled to customize and build one time only.

HOW TO ORDER

**ORDER BY PHONE
1-800-718-7526**

ORDER ONLINE
www.saterdesign.com

SATER DESIGN COLLECTION
25241 Elementary Way, Suite 102
Bonita Springs, FL 34135

WHAT SETS A SATER PLAN APART?

In order to ensure that your home is built to look just as spectacular as the homes shown in this magazine, we have created highly detailed construction drawings. Our plans are the ultimate guide to building the home of your dreams. Some of the features that you'll find in Sater plans, but not other plans, are:

	SATER	OTHERS
Extensive Interior Elevations *Interior design-quality drawings, showing highly detailed elevations of architectural built-ins and cabinetry*	YES	NO
Detailed Materials List *To assist the owner and builder with estimating building costs (Some offer this for a fee, but with us it's free!)*	YES	NO
Reflected Ceiling Plans *With detailed sections of the numerous ceiling and soffit designs*	YES	NO
Separate Electrical Plans *Carefully designed lighting plans that contemplate your family's use and enjoyment*	YES	NO
Green Brochure *To help you make decisions about implementing green building practices in your home's construction .*	YES	NO
Unparalleled Customer Support *Our dedicated staff is committed to helping you in the decision process*	YES	NO

PLAN CUSTOMIZATION SERVICES

If you want to tweak the plan to better suit you and your family, we certainly understand and hope you'll let us make the changes for you. That way we can ensure that the plan with the changes is just as beautiful as the plan before the changes and that all changes are properly made. Call 1-800-718-7526 to speak with a customer service representative about your needs, we're happy to help!

We DO NOT sell photography shown in this book for any purpose.
Prices of plans are subject to change without notice.